THE DECLINING HEGEMON

**Recent Titles in
Contributions in Military Studies**

The Culture of War: Invention and Early Development
Richard A. Gabriel

Prisoners, Diplomats, and the Great War: A Study in the Diplomacy of Captivity
Richard Berry Speed III

Military Crisis Management: U.S. Intervention in the Dominican Republic, 1965
Herbert G. Schoonmaker

The Persian Gulf War: Lessons for Strategy, Law, and Diplomacy
Christopher C. Joyner, editor

Where Eagles Land: Planning and Development of U.S. Army Airfields, 1910–1941
Jerold E. Brown

First Strike Stability: Deterrence after Containment
Stephen J. Cimbala

Legitimacy and Commitment in the Military
Thomas C. Wyatt and Reuven Gal, editors

The Army's Nuclear Power Program: The Evolution of a Support Agency
Lawrence H. Suid

Russian Imperial Military Doctrine and Education, 1832–1914
Carl Van Dyke

The Eagle and the Dragon: The United States Military in China, 1901–1937
Dennis L. Noble

An Eyewitness Account of the American Revolution and New England Life: The
Journal of J.F. Wasmus, German Company Surgeon, 1776–1783
Helga Doblin, translator, and Mary C. Lynn, editor

THE DECLINING HEGEMON

The United States and European Defense, 1960–1990

JOSEPH LEPGOLD

Contributions in Military Studies, Number 103
Colin Gray, Series Adviser

GREENWOOD PRESS
New York • Westport, Connecticut • London

Library of Congress Cataloging-in-Publication Data

Lepgold, Joseph.
  The declining hegemon : the United States and European defense,
1960–1990 / Joseph Lepgold.
    p.   cm.—(Contributions in military studies, ISSN 0883–6884
; no. 103)
  Includes bibliographical references.
  ISBN 0–313–26373–6 (lib. bdg. : alk. paper)
  1. United States—Military policy.   2. Europe—Defenses.
3. United States—Military relations—Europe.   4. Europe—Military
relations—United States.   I. Title.   II. Series.
UA23.L484   1990
355'.033573—dc20   90–3132

British Library Cataloguing in Publication Data is available.

A paperback edition of *The Declining Hegemon* is available from
Praeger Publishers (ISBN 0–275–93657–0)

Library of Congress Catalog Card Number: 90–3132
ISBN: 0–313–26373–6
ISSN: 0883–6884

First published in 1990

Greenwood Press, 88 Post Road West, Westport, CT 06881
An imprint of Greenwood Publishing Group, Inc.

Printed in the United States of America

The paper used in this book complies with the
Permanent Paper Standard issued by the National
Information Standards Organization (Z39.48–1984).

10 9 8 7 6 5 4 3 2 1

Copyright Acknowledgments

The author and publisher gratefully acknowledge permission to use the following:

Kaufman, David J., Jeffrey S. McKitrick, and Thomas J. Leney, eds. *U.S. National
Security*. Lexington, Mass.: Lexington Books, D.C. Heath and Company. Copyright
© 1985 by D.C. Heath and Company. Reprinted by permission of D.C. Heath and
Company.

Smoke, Richard. "Extended Deterrence: Some Observations." *Naval War College
Review* 36, no. 5 (September-October 1983): 42.

To Nicki and Meghan, who were there
when it mattered, and to
Jordan, who arrived at the end.

Contents

Illustrations   ix

Acknowledgments   xi

1. The United States and Europe in the 1980s: Four Debates   1

2. Hegemonic Stability and Adaptation   33

3. Explaining Hegemonic Adaptation   69

4. The United States and European Defense, 1961–1965   111

5. The United States and European Defense, 1966–1973   137

6. The United States and European Defense, 1974–1980   163

7. Conclusions and Implications   195

   Bibliographic Essay   213

   Index   219

Illustrations

Table 1.1   U.S. Military Personnel in EUCOM Geographical Area   10

Table 1.2   Evolution of U.S. Extended Deterrence Strategies   12

Table 1.3   Ratio of U.S. Power Capabilities to World Total   14

Figure 1.1   Soviet and Western Nuclear Delivery Vehicles   15

Figure 2.1   Ikenberry's Typology of National Adjustment Strategies   35

Figure 2.2   An Amended Adjustment Typology   36

Figure 2.3   The Lag Between Economic and Military Ascendance   51

Figure 2.4   Adjusting Foreign Policy Commitments   60

Figure 3.1   Geopolitical Determinants of State Expansionism   78

Figure 3.2   International Goods and Hegemonic Control   100

Acknowledgments

This book owes much to many people. For help in locating a vast amount of secondary literature, I am in debt to the interlibrary loan staffs at the University of Louisville and Lawrence University. Several staff members of congressional committees provided reprints of important hearings. The reference staffs of the Kennedy, Johnson, and Ford libraries helped me find and get access to some important executive branch documents. Tom Sykes at the Lawrence Media Center did a splendid job preparing the graphics. I would particularly like to thank the many former government officials who took time from busy schedules for interviews. Several talked to me more than once, and some answered detailed follow-up questions in writing. Their candor helped me to sort through several confusing episodes.

I also owe thanks to my mentors. Stephen Krasner made certain that I kept my eye on the big picture. I also learned a lot from his own superb expository style. Alexander George helped me a good deal in thinking about the role that images and beliefs play in policy process. I would also like to thank Robert Jervis for helping me with this problem and David Lake and Rich Friman for very useful critiques of an early chapter draft.

My former teacher and colleague David Garnham was a tremendous source of help and inspiration. His knowledge of and interest in the issues dealt with in this book was, at times, a nearly bottomless resource. He was always willing to listen to an idea or read a draft, and his suggestions were invariably insightful and useful.

My family put up with this book longer than any of them care to remember, and I am deeply grateful. My parents were there at early stages financially and at later stages emotionally. My wife, Nicki Dean, and stepdaughter, Meghan Kline, had no idea when we met that American NATO policy would consume most of my time and thoughts for the next six years. I appreciate greatly their love, patience, and sense of perspective.

1 The United States and Europe in the 1980s: Four Debates

For over forty years, the United States has been committed to defending Western Europe, if necessary through nuclear warfare. Since 1951, that pledge has included at least 300,000 troops stationed on and offshore European territory. Assumption of these costs and risks marked a historic transition from peacetime isolationism to a very different role, that of sustaining the post–World War II non-Communist order. This was not an act of altruism: though no longer great powers, Europe's states controlled resources that made them the main geopolitical stakes of the Cold War. Keeping them anchored to America remains a key objective. Forward defense, required by Europe's location adjacent to Soviet-controlled territory, became the means to this end.

By a number of indicators, Europe is America's principal security commitment. Over one-half of the defense budget is spent on forces in or earmarked for Europe.[1] U.S. force structures and operational strategies, including those for large-scale nuclear war, are oriented mainly to the kind of conflict that would be fought in Europe, even though such a war is particularly unlikely. These priorities have changed little since the 1950s, although America's world position is now markedly different. The United States then had or approached first-strike nuclear capability vis-à-vis the Soviet Union, an unchallenged economic position within the Western bloc, and was fiscally sound. None of these was true thirty years later. Yet, as former Defense Secretary Schlesinger told Congress, "the degree of American commitment worldwide has not altered." Great powers, he said, cannot easily walk away from commitments; the corresponding risk—insufficient capabilities to meet them—must be accepted. "Try as we will, there is no acceptable way that we can escape from either these responsibilities or these risks."[2]

Neither these problems nor Schlesinger's response developed overnight. The first six chapters of this book examines the substance of and rationale for the American defense commitment to Europe between 1960 and 1980, a period of marked change in the U.S. world position. While there is spirited debate about the significance of these changes, few deny that America has lost the military, technological, and economic primacy of the 1950s. Partly as a result of such changes, commentators now ask whether the United States will remain a European power. The question is ironic in view of the Reagan administration's substantial efforts to revive American confidence, prestige, and leadership on East–West issues, but understandable in light of numerous problems and attitudes that erode the perceived community of American and European interests.[3]

Two substantive questions are explored in this study: how have political leaders adapted to these changes, and why? The latter is addressed as part of a second, broader objective, analysis of a "hegemonic" state's foreign policy adaptation. If, as Schlesinger suggests, policymakers have not adjusted basic policy priorities, what other tradeoffs have been made? Do these constitute meaningful patterns? Some of the answers to these questions depend on how policymakers treat interstate commitments. Are commitments tied to specific circumstances of time and power position, or are they more context-dependent and supple?

This chapter provides background for the analytic discussion of policy adaptation in chapters 2 and 3 and the case study of U.S. policy in chapters 4 through 6. After a brief discussion of what the American role in Europe entails, I summarize how it evolved before 1960. I then examine four debates that took place within the policy community—of policymakers, academicians, and other commentators—during the late 1970s and 1980s. These debates frame interpretations of past adaptation as well as future choices. One concerns the decline of U.S. power: there has been disagreement about indicators, the meaning of power, and policy implications. Since this book assumes that there has been an important decline, my position and those that refute it should be clear. Two others concern the future U.S. role in Europe. The issue here is which, if any, of the commitments undertaken in the early 1950s should be adjusted under present circumstances. Policy positions depend on assessments of stakes as well as burdens: do the advantages of present NATO arrangements outweigh the benefits of others that might cost significantly less? Such costs are assessed in light of differing perceptions of power, preferences, and expected outcomes. Each of these debates is related to a fourth: what is the appropriate relationship between foreign-policy commitments and resources? Should they decline together, just as they often grow together? This question is the leitmotif of the study as a whole.

THE U.S. DEFENSE ROLE IN EUROPE

Extended nuclear deterrence and a peacetime commitment of several hundred thousand troops are America's principal contributions to Europe's defense. While neither is formally specified in the North Atlantic Treaty or bilateral agreements, both are intrinsic components of the U.S. role in Europe. Extended deterrence is a conditional pledge to initiate nuclear war rather than permit NATO Europe to be defeated. In recent years, the "height" of the nuclear threshold—the level of conflict at which the pledge would be executed—has been debated in various fora. For reasons discussed throughout the book, North Atlantic Treaty Organization (NATO) government officials strongly oppose a "no first use" pledge. Another sensitive issue is troop deployment: numerous U.S. congressional representatives, some of them hard-liners, have linked it to greater European military contributions. If either commitment were significantly altered, the U.S. role would be redefined.

Extended Nuclear Deterrence

Extended deterrence policies threaten retaliation for attacks on allies; basic deterrence, in contrast, dissuades attacks on one's own territory. Since the 1940s, U.S. policy has compensated for conventional-forces shortfalls through the former. Partly because the Soviet Union is within easy reach of many American allies, and partly because the United States was largely invulnerable to a Soviet nuclear strike until the mid–1950s, extended deterrence preoccupied U.S. policymakers long before basic deterrence was perceived as problematic.[4] Almost by definition, threats that cover allies are less credible than basic deterrence. Since the United States has continued to rely on nuclear threats more than its adversaries,[5] extended deterrence has been and continues to be a major American strategic problem.

Two distinctions define the scope of first-nuclear-use commitments. One involves *what* is deterred: do nuclear responses cover conventional as well as nuclear attacks? This is a threshold issue; Flexible Response, which has been American policy since 1961, fudges the matter. But first use essentially obligates the United States to wage nuclear war rather than accept conventional defeat, and makes the deterrent against major conventional attack identical to that against all-out nuclear war.[6]

A second distinction involves the *degree* of military "coupling" between the deterrer's territory and others under the nuclear umbrella. Coupling denotes the probability that fighting in the forward theater will spread to the deterrer's homeland. (In purely military terms, this probability, ceterus paribus, is inversely related to the adequacy of the local defense.) U.S. allies have demanded tight coupling as a form of assurance, and American policymakers, largely out of fear that they would otherwise become neutralized (or worse), have acceded. One response has been thousands of nuclear weapons in Europe and others targeted on Soviet assets usable in a European war. Tight coupling increases the likelihood of nuclear escalation if deterrence fails.

First nuclear use implies willingness to launch a preemptive strike under some circumstances. Preemption has always been a key element of extended deterrence. Although it was most obvious during the 1950s, when U.S. declaratory policy suggested that the nuclear threshold was low, it remained an option under the Kennedy-McNamara posture of "flexible response."[7] First-strike options degrade nuclear stability—the absence of incentives for either side to preempt in a crisis—and thus work against other, important U.S. goals. First-use policies, based on the belief that a local conventional defense is impossible, thereby require preemptive attack on Soviet hard targets to limit damage from a retaliatory strike. Were Washington to agree with Moscow on an operational definition of nuclear ability, it would probably weaken extended deterrence.[8]

The Conventional Troop Deployment

American soldiers and airmen in Europe have served two roles. Only one has been military. During the Cold War, U.S. Seventh Army guarded 30 percent of the inter-German and Czech border and played a key role in defending critical central-front invasion routes from the east. Other major missions have included air defense and air support: U.S. Army units have manned much of the Alliance's air defense belt in southern Germany, and American tactical air units have played a key role in countering opposing Warsaw Pact tank formations. These missions have loomed large in view of NATO's repeated failures to meet its troop goals. Significant U.S. withdrawals that were not compensated by allied force additions would compromise forward defense and lower the nuclear threshold.[9]

U.S. troops have also performed two political functions. One applies to extended deterrence as well, especially if U.S.–European coupling is tight. To Europeans, the forces symbolize shared risk: the allies will not have to face an aggressor alone. Although it is bad form to call American forces hostages to full U.S. involvement, one of their political purposes has been to send this signal to Europe.

Sending the message to Moscow is another political function. While the Soviets have little doubt that Western Europe is a vital American interest, this is presumably reinforced by knowledge that U.S. troops would be immediately involved in virtually any military engagement. Some analysts interpret this dependence alarmingly: if significant numbers of U.S. troops were withdrawn and not replaced by local forces, NATO could be forced back to a form of massive nuclear retaliation. "[This] . . . would send a signal to Moscow that would not be ignored. By weakening NATO's conventional defenses, it would provide the Soviets a plausible way to inflict a quick military defeat on the alliance short of nuclear war."[10]

THE EVOLUTION OF THE NATO COMMITMENT: AN OVERVIEW

Present U.S. defense commitments to Europe did not develop easily. This was hardly surprising, given the strong tradition of non-entanglement in European affairs. In fact, the initial pledge was made under assumptions quite different from those that emerged after 1950. Recent historical work has emphasized this point: Until the creation of an organizational structure for the North Atlantic Treaty (NAT) and the deployment of additional U.S. forces that underpinned it, American military involvement in Europe was hesitant and sharply limited in scope.

Both the treaty itself and U.S. policy before the Korean War bespoke a limited effort. Few saw evidence of Soviet intent to attack Western Europe: the Russians had torn out their rail links through Poland to Germany. Even so, military planners, seeking to play it safe and avoid a World War II–type liberation operation, favored forward defense and, and as a prerequisite, automatic, large-scale U.S. military involvement. The State Department, White House, and Congress disagreed. The political consensus in Washington was that Europe's problem was mainly a lack of will, which could be reinforced by economic recovery. A full-scale U.S. military commitment was not required.[11]

But Moscow's forces in the center of the continent were intimidating and called for an interim military response. Until the Europeans could recover economically and do more for themselves, the Alliance relied on the nuclear guarantee. Linking the bomb to Europe's defense was the point of the NAT. During the late 1940s, U.S. leaders foresaw neither a standing, integrated army nor an American as Supreme Commander in Europe during peacetime.[12] Most professed to believe that the nuclear pledge was sufficient. Even at this early stage, first nuclear use, focused on European contingencies, was the basis of the Strategic Air Command's (SAC) war plans.[13]

These lopsided plans were largely dictated by congressional sentiment. Many legislators saw the European Recovery Program and the NAT as methods of bringing West Germany into the evolving Western security system and thus limiting U.S. efforts. They were thus interpreted as emergency measures rather than adjustments to a long-term shift in the distribution of power.[14]

In these circumstances, the Truman administration had to proceed slowly. The NAT itself, as an "entangling" alliance, went far enough for a Congress that was still largely isolationist. The Europeans had to settle for a loose pledge that each member would respond to an attack as it saw fit—considerably less than they wanted. France was especially adamant that Washington guarantee, through a substantial presence in Europe, against German as well as Soviet aggression. The treaty, however, specified neither the U.S. military contribution nor West Germany's role in the future military framework.[15] Since elements of the Truman administration and especially the Senate had priorities in both areas that differed sharply from the allies', the U.S. commitment was very vague during the late 1940s.

During these years the United States emerged from a century and a half of isolationism, pulled along by leaders determined to keep at least half of Europe out of hostile hands. Most soon concluded that the task would require German resources. For obvious reasons, the French strongly opposed German rearmament. U.S. officials, including Secretary of State Dean Acheson, thought this "all wrong,"[16] but were divided about how quickly to press the issue. The State Department feared that collective defense could be jeopardized if German participation led to noncooperation from Paris. In return for a U.S. ground-force contribution, the Pentagon demanded a viable defense posture, which was interpreted to include German troops. Without an emergency, this deadlock might have gone unresolved.

U.S. security policies and assumptions during this period were thus incoherent. On the one hand, while U.S. forces in Europe were weak, the real objective of the American guarantee was to restore European self-confidence. In this view, deterrence by punishment (the nuclear threat) was sufficient and a high-confidence defense was unnecessary. But few were certain about Soviet intentions or American ability to contain future probes. "Many decision makers realized, at least at times, that their beliefs implied the need for something more substantial. . . . Because the Soviet military threat could not be dismissed, the ability to protect Western Europe was a desired goal, albeit one that could not be reached because of the public's refusal to pay the price."[17] In early 1950, NSC–68, the policy memorandum that defined the security threat in global terms, catalogued the perceived mismatch between threats and defense preparedness. That document argued that a Soviet nuclear weapons capability would require a Western theater defense in Europe and much higher defense spending.

The Korean War resolved some of the incoherence between ends and means in two ways.[18] One was a sizable increase in defense spending, which allowed the administration to begin implementing the program contained in NSC–68. Korea produced this result because the Communist threat suddenly seemed much more tangible and more money was needed to fight the war. Once this happened, the fiscal and political arguments against a larger defense effort lost much of their force.

Korea also led to the second component of the U.S. commitment: forces-in-being to complement the nuclear guarantee. While the Asian war had little direct relevance to Europe, it considerably heightened the sense of threat. The attack came less than a year after Moscow acquired nuclear weapons and ended the U.S. monopoly, which gave force to the position taken in NSC–68. Divided Korea also bore an unpleasant resemblance to Germany, and some saw the invasion as a potential diversion for aggression in Europe. The allies soon appraised the situation more calmly, and thereafter failed to meet agreed-upon conventional forces goals. Nevertheless, East-West battle lines had become more sharply drawn. As Acheson later put it, security threats now had to be met by credible deterrence, not the promise of liberation.[19]

Some observers, including former policymakers, have argued that the extra ground forces were unnecessary or even needlessly provocative. The latter is true to the extent that the ensuing buildup solidified the division of Europe and intensified mutual security fears. These outcomes, though, may have been unavoidable at the time. A stronger case might be made for the former: Charles

Bohlen later claimed that a small increase in the U.S. defense budget could have substituted for the standing army.[20] The proposition turns partly on Moscow's intentions at the time, which are unknown even with forty years' hindsight. Decision makers were, in any case, mainly interested in reassuring Europe. Acheson and others worried about allied "will to resist" and nonmilitary conquest.[21] A consensus was soon reached that only U.S. troops could provide the necessary reassurances. As will be seen in subsequent chapters, the U.S. commitment continues to rest largely on this rationale.

These considerations, heightened by the Korean attack, made German rearmament more urgent than before. Neither Washington nor London believed that Europe could be protected without a German contribution; both also felt that the German people required a psychological stake in their own defense. The Truman administration pressed the issue because it decided that defense on the ground had to supplement the nuclear guarantee. Had it calculated differently, Bohlen's retrospective advice might have been taken.

Given French sensitivities, this decision made a substantial U.S. contribution even more necessary to balance the Germans. Domestic U.S. politics, on the other hand, demanded that the Europeans appear to be making a comparable effort. For Congress, this meant a meaningful German role.[22]

The precise link was shaped by months of hard bargaining. Acheson was keenly sensitive to France's German phobia and favored only loose strings on a U.S. deployment. Moreover, Korea convinced him that forward defense, using German resources, had become urgent. In September 1950, in response to the president's demand for a coherent policy, he agreed to the Pentagon's demand for a package plan that linked German and American troop participation. When the French response—the Pleven Plan for a fully integrated European army— seemed only a delaying tactic, Washington caved in to Paris, setting a pattern in which U.S. officials made tangible commitments in return for promises of future cooperation.

Under what became known as the Spofford Compromise (named for the deputy U.S. representative to the North Atlantic Council), the United States decoupled its troop commitment from immediate German rearmament. An American Supreme Commander and four additional divisions would be provided immediately; in return, France accepted the eventual participation of German units below division size. President Truman announced the pledge in September; in December, the North Atlantic Council, the Alliance's highest decision-making body, finalized the agreement. Paris and Washington each achieved its minimum objectives: The former got U.S. troops and a delay in German rearmament, while the latter got NATO agreement on eventual German participation. This bargain, rather than the initial North Atlantic Treaty, established an integrated NATO command structure and set the size of the American conventional contribution.[23]

The Senate also had to agree to this arrangement, and there was resistance. Some came from committed isolationists opposed to any deepening of the original, vague guarantee. This was overcome fairly easily, but a second faction, represented by such traditional conservatives as Robert Taft and Richard Russell, worried that if U.S. troops were placed in an integrated command, they could not be removed.[24] It seems that the administration, having just appeased France over the timing of German rearmament, withheld information regarding the impact of the German factor in defining the four-division commitment. That pledge, as part of a three-sided deal, was far deeper than publicly admitted at the time. The administration skirted the issue by focusing exclusively on the Soviet threat. This, too, would set a long-term pattern. In this way, the Senate was led to interpret the move as temporary—to use a concept introduced in Chapter 2, a "situational" commitment.[25]

On April 5, 1951, two years after approval of the NAT, the Senate approved General Dwight D. Eisenhower as Supreme Allied Commander Europe (SACEUR) and declared that Western security required the deployment of "such units of our armed forces as may be necessary and appropriate to contribute our fair share . . . for the joint defense of the North Atlantic area."[26] The resolution, however, also stipulated that no additional ground troops could be sent without further legislative approval.

As this suggests, the troop commitment raised the issue of relative effort. It has remained a sore spot with Congress for forty years. Most senators were sensitive about it, and a few pressed administration witnesses about how the adequacy or fairness of European defense contributions would be determined. Eisenhower and Secretary of Defense George Marshall tried to deflect them by arguing that U.S. troops were mainly intended to build the Europeans' morale and give them incentives to do more for themselves. According to NSC–82, officials "hoped that the United States will be able to leave to European nation-members [of NATO] the primary responsibility of maintaining and commanding such a force."[27] Eisenhower also said that if the allies did not "measure up . . . I think we would have to take steps." Such options, however, were left unspecified, and the administration signaled its priorities by refusing to state a fixed ratio of American participation.[28] The executive branch's perspective clearly differed from Congress's. Reassurances and forward defense were more important to the former than burden sharing; legislators weighed them more equally.

These differences were understandable. A viable forward defense would require substantial European efforts. U.S. officials have therefore continued to press the issue on strategic grounds; as seen in Chapter 4, this caused much trans-Atlantic friction during the early 1960s. But this has not been the norm: between 1950 and 1980, reassuring Europe was usually more important to central decision makers. It has inclined them to emphasize the continuity of the conventional commitment as a symbol of U.S. staying power. Better burden-sharing arrangements are thus seen more as ways to pacify Congress than as ends in themselves. These contrasting perspectives are emphasized here both because they explain much of U.S. policy and because the allies have often behaved in ways that cause political problems for their natural allies in the executive branch. In the early 1950s, "the Europeans were willing to promise to increase their defense spending and to agree in principle to German rearmament, not so much because they thought it was feasible or necessary to defend Europe, but because they wanted to deepen the American commitment."[29] This continues to be true: Europeans will not do more so long as U.S. policymakers hold present priorities.

This is a continuing source of tension within the alliance because Americans, especially congressional representatives, are more sensitive to the costs of the conventional troops than the risks of first use. These pressures may be mitigated in either of two ways during the early 1990s. At NATO's fortieth anniversary summit in mid–1989, President George Bush proposed a common ceiling of 275,000 U.S. and Soviet troops in Europe, a 20 percent cut in American combat forces. More recently, the Bush administration has set a target of 195,000 American troops. While an accord would require proportionately larger Soviet reductions, Moscow's interest appears strong. Furthermore, as discussed later in this chapter, long-term domestic support for the deployment is more tenuous in the early 1990s than it has been in nearly twenty years. Late in the Reagan administration, Defense Secretary Frank Carlucci, in contrast to his predecessor, chose to accommodate shrinking real defense budgets by pruning force size—100,000 personnel over five years—rather than degrade combat readiness. While no immediate cuts were planned for Europe, those commitments will almost certainly be reduced if budgetary pressures continue.[30] As Table 1.1 indicates, this Europe-first priority has characterized U.S. defense allocations for nearly forty years.

Despite cuts during the Vietnam era, this indicates a commitment of significant size and continuity. The number of troops in Europe at the beginning of the 1980s was 77 percent of the greatest number, and only 17,000 less than the mean of 345,875. Considering just ground forces, there were four divisions, several brigades, and two armored cavalry regiments in Europe during the late 1970s, for a total of almost six divisions—fairly close to the original deployment. No major cuts have been made in these forces since the late 1960s. The initial wartime commitment is ten divisions. All these units are "heavy," that is, composed of either armored or mechanized battalions using large numbers of antitank weapons, artillery, and personnel carriers. The twelve divisions pledged to Europe after a first-wave reinforcement were three-fourths of the sixteen total Army active force divisions maintained in the late 1970s. The garrison also included, before reinforcement, approximately 500 tactical aircraft, of a total of 1,680 in 1980.[31]

Extended deterrence in Europe involves neither expensive nor highly visible troop deployments, and thus has been less controversial in the United States. Nevertheless, U.S. crisis behavior has apparently exacerbated the obvious risks of first-use policies. Drawing on newly available primary documents, Richard Betts shows that American presidents have made nuclear threats without thinking through the consequences. Although no president after Truman doubted America's vulnerability to devastating Soviet retaliation, most exhibited a "peculiarly facile" tendency to use nuclear threats where at least *they* perceived vital interests

Table 1.1
U.S. Military Personnel in EUCOM Geographical Area* (Nearest Thousand—Approximate)

End 1950	145
End 1951	346
End 1952	405
End 1953	427
End 1954	404
End 1955	405
End 1956	398
End 1957	393
End 1958	380
End 1959	380
End 1960	379
End 1961	417
End 1962	416
End 1963	380
End 1964	374
End 1965	363
End 1966	366
End 1967	337
End 1968	316
End 1969	300
End 1970	291
End 1971	303
End 1972	307
End 1973	300
End 1974	300
End 1975	303
End 1976	308
End 1977	318
End 1978	325
End 1979	330
End 1980	323
End 1981	329

* Includes Army, Air Force, Navy, and Marines Corps (ashore and afloat) and small numbers of military personnel in non-NATO countries in the EUCOM geographical area (e.g., Austria and Switzerland). In 1982, Congress established a ceiling on U.S. military personnel ashore in NATO Europe of 326,414.

Source: U.S. Department of Defense, mimeo, no date.

at stake: "in a sense, the people at the top sometimes appeared to grit their teeth, close their eyes, and forge ahead."[32]

This crutch has been less affected by Soviet achievement of nuclear parity than might be assumed. Although the U.S. nuclear threshold is certainly higher than it was in the 1950s, *any* first-use commitment might logically presuppose

U.S. ability to limit damage from the Soviet counterstrike. Since Soviet capabilities have long made this impossible, what explains such risky behavior?

Three factors stand out. First, official definitions of nuclear parity have been deliberately left vague. The Carter and Ford administrations, both of which tried to codify the offensive strategic balance in arms treaties, preferred the more flexible term "essential nuclear equivalence." Such latitude was necessary to find a package of offsetting asymmetries in the two sides' arsenals that could be sold to domestic hawks as well as Moscow. Whether the Soviets in fact ever achieved parity depended on which of several definitions was used; some preserved residual U.S. advantages into the mid–1970s.[33]

Second, while most Europeans pay little attention to technical indices of nuclear capabilities and much more to the general state of the trans-Atlantic relationship and U.S. self-confidence, U.S. policymakers lack confidence in this. Americans have assumed that Europe's resolve to resist Soviet pressure depends largely on U.S. strength and staying power. This makes it important to examine U.S. images of weak European resolve, discussed in chapters 5 and 6. Finally, as Betts emphasizes, U.S. leaders have been fortified by assumptions that what strategists call the "balance of resolve" would continue to favor them in the East-West competition. Since they viewed themselves as the status quo power and their adversaries as revisionists, they believed that the latter would more readily back down. Betts is not optimistic about the outcome of any future crises, since an advantageous balance of nuclear power is no longer available as a prop.

In sum, even though the commitment has been incrementally adjusted, U.S. policy remains pledged to conditional first nuclear use. Table 1.2 summarizes the evolution of American extended deterrence concepts.

First use has been strategically problematic since Moscow acquired nuclear weapons. One response has been to make plans for limited, theater use of nuclear weapons that could, perhaps, render U.S. threats less than completely catastrophic and therefore minimally credible. What follows refers to the theater weapons that link Europe to the U.S. strategic arsenal and would likely be used early in a major European conflict.

From its first year in office, the Eisenhower administration nuclearized U.S. combat units with virtually no public debate at home or in Europe. As of mid–1989, about 4,000 short-range nuclear weapons were stored on the territories of seven NATO allies; this reflected unilateral reductions of over 2,400 weapons during the 1980s and the smallest tactical nuclear arsenal in Europe since the early 1960s.[34] If NATO abandons flexible response to ease Soviet acceptance of a united Germany in the alliance, removal of all such weapons from Europe would likely follow. Nevertheless, they remain thoroughly integrated into battlefield planning; despite NATO's adoption of flexible response in 1967, intended by U.S. civilian officials to raise the nuclear threshold, " there have been no fundamental changes in NATO nuclear procedures since the early 1950s."[35]

Consequently, what began as cheap deterrence evolved into efforts to reinforce a fairly low nuclear threshold. By the late 1950s tactical nuclear war in Europe

Table 1.2

Evolution of U.S. Extended Deterrence Strategies

Significant Soviet attack on U.S. allies deterred by	Principal requirements for credible deterrent threat
1. Massive strategic attacks on opponent's territory	1. Substantial strategic superiority: the opponent's counter-strike can do modest damage at most
2. Initiation of theater nuclear war	2. Substantial theater nuclear force superiority: opponent has only few or soft TNF capabilities in the theater
3. Flexible Response	
(a) Conventional defense is sufficient: nuclear threshold nuclear threshold need not be crossed. (Most theaters well outside Soviet periphery.)	(a) Conventional force superiority, at least after reinforcements arrive in theater. Presumes no defeat in in theater before they arrive.
(b) Uncertain or likely losing conventional defense, with the threat of controlled or uncontrolled escalation thereafter. (Most theaters on the Soviet periphery)	(b) Some interpretations require escalation dominance: superiority or at least parity at each level of violence Other interpretations require only mutual second-strike capability, with explicit threats to escalate, perhaps uncontrollably, if as the level of violence increases.
4. Limited Nuclear Options few accurate weapons.	4. No requirements beyond a few accurate weapons. Advocates claim that it is more credible than threatening all-out nuclear war.

Source: Adapted from Richard Smoke, "Extended Deterrence: Some Observations," *Naval War College Review* (September/October 1983), p. 42.

appeared preferable to an intercontinental exchange, even though NATO would thereby destroy what it was trying to defend. U.S. allies were threatened with troop withdrawals unless they gave blanket permission for use of the weapons and kept quiet about it.[36] As more recent developments have shown, allied governments have always been torn over this issue: their people would neither pay for an adequate conventional defense nor welcome the prospect of becoming nuclear battlegrounds.

The results predispose NATO toward early use of nuclear weapons in a conflict. Its commanders have never believed that the Alliance could resist an all-out Warsaw Pact thrust without them and presumably have calculated accordingly.

Since many of the theater delivery systems are dual-capable (i.e., can fire both nuclear and conventional munitions), some commanders might withhold them early in a conflict, expecting authorization to use nuclear weapons. Furthermore, NATO's complex consultation procedures make it likely that a decision to cross the nuclear threshold would be made before the Alliance's conventional defenses had been fully tested.[37]

Political leaders judge these risks to be tolerable because America's first-use pledge has kept the Alliance together, the prospect of a European war is very low, and there has been no politically acceptable alternative. NATO's nonnuclear defenses are more than simply a "plate glass": though this may have been true in the 1950s, it is not today. But as long as nuclear and conventional weapons are so thoroughly mixed on the battlefield, the nuclear threshold remains too low for many and a risk to the United States.

This review indicates that commitments to Europe have remained largely the same since the early 1950s. Yet many assert that relative capabilities have declined and that the two are mismatched. This is not a new idea; Eisenhower feared lest America become overcommitted and did not favor a long-term troop commitment.[38] Yet U.S. pledges, for reasons explained in later chapters, quickly became rigid. Declining hegemony led to less policy change than might have been assumed, and the American policy community is now debating some of the consequences.

FOUR POLICY DEBATES

Despite Ronald Reagan's attempts to bolster U.S. military capabilities and self-confidence, many Americans remained dubious about the costs and long-term prospects of standing tall. Four related debates that bear on the U.S. role in Europe took place during Reagan's presidency. Each involved both academicians and practitioners. Each is the subject of an extensive literature, and many readers will be familiar with them. Brief summaries and critiques will indicate that they frame the major issues of this book.

Has Hegemonic Decline Taken Place?

America's global position during the 1970s and 1980s was undeniably weaker than it had been a generation earlier. The real issue in all the debates was whether it remained a "hegemonic" power—a "state powerful enough to maintain the essential rules governing interstate relations, and willing to do so."[39] Within NATO, these rules amount to the existing distribution of burdens and responsibilities: Europeans provide most of the alliance's peacetime personnel, tanks, aircraft, and reserves, but America contributes virtually all the nuclear weapons, shares the risks of first use, and keeps six divisions in Europe.

Long-term, irreversible decline is clearest from resource-base indicators. As

Table 1.3
Ratio of U.S. Power Capabilities to World Total

	1950	1960	1970	1976
National Income	.52	.45	.39	.31
Crude Petroleum Production	.53	.33	.21	.14
Crude Steel Production	.45	.26	.20	.17
Iron Ore Production	.42	.19	.13	.10
Wheat Production	.17	.15	.12	.14
International Financial Reserves	.49	.21	.16	.07
Military Expenditures	.32	.48	.35	.27
Exports	.18	.16	.14	.11
Foreign Aid		.58	.45	.32

Sources: Stephen Krasner, '' American Policy and Global Economic Stability,'' in William P. Avery and David P. Rapkin, eds. *America in a Changing World Political Economy* (New York: Longman, 1982), p. 38: Henry Kissinger, *Years of Upheaval* (Boston: Little, Brown, 1982), p. 238.

Table 1.3 and Figure 1.1 indicate, U.S. relative capabilities declined in every category from 1950 to the 1970s. Even as Soviet attainment of nuclear parity made the conventional balance more important, Soviet long-range projection capabilities grew significantly during the 1970s. Most important, however, was the loss of America's huge productive and technological advantages. Modern weapons are so capital intensive that cutting-edge technology is necessary to continuing military advantage. The U.S. position as alliance leader was thus threatened as its share of GNP and GDP among the top seven industrial states shrunk from about 70 percent to about 43 percent between 1950 and 1987.[40]

Some argue that this is less than meets the eye. If the essence of power is the ability to control outcomes, relative resource erosion may not be directly relevant. This fundamentally is the claim of those who assert that America can still play leadership roles in international politics, particularly in its major alliance relationships.

Bruce Russett, Susan Strange, and Samuel Huntington have taken this position. None denies that U.S. capabilities have declined relative to others', but all note how skewed global resources were just after 1945. America is still, in this view, a very strong country by virtually every quantitative indicator. But this line of argument rests on the distinction between power resources and favorable results, not relative advantages in resources. The United States effectively reordered the international system after World War II, and continues to reap substantial benefits from the resulting arrangements.

Each of these scholars emphasizes the importance of structural power, that is, "the ability to define the context in which others must make decisions."[41]

Figure 1.1
Soviet and Western Nuclear Delivery Vehicles

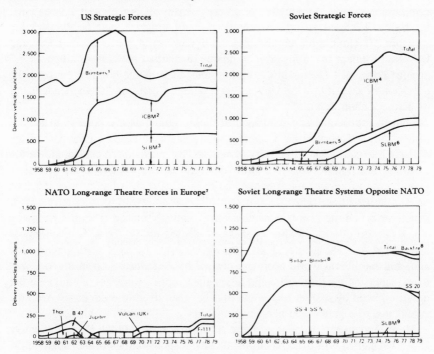

Source: Modified from DOD data of October 1979 by the author.

[1]B-47 and B-52 bombers, excluding B-47 based in Europe.

[2]*Atlas, Titan* and *Minuteman.*

[3]Number of tubes on U.S. *Polaris* and *Poseidon* SSBN. Includes SLBM dedicated to SACEUR.

[4]SS-7, -8, -9, -11, -13, -17, -18 and -19.

[5]*Bear* and *Bison.*

[6]SLBM tubes on active submarines.

[7]Does not include French Forces or 400 *Polaris/Poseidon* warheads assigned to SACEUR or British SLBM.

[8]Excluding naval versions.

[9]SLBM tubes directed against NATO.

Source: From Daniel J. Kaufman, Jeffrey S. McKitrick, and Thomas J. Leney, eds., *U.S. National Security: A Framework for Analysis* (Lexington, Mass.: Lexington Books, 1985).

The results include "stable peace" within the non-Communist industrialized world, which supports a thriving world economy and Western containment policies; open world economic arrangements for trade, capital, and investment, which have certainly benefited the United States; and, less tangibly, pervasive American cultural influence. As compared to the pre–1945 international environment, these changes served key United States interests, often without application of direct leverage.[42] Strange highlights the structural power derived from the "security structure" (allied dependence on U.S. nuclear and conventional commitments), the "production structure" (many of the biggest international firms are still American), the international credit structure, and the "knowledge structure."[43] Huntington emphasizes the dynamism of the U.S. economy and U.S. involvement in "a historically unique diversified network of alliances."[44] Strange concurs: "always in the background, there is the contrast between the provision of security by the United States defense forces and the dependence of its partners upon them."[45]

Both the substance and relevance of these arguments are open to criticism. Robert Gilpin observes that U.S. hegemony has been based on the role of the dollar in the international monetary system and the provision of nuclear protection to allies. The dollar's role has surely declined as compared with the pre–1971 period, when foreign central banks had to hold it; such behavior now depends on its relative attractiveness compared with other assets. In broader terms, U.S. structural economic power depended on a relatively closed domestic economy and access to others. Neither of these is assured today: the U.S. economy is disciplined to a far greater degree by international markets than a generation ago, and the liberal world economy desired by American elites has given way to an increasingly nationalistic and regionalized one.[46] Nuclear commitments are not disciplined by market forces and thus have survived, though hardly with the confidence of a generation ago.

More fundamentally, none of these arguments addresses the kind of adaptive choices America will make about its alliance responsibilities or has made in the past. For three reasons, structural power is irrelevant to these issues.

First, structural power is valuable only if others' vulnerability is turned to political advantage. Indeed, America and Western Europe are politically closer than they would be without the security guarantee, and this benefits the United States. But as I show in later chapters, U.S. leaders have been so afraid of allied "Finlandization"—Europe's alleged willingness to meet certain Soviet foreign-policy demands in return for negligible defense requirements and domestic autonomy—that they have been reluctant to use Europe's dependence as a lever to shift relative burdens. They hesitated even to pressure allies to compensate for U.S. out-of-area efforts in the Persian Gulf until congressional demands made the problem impossible for them to ignore. Direct nuclear risks to the U.S. have been somewhat reduced by a higher threshold over the past 25 years, but not enough to reduce the felt need for early nuclear use in a war. This contrasts sharply with the evolution of America's role in the postwar economic regime. Here, as the margin of advantage discussed earlier eroded, U.S. policy priorities shifted: beginning in the late 1960s, national commercial and monetary interests began to supercede concern for the system as a whole.[47] American willingness to maintain costly essential rules (such as an overvalued dollar) and pay for collective goods has declined. Comparable adjustments will occur within NATO, but U.S. leaders have not thus far expedited them.

Second, a declining hegemon's relative opportunity costs will grow even if its structural power remains intact. A military establishment large enough to permit *peacetime* deployment of 300,000 troops in Europe posed more severe tradeoffs in the 1970s and 1980s than a decade or two earlier. Because the countries benefiting from this protection are some of America's principal commercial and technological competitors and they have been able to hold military spending significantly below U.S. rates, these opportunity costs have increased as American technological advantages and share of world markets have declined.[48]

A third reason involves distinctive requirements of alliance or bloc leaders. William T. R. Fox, who coined the term "superpower," identified two requirements: "great power plus great mobility of power."[49] The importance of the latter—capacity to project one's presence and, if necessary, to apply force for sustained periods at various geographic points—casts doubt on Strange's claims that structural power now decides outcomes more than "relational" power, and that since the former has actually increased in certain respects since 1945, America's position has improved. Relational power is control over others' specific behavior. Since the 1960s, the United States has faced increasing difficulty in getting allies' support for its preferences in a variety of areas.[50] Insofar as U.S. mobility requires sustained cooperation from others, particularly for access to bases and overflight permits, relational power is especially important.[51]

Despite their complexity, some conclusions can be drawn about these issues. Relative capabilities have eroded, though this has been exaggerated by swings in America's public mood.[52] The U.S. has less day-to-day leverage over others, including allies, than a generation ago, but perhaps considerable unused structural leverage. America *acts* less as a beneficent hegemon than it did a generation ago, though this has affected economic more than security commitments.

Since this book discusses policy adaptation during the 1960s and 1970s, the debate about hegemonic decline might appear relevant only in hindsight. This is mistaken. While evidence of economic erosion became inescapable only during the Carter and Reagan administrations, the foundations of U.S. primacy, including military superiority over the Soviet Union, had been deteriorating for some time. The issue has never been one of absolute capability, but whether the country was growing or selling abroad enough to afford its external obligations without higher domestic costs. Chapter 4 shows that John F. Kennedy worried about this during the early 1960s. As Western Europe and Japan recovered from World War II and some less developed countries went through the take-off growth phase, America's share of world product declined much more in the first two postwar decades than in the 1970s and 1980s.[53] Likewise, the first-use commitment had lost considerable credibility by the mid–1960s; since then, "all that has changed is the *degree* of doubt in extended deterrence."[54] In consequence, no administration after Kennedy's could prudently assume that America's extraordinary dominance would last; the question for each was how to manage or cushion the decline.

Do Commitments Exceed Available Capabilities?

The first debate has been inconclusive, largely because the criteria against which to assess U.S. decline are rarely specified. Perhaps they cannot be. "If 'hegemony' means having 40 percent or more of world economic activity . . . American hegemony disappeared long ago. If hegemony means producing 20 to 25 percent of the world product and twice as much as any individual country, American hegemony looks quite secure."[55] America's usable nuclear-weapons capability is likewise hard to specify: aside from homeland invulnerability, which cannot be regained, what does first use require? Is escalation dominance—the ability to prevail at higher levels of conflict if defeat at lower levels is likely— necessary? General assessments are difficult because the requirements of some commitments, such as deterrence, are indeterminate; others, such as those needed for economic leadership, depend a good deal on domestic perceptions of cost and benefit.

Analytically, there are two problems. First, few if any countries have had America's degree of dominance or nearly so ambitious a foreign policy. Historical analogies about other overextended hegemons thus have to be interpreted cautiously. Second, there is no isomorphic relationship between tangible capabilities and a hegemon's leadership role. Much depends on mutual feelings of confidence (the hegemon's self-assurance and others' willingness to depend on it) and a broad sense of national interests in the leading state.

Nevertheless, by the 1980s America was commonly characterized as overextended. Foreign commitments were seen to exceed available fiscal and military means. In this view, ends had to be matched to available resources: reduced foreign obligations and more investment at home were common prescriptions.

Even those who disagreed usually began from a familiar reference point. In 1943 Walter Lippmann asserted "the controlling principle that the nation must maintain its objectives and its power in equilibrium . . . its commitments related to its resources and its resources adequate to its commitments."[56] Three basic positions emerged in this debate. One held that external retrenchment, preferably in Europe, was necessary to meet Lippmann's criterion. Another claimed that Americans could easily afford the 7 percent (or less) of GNP they spent on external security. A third, perhaps more cynical, view held that Lippmann's desideratum had no policy relevance: great powers always overextend themselves.

The most sweeping and best known version of the first position came from Paul Kennedy. American grand strategy—the relationship between ends (security, wealth, future growth) and means (achievable military, economic, and diplomatic capability)—had become seriously unbalanced. Except for Vietnam, the United States had about the same defense commitments in the 1980s as two decades earlier, when its shares of world product, military spending, and forces under arms were much higher. America had thus fallen victim to "imperial overstretch," the tendency of declining hegemons to maintain their military position at the expense of long-term investment and productive capacity.[57] The implication—what Kennedy calls "sensible" adjustment "to the new world order"—is devolution of some commitments to allies.

Abundant evidence supported this argument, as was evident from the Reagan administration's peacetime plans for foreign troop deployments:

Overseas basing of United States forces will continue in Europe, the Western Pacific, Latin America, and, when circumstances permit, in Southwest Asia. Naval and air forces will provide for a continuous presence of combatant forces in the North Atlantic, Caribbean, Mediterranean, Western Pacific, and Indian Ocean/Southwest Asia regions. Selective deployments of significant forces will be made to South America, Africa, Southeast Asia and the Southwest Pacific. Ground and air deployments will periodically be made to Southwest Asia, as political considerations permit.[58]

Many strategists found this indiscriminate, even as a wish list. Jeffrey Record attacked the "vast and disparate accumulation of old and new military obligations unattended by the military means sufficient to fill them. The heart of the problem lies less in the obligations themselves . . . [than] in the unwillingness of the United States to match its declared military ends with commensurate military means."[59] This pattern existed long before Reagan took office. Military officers, well aware of constraints on spending and force size, have repeatedly made these points to civilians. Commitments, such as defense of the Persian Gulf, are typically added without the means to honor them; ammunition, training, fuel, and spare parts get short-changed. Whether these are acceptable tradeoffs is discussed below, but the consequences are sobering. In the mid–1980s, NATO Commander Bernard Rogers said that low ammunition stocks would force a decision to use nuclear weapons early in a major war— disturbing, to say the least, in view of long U.S. efforts to raise the nuclear threshold.[60]

Chronic shortfalls in personnel and equipment are accompanied by a persistent fiscal gap. Both are part of a larger pattern: just as Americans will not provide forces adequate to commitments, they won't pay for the forces they do buy. In this line of reasoning, NATO's claim on the U.S. defense budget make it part of the problem.

As David Calleo sees it, Americans have not been willing to pay enough taxes to support defense and entitlement programs. History has taught them to view defense preparation as an emergency measure that can be financed by debt. Since no country, however powerful, can sustain this indefinitely, and the U.S. defense role is easier to change than internal characteristics such as an aversion to fiscal collectivism, devolution of some defense commitments is suggested. "Once the pretension to run European defense is abandoned, America's standing contribution to Europe's territorial defense can be limited to the equivalent of two or three heavy divisions, with perhaps another division or two in the continental United States earmarked for Europe. . . . a refashioned American army might total around ten divisions, a drastic cut from the traditional sixteen."[61]

Others acknowledge a gap but do not believe it demands such far-reaching measures. Huntington advocates a variety of steps that could cumulatively strengthen the U.S. position. On cost-effectiveness grounds, nuclear deterrence should be strengthened, not weakened; the same applies to offensive conventional strategies in Europe and liberal use of security assistance. The Pentagon should be reorganized to emphasize major strategic missions; the services should be allowed only to "bid" for them. Over the longer term, the budget deficit and underinvestment in technology and human resources must be reversed. Meanwhile, he rejects cuts in commitments. The allies will probably not fill the shortfall, and America can perform these same tasks more efficiently. Instead, the allies should pay the U.S. some significant share of the costs of existing obligations.[62]

Richard Kugler takes issue with Calleo more directly. Kugler emphasizes several factors: Europe's overriding strategic value, which, he asserts, has kept the basic commitment intact during other austerity periods; the relatively low annual operating costs ($2 billion) of U.S. troops in Europe; the improved readiness and mobility of U.S. forces available for other contingencies, due largely to the Reagan buildup. In his view, "uncovering" Europe would weaken deterrence there and, if the forces were disbanded, worldwide. On the other hand, since the Reagan defense buildup "had its desired strategic effect of keeping U.S. defense capabilities aligned with their global requirements,"[63] withdrawals are unnecessary.

Aaron Friedberg critiques Calleo's and Kennedy's positions on broader grounds. Calleo's fiscal arguments, he claims, do not stand up: since the budget deficits were not produced by defense spending alone, major cuts in military commitments are not fiscally imperative. On a number of counts, Friedberg likewise disputes Kennedy's contention that declining hegemons face progressively higher defense opportunity costs. Defense spending neither necessarily crowds out private investment nor causes a brain drain from the civilian to the military sector. Because American culture is hostile to statist economic management, there is also little reason to believe that lower defense spending alone would lead to more government-sponsored nondefense research.[64]

Finally, according to William Kaufmann, whose views are close to Schlesinger's and whom he advised as Defense Secretary, a "minimum-risk" force posture is too expensive. A smaller force entails added risks, albeit tolerable ones. The idea that capabilities must match commitments is thus a "myth." The real issue is how much decision makers are willing or able to pay to reduce those risks.[65]

Huntington's and Kugler's arguments are quite different from Kaufmann's, though all reject major cuts in commitments. Through overly optimistic or misleading assumptions, Huntington and Kugler either exaggerate the likelihood of reducing costs or minimize existing costs. In Huntington's case, how the U.S. will extract greater contributions from its allies when it has largely failed to do so for 40 years is unclear. He admits that "the relative decline in American power both enhances the need for allies to increase their contribution to the common defense and reduces the ability of the United States to persuade them to do so."[66] On the other hand, by pricing U.S. forces in Europe at $2 billion a year, Kugler notes only the direct operating costs of forces deployed there; he ignores the far larger share of the defense budget (estimated by the Pentagon itself as over half) that directly or indirectly supports U.S. obligations.

Friedberg's analysis, less tied to immediate policy issues than Kugler's or Huntington's, is closely reasoned but not entirely convincing. He admits that America's postwar economic performance was generally less impressive than Europe's and Japan's even after the latter passed the steep phase of the growth curve, and that U.S. investment has suffered due both to defense spending and private consumption.[67] And even if high U.S. civilian consumption was largely responsible for low investment and growth, would a consumption tax, an alternative to defense cuts, be as politically acceptable as the latter? Surely America's aversion to taxes, a point Calleo makes quite convincingly, is as much a part of the country's individualistic culture as opposition to centralized planning.

Political leaders whose citizens do not want to fight might seem too risk-averse to accept Kaufmann's position. If so, the constraints on national security planners during the 1970s—significant growth in Soviet capabilities and declining defense budgets—should have led to reduced defense responsibilities, not new ones. But this was not the case: new commitments in the Persian Gulf were guaranteed by some of the same forces pledged to NATO. Given Moscow's greater proximity to both theaters, its interior lines of communication, and its larger forces, the Carter Doctrine (which explicitly committed the United States to safeguard the Persian Gulf) exemplifies Kaufmann's viewpoint.

As discussed in chapter 2, accepting higher risks is one way of adjusting to increased constraints. This is not without precedent and perhaps justification. Great powers by definition have system-wide interests, and few have maintained sufficient forces in peacetime to cover them all. The costs are clearly prohibitive. Policymakers also assume that they will not have to defend every commitment simultaneously, certainly not unilaterally.[68] Still, by the 1970s, earlier adaptive strategies had become more problematic. Nuclear parity precluded Eisenhower's policy of substituting nuclear for conventional strength, and, as indicated above, American leverage over allies was also weaker. In short, the United States has had increasing difficulty maintaining its systematic position as relative capabilities have declined.

Should Commitments to Europe Be Revised?

These considerations fed two other debates: for the first time since 1950, both the nuclear and conventional commitments were seriously questioned by Amer-

ican elites. NATO watchers are usually self-critical, but the degree of dissatis-
faction during the 1980s was unusual. Moreover, there was significant overlap
with the first two debates—that is, with broader issues of American capability
and willingness to lead the Alliance. Nevertheless, nuclear risks and allied
burden-sharing were discussed largely in isolation from one another.

For many Americans, particularly congressional representatives, burden-sharing had become a domestic political issue. It involved broad societal priorities,
not specific allied defense contributions. They argued that by the most common
measure, share of GNP devoted to defense, America did substantially and consistently more than its allies. Virtually everyone agreed that other NATO members needed to rectify the imbalance. Beyond this, however, there were key
differences in goals and tactics. Some, mainly in the executive branch, wanted
Europe to do more mainly to keep the existing U.S. contribution intact. A
growing group believed that Europeans would have no incentive to do more
unless the U.S. did less.

By the mid-1980s, many legislators were frustrated by the division of defense
burdens. A few statistics indicate why. The U.S. share of GNP spent on defense
was at least one percentage point higher than every other NATO member except
Greece (whose effort is mainly directed against Turkey) and, at 6–6.5 percent
for most of the decade, nearly twice the NATO average.[69] In financing much of
the U.S. budget deficits, some allies, in effect, were borrowing from America
the money to protect them.[70] Most politically unpalatable was a realization that
the United States was spending more to protect the allies than most were spending
to defend themselves.[71] By most measures, U.S. defense spending on NATO is
significantly higher in absolute terms than the combined contributions of all other
members.[72]

Senator Sam Nunn, hardly an isolationist or anti-NATO, was a bellwether of
congressional sentiment. In 1984 he proposed withdrawal of 90,000 troops unless
the Europeans met force-improvement targets that would prevent early nuclear
use. His amendment was defeated by only seven votes. By 1988, he was emphasizing relative effort: he wrote that "despite the shift in relative economic
power to our allies, the cost of defense has remained disproportionately on
American shoulders. Adjustments are long overdue."[73] In 1986, Representative
Patricia Schroeder got 90 votes for an amendment to halve the deployment; more
recently, she has proposed a country-by-country import duty equal to the percentage difference between the U.S. and others' share of GNP spent on defense.

Not everyone sought the same ends. Nunn's record suggested that he desired
a stronger NATO conventional posture and firmer domestic support for the
alliance. Schroeder seemed more interested in reducing U.S. efforts: since the
U.S. presumably derives benefits from its commitments outside Europe, and
Americans view the Soviets more ominously than most Europeans, it was likely
that U.S. defense budgets would be proportionately higher for the indefinite
future. Some who argued for troop cuts thus wanted to save money[74] or perhaps

punish Europe. Others, mainly outside Congress, wished to enhance U.S. flexibility for other contingencies.[75]

Still, it was significant that pressure on Europe came from all directions—hard-liners as well as doves, traditional internationalists as well as neoconservatives—and that most who raised these issues touched similar themes. Many neoconservatives were redolent of Robert Taft in their nationalism and scarcely concealed unilateralism. A House Armed Services subcommittee reported that "Many Americans feel that we are competing 100 percent militarily with the Soviets and 100 percent economically with our defense allies. Some have said that the United States has incurred all the burdens of empire and few, if any, of the benefits."[76] The panel's ranking Republican, a self-proclaimed hawk, argued that "we can't go on as though it's still 1949."[77]

Some saw America's isolationist tradition as a deeper source of such resentments. If so, NATO's base of support in the United States was wide but shallow, and tinkering with military arrangements could unravel other ties with Europe.[78] Henry Kissinger perceived similar problems but had a different solution. NATO would work only if the United States and Europe had independent options; allied dependence bred resentment in America and irresponsibility in Europe. Europeans therefore needed to determine their own security requirements and provide a sufficient conventional defense. Up to half the U.S. ground forces should be cut if they fail to do so. More preferable was a new division of labor within the Western coalition, with America concentrating on nuclear deterrence and Third World contingencies.[79]

By the end of the decade the Cold War had eased enough to make troop cuts virtually certain. When some congressional representatives proposed withdrawing up to 15,000 troops either in Europe or scheduled to service weapons eliminated by the Intermediate Nuclear Forces (INF) Treaty, there was little controversy. In mid-1989 President Bush proposed a common ceiling of 275,000 on superpower troops in Europe as part of the Conventional Forces in Europe (CFE) negotiations, and later revised that number downward. Although the president stated that a treaty might be completed in six months and take effect by 1992, the ceiling would require Moscow to withdraw about ten times as many troops as Washington. The Soviets appeared ready for large asymmetric cuts, but demanded compensation for French, British, and Canadian troops in the Federal Republic of Germany. Few were optimistic that a comprehensive accord could be reached so quickly.

Meanwhile, NATO was again split over nuclear risk-taking. This time, unlike the 1960s and 1970s, doubts were raised about Bonn rather than Washington. Germany and several other alliance members had deployed intermediate-range nuclear weapons in the early 1980s only over considerable popular opposition. After these were removed by the 1987 INF Treaty, short-range weapons such as the U.S. Lance became the only option for initiating flexible response below the intercontinental level. More important, NATO diplomats agreed that battlefield weapons had come to symbolize Europe's willingness to share nuclear risks. But Soviet offers to eliminate both sides' systems were attractive in Germany, and the Helmut Kohl government felt considerable pressure to begin such talks. U.S. congressional representatives, meanwhile, strongly hinted that American troops would not remain in Europe without nuclear protection.

The 1980s also saw basic critiques of the first-use pledge. Unlike defense burden sharing, extended deterrence issues were arcane and did not usually tap resentments about allied free-riding. Consequently, they were raised mainly by outside analysts, some of them former high-level officials, rather than in Congress.

While few were satisfied with NATO's low nuclear threshold, the speed and extent to which it can be raised have been much more controversial. By the early 1980s some were impatient. They claimed that NATO's nuclear posture, designed to deal with Soviet conventional advantages in Eurasia, was anachronistic in an era of massive nuclear arsenals. No First Use (NFU), the most radical alternative, would instead reserve nuclear weapons for retaliation against nuclear attack. In this view, controlled nuclear use was a chimera and NATO had no coherent, agreed strategy for such use. The implication was that none was possible; the alliance would be politically stronger with a believable, high-confidence conventional defense.[80]

These arguments emphasized risk-aversion, crisis stability, and credible (i.e., nonnuclear) military options. A high nuclear threshold would increase American options at the allies' expense.[81] Even though these goals figured prominently in U.S. policy after 1961, policymakers eschewed the political adjustments that far-reaching military changes would inevitably have entailed. Partly as a result, the nuclear threshold has not been raised significantly and battlefield nuclear options remained tightly linked to conventional operations. One former official thus suggested an entirely separate NATO nuclear command, freeing the main combat unit for conventional operations.[82]

The counterarguments emphasize different risks. Many claimed that Soviet leaders would be less restrained if NATO appeared ready to accept conventional defeat rather than initiate nuclear use. In this argument, the major "firebreak" is the onset of superpower war, not the nuclear threshold.[83] But unless first use were pure bluff—and battlefield deployments make that unlikely—the threat made sense only if a nuclear was *might* be controllable. Some opponents of NFU argued that it could be.[84] Another analysis claimed that first use was the essence of stable peace: "by sparing the West Europeans the necessity of autonomous choice in matters of defense, the United States removed the systemic cause of conflict that had underlain so many of Europe's past wars."[85]

A detailed analysis of the NFU debate is unnecessary here, but a few points pertain to the substantive themes of this book. Extended deterrence has largely defined the postwar Atlantic security relationship. Consensus first-use policies have held NATO's governments together, whatever their strategic incoherence. Since the conventional improvements needed to obviate the nuclear umbrella would be a European responsibility, NFU would effectively end America's leading role in NATO. NFU therefore implies substantial devolution and must be assessed accordingly. (Soviet conventional troop reductions could facilitate a non-nuclear defense of Europe, a possibility discussed in chapter 7.) On the other hand, ex cathedra pronouncements on the controllability of nuclear war cannot make first-use any more rational a threat for Americans. As discussed in Chapter 6, limited nuclear war scenarios are implausible; Americans must either accept the direct physical risks of present policies or raise the threshold substantially.

Finally, is U.S. protection indeed indispensable to peace *within* Western Europe? It may have been in the late 1940s, but time and the structural transformation of the international system make it less so in the 1990s. Before 1945, the international system was Eurocentric and the security dilemma therefore operated among the European great powers. Neither is true today. European governments would now have reason to form a local balance against Soviet power, if it were again to threaten them, not to fear each other. "Stable peace," in Russett's terms, was harder to create than it would be to maintain. The end of American nuclear hegemony would not ensure its demise.[86]

These four controversies took on new urgency during the decade after the Soviet invasion of Afghanistan, but all, especially the last three, were part of the broader, ongoing debate about national strategy that began in the late 1940s. Issues such as the degree of acceptable risk in extended deterrence, the costs of reducing such risks, support for troops in Europe, and the match between commitments and capabilities were inherent in U.S. obligations to NATO. Hegemonic decline has simply sharpened the constraints and tradeoffs. The next two chapters present a framework for analyzing policy adaptation, and the following three interpret U.S. policy between 1960 and 1980.

ANALYTIC APPROACH

The nature and limitations of the case study deserve discussion at this point. It begins in 1960, when the outgoing Eisenhower administration had begun to acknowledge weaknesses in the U.S. external position, and ends in 1980, when Reagan's election was interpreted as a mandate for strong international leadership. Although I do not discuss decision making in detail either before or after that period, the book as a whole assesses the American role from the late 1940s through the early 1990s. Reagan claimed that much of the period of the 1960s and 1970s was marked by retreat and compromise. He was partly correct: to varying degrees, each administration adjusted to constrains that were symptomatic of hegemonic decline.

Firmer temporal parameters are available, however. If the period between 1947 and 1963 was a "long decade" of U.S. hegemonic leadership in the international economy,[87] is a comparable periodization appropriate for security affairs? During the long decade, U.S. officials emphasized stable regimes rather than short-term advantage; national and cosmopolitan interests were often seen as inseparable. This began to change as policymakers found themselves constrained under existing rules. The early 1960s thus roughly marks the end of economic leadership. Although there was less change in NATO policy, comparable indicators of adjustment are evident. These factors suggest that the Kennedy administration was the first to confront decline upon taking office and that this period is a pertinent one for evidence of early adjustment.

The method of analysis is controlled case comparison. Explicit, theoretically grounded hypotheses are examined. The case study is a focused comparison across time between two issue areas, extended deterrence and provision of conventional forces. The narrative chapters frame chronological accounts around the predictions made by these hypotheses.

Yet hypotheses can rarely, if ever, be rigorously tested by in-depth case studies, and this book does not do so. In international relations generally, there are too few truly independent events and too many causes of behavior at different levels of analysis.[88] The story in Chapters 4 through 6 is therefore what Eckstein calls "disciplined configurative": "the chain of inquiry in disciplined-configurative studies runs from comparatively tested theory to case interpretation, and thence, perhaps, via *ad hoc* additions, newly discovered puzzles, and systematized prudence, to new candidate-theories."[89] The hypotheses are plausible enough to be probed thoroughly in a close study of one country's adaptation; anomalies and refinements can be used to amend the original argument and, perhaps, tested in other studies.

CONCLUSION

America's major strategic problem of the 1970s and 1980s was adjustment to relative decline caused by the growth of partners as well as adversaries. Even those who downplayed its significance largely agreed that the United States had lost global weight. Consequently, the opportunity costs of major commitments have steadily grown. Although military and especially economic capabilities have diffused considerably since the 1950s, "Washington still attempts to play the same global geopolitical role it did in the 1950s."[90] This applied particularly to NATO commitments, which constituted a larger share of U.S. military outlays in the 1970s than a decade earlier. Three of four key policy debates during the Reagan years thus focused on the U.S. role in NATO, further politicizing issues of long concern in the foreign-affairs community.

Even more than nuclear risks, disparities in defense burdens touched a raw nerve in Washington during the 1980s. Europe's growth and potential strength were frequently contrasted to its self-indulgence; until U.S. support was reduced or at least made more conditional, Europeans had little reason to do more for themselves. This sentiment—strong in Congress but increasingly evident among a broad range of opinion makers as well—seemed to presage significant devolution during the 1990s.

Yet even in decline, America remained tremendously powerful; only a hegemon can aspire to world leadership. This was the larger purpose of NATO, an instrument that gave U.S. leaders leverage to shape much of the postwar order.[91] As many emphasized, borrowing immensely abroad—the price of the U.S. world role in the 1980s—evinced residual structural power, even if the long-term result would be further decline.

Despite this power and generally stable priorities, U.S. policy has changed in significant ways and has often been under strain. Favorable conditions during the first postwar decade gave way to major external and internal constraints during the 1960s and 1970s. Much of the case study catalogs the efforts required just to stay in the same place. Surely this constitutes adaptation, even if major policies remained recognizably similar. The next two chapters argue that those tradeoffs and adjustments constitute meaningful patterns.

NOTES

1. Richard Halloran, "Two Studies Say Defense of Western Europe is Biggest U.S. Military Cost," *The New York Times*, July 20, 1984, p. A-2.

2. "Excerpts from Senate Testimony by Schlesinger on Foreign Policy," *The New York Times*, February 7, 1985, p. A-14.

3. Robert E. Hunter, "Will the United States Remain a European Power?" *Survival* 7 (May-June 1988).

4. Albert Carnesale et al., *Living With Nuclear Weapons* (New York: Bantam Books, 1983), p. 140.

5. Richard K. Betts, *Nuclear Blackmail and Nuclear Balance* (Washington, D.C.: Brookings Institution, 1987), p. 11. Betts's more specific definition of extended deterrence—"[prevention of] an attack by Soviet conventional forces against Western Europe, through the threat of retaliation by first use of nuclear weapons if NATO's conventional defense falters"—signifies the centrality of Europe in postwar U.S. defense planning. See page 10.

6. Fred C. Ikle and Albert Wohlstetter, *Discriminate Deterrence: Report of the Commission on Integrated Long-Term Strategy* (Washington, D.C.: U.S. Government Printing Office, 1988), p. 33.

7. Betts, *Nuclear Blackmail and Nuclear Balance*, p. 161.

8. See Earl C. Ravenal, "Counterforce and Alliance: The Ultimate Connection," *International Security* 6, no. 4 (Spring 1982), and Richard K. Betts, "Elusive Equivalence: The Political and Military Meaning of the Nuclear Balance," in Samuel P. Huntington, ed., *The Strategic Imperative: New Policies for American Security* (Cambridge, Mass.: Ballinger, 1982), p. 133.

9. Richard L. Kugler, "Theater Forces: The Future of the U.S. Military Presence in Europe," in Joseph Kruzel, ed., *American Defense Annual 1988–89* (Lexington, Mass.: D. C. Heath, 1988), pp. 94–95.

10. Kugler, "Theater Forces," p. 96.

11. James A. Nathan and James K. Oliver, *United States Foreign Policy and World Order*, 2nd ed. (Boston: Little, Brown, 1981), pp. 95–96.

12. Charles E. Bohlen, *Witness to History, 1929–1969* (New York: Norton, 1973), pp. 303–304.

13. Gregg Herken, *Counsels of War*, expanded edition (New York: Oxford University Press, 1987), p. 96.

14. Timothy P. Ireland, *Creating the Entangling Alliance: The Origins of the North Atlantic Treaty Organization* (Westport, Conn.: Greenwood Press, 1981), pp. 225–226; Phil Williams, *U.S. Troops in Europe* (London: Routledge and Kegan Paul, 1984), p. 12.

15. Stanley R. Sloan, *NATO's Future: Toward a New Transatlantic Bargain* (Washington, D.C.: National Defense University Press, 1985), p. 390.

16. Dean Acheson, *Present at the Creation: My Years in the State Department* (New York: Norton, 1969), p. 390.

17. Robert Jervis, "The Impact of the Korean War on the Cold War," *Journal of Conflict Resolution* 24, No. 4 (December 1980): 569–571.

18. The paragraph draws on Ibid., pp. 579–580.

19. Acheson, *Present at the Creation*, p. 494. See also Williams, *U.S. Troops in Europe*, pp. 12–13.

20. Bohlen, *Witness to History*, p. 304.

21. The quoted phrase was in a memo from Acheson and Truman and Secretary of Defense Louis Johnson; see Ireland, *Creating the Entangling Alliance*, p. 194. See also Acheson, *Present at the Creation*, p. 495.

22. Ireland, *Creating the Entangling Alliance*, p. 214.

23. Ibid., p. 207.

24. U.S. Congress, Senate, Committee on Foreign Relations, *Assignment of Ground Forces in the European Area: Hearings Before the Senate Committee on Foreign Relations*, 82nd. Cong., 1st sess., 1951, p. 13.

25. Ireland, *Creating the Entangling Alliance*, pp. 226, 215. Jeffrey Record, in *Beyond Military Reform: America's Defense Dilemmas* (Washington: Pergamon-Brassey's, 1988), p. 23, claims that Truman and Eisenhower viewed the troop commitment as temporary, to be terminated after Europe recovered from the war. This was true of Eisenhower; at an early National Security Council Meeting, he interpreted the commitment this way but noted that the allies did not. See Zbigniew Brzezinski, *Game Plan: How to Conduct the U.S.-Soviet Contest* (Boston: Atlantic Monthly Press, 1986), p. 176. But Record provides no direct evidence about Truman's intentions. Truman himself apparently did not put a time limit on the commitment, and the complexity of the original bargain suggested that he was in no position to do so.

26. U.S. Congress, Senate, *Text of Joint Resolution 99*, 82nd Cong. 1st sess., April 4, 1951; see *Congressional Record* 97, p. 3282.

27. Richard Halloran, *To Arm a Nation: Rebuilding America's Endangered Defenses* (New York: Macmillan, 1986), p. 215.

28. *Assignment of Ground Forces in the European Area*, p. 22. See also Ireland, *Creating the Entangling Alliance*, p. 209.

29. Jervis, "The Impact of the Korean War on the Cold War," p. 581.

30. David Garnham, *The Politics of European Defense Cooperation: Germany, France, Britain, and America* (Boston: Ballinger, 1988), p. 19.

31. See William P. Mako, *U.S. Ground Forces and the Defense of Central Europe* (Washington, D.C.: Brookings Institution, 1983), pp. 1–2; The Boston Study Group,

The Price of Defense: A New Strategy for Military Spending (New York: New York Times, 1979), p. 156; William W. Kaufmann, *A Reasonable Defense* (Washington, D.C.: Brookings Institution, 1986), p. 42.

32. Betts, *Nuclear Blackmail and Nuclear Balance*, p. 9. Whether these threats were bluffs is discussed extensively below.

33. Ibid., pp. 187, 188, 190, 197. The Carter administration saw its revised nuclear war fighting options as preserving "escalatory equity" even if reliable escalation dominance was no longer available.

34. Thomas L. Friedman, "Gorbachev Hands a Surprised Baker an Arms Proposal," *New York Times*, May 12, 1989, pp. 1, 6. Under current plans, without further negotiated reductions, there will be only about 3,250 U.S. nuclear warheads in Europe by 1993.

35. Morton H. Halperin, *Nuclear Fallacy: Dispelling the Myth of Nuclear Strategy* (Cambridge, Mass.: Ballinger, 1987), p. 91.

36. Ibid., pp. 12–13.

37. Ibid., pp. 93–94.

38. Williams, *U.S. Troops in Europe*, p. 14.

39. Robert O. Keohane and Joseph S. Nye, *Power and Interdependence: World Politics in Transition* (Boston: Little, Brown, 1977), p. 44.

40. Mark E. Rupert and David P. Rapkin, "The Erosion of U.S. Leadership Capabilities," in Paul M. Johnson and William R. Thompson, eds., *Rhythms in Politics and Economics* (New York: Praeger, 1985), p. 163; David Garnham, "The United States in Decline?" in Christopher Coker, ed., *Shifting into Neutral: The Burden Sharing Defence Debate in the Western Alliance* (London: Brassey's Defense Publishers, 1989).

41. Bruce Russett, "The Mysterious Case of Vanishing Hegemony; or, is Mark Twain Really Dead?" *International Organization* 39, no. 2 (Spring 1985): 211.

42. Russett, "The Mysterious Case of Vanishing Hegemony," pp. 217–221, 229.

43. Susan Strange, "The Persistent Myth of Lost Hegemony," *International Organization* 41, no. 4 (Autumn 1987): 565–571.

44. Samuel P. Huntington, "The U.S.—Decline or Renewal?" *Foreign Affairs* 67, no. 2 (Winter 1988/89): 91.

45. Strange, "The Persistent Myth of Lost Hegemony," p. 566.

46. See Robert Gilpin, *The Political Economy of International Relations* (Princeton, N.J.: Princeton University Press, 1987), p. 134; Gilpin, "American Policy in the Post-Reagan Era," *Daedalus* 116, no. 3 (Summer 1987): 33.

47. Stephen D. Krasner, "American Policy and Global Economic Stability," in William P. Avery and David P. Rapkin, eds., *America in a Changing World Political Economy* (New York: Longman, 1982), pp. 31–43.

48. I thank David Garnham for pointing this out to me.

49. William T. R. Fox, *The Superpowers* (New York: Harcourt, Brace and Co., 1944), p. 21.

50. Theodore Geiger, *The Future of the International System: The United States and the World Political Economy* (Boston: Unwin Hyman, 1988), pp. 35–39.

51. This is illustrated by access to foreign bases, a sine qua non for mobility. Bases have become progressively harder for both superpowers to acquire and maintain. This has been evident not just in the Philippines but in Greece, Spain, and, for nuclear weapons, New Zealand. In contrast to the early postwar years, access to bases now depends less on fixed client-patron ties and more on specific, increasingly restrictive bargains. Even as the superpower competition for bases has become genuinely two-sided and moved to

the heart of the rivalry, the balance of leverage between users and hosts has decisively changed to the latter's advantage. See Robert E. Harkavy, "Global Bases: Major Power Rivalry," *Phi Kappa Phi Journal*, Fall 1986. Fred C. Ikle is more optimistic. In arguing for a strategic "dyad" of increasingly accurate submarine-based missiles and the stealth bomber, he claims that strategic bombers might reduce U.S. dependence on aircraft carriers and overseas bases. He cites the 1986 raid against Libya as an example of such use. But bases and carriers are necessary if power is to be projected for any sustained period, especially in areas like the Persian Gulf where control over territory might be the objective. See "Riding ICBM's into the Past," *New York Times*, March 27, 1989, p. 23.

52. Joseph S. Nye, Jr., "Understating U.S. Strength," *Foreign Policy*, no. 72 (Fall 1988), p. 109.

53. Huntington, "The U.S.—Decline or Renewal?" pp. 81–82.

54. Betts, "Elusive Equivalence," p. 118. Emphasis in the original. In Henry Kissinger's words, "the late 1960s marked the end of the period of American predominance based on overwhelming nuclear and economic supremacy." See Kissinger, *Years of Upheaval* (Boston: Little, Brown, 1982), p. 238.

55. Huntington, "The U.S.—Decline or Renewal?" p. 84. Russett, in "The Mysterious Case of Vanishing Hegemony," p. 209, makes a similar point.

56. Walter Lippmann, *U.S. Foreign Policy: Shield of the Republic* (New York: Pocket Books, 1943), p. 4.

57. Paul Kennedy, "The (Relative) Decline of America," *The Atlantic*, August 1987, pp. 36, 34; Paul Kennedy, *The Rise and Fall of the Great Powers: Economic Change and Military Conflict from 1500 to 2000* (New York: Random House, 1987), pp. 395–540.

58. United States Department of Defense, *Defense Guidance* for Fiscal Year 1984. Quoted in Richard Halloran, *To Arm a Nation: Rebuilding America's Endangered Defenses* (New York: Macmillan, 1986).

59. Record, *Beyond Military Reform: America's Defense Dilemmas* (Washington, D.C.: Pergamon-Brassey's, 1988), pp. 20–21.

60. Bernard W. Rodgers, "Supreme Commander Pessimistic on Defense Buildup," *The Wall Street Journal*, June 5, 1984.

61. David P. Calleo, *Beyond American Hegemony: The Future of the Western Alliance* (New York: Basic Books, 1987), p. 124, and Chapter 7, passim. As Calleo wrote elsewhere:

West Europeans cannot ignore easily the link between massive U.S. domestic budget and trade deficits and the costs of America's military protectorate in Western Europe. Thus a kind of systemic justice permits the United States to manipulate the world monetary system so that the rich allies pay, at least indirectly, the costs of their own defense. Unfortunately, America's comparative disadvantage in sending forces to Europe means that the whole arrangement is neither militarily efficient nor economically cost-effective. The ensuing monetary instability imposes heavy burdens on the global economy. In short, the NATO relationship, central to the whole postwar structure, has gradually become a critical mechanism for its disintegration.

See "NATO's Middle Course," *Foreign Policy*, no. 69 (Winter 1987–88), p. 141.

62. Samuel P. Huntington, "Coping With the Lippmann Gap," *Foreign Affairs* 66, no. 3 (*America and the World 1987/88*).

63. Kugler, "Theater Forces," p. 103 and pp. 100–102.

64. Aaron L. Friedberg, "The Political Economy of American Strategy," *World Politics* 41, no. 3 (April 1989).

65. William W. Kaufmann, *The 1986 Defense Budget* (Washington, D.C.: Brookings Institution, 1986), p. 3.

66. Huntington, "Coping With the Lippmann Gap," p. 472.

67. Friedberg, "The Political Economy of American Strategy," p. 398.

68. Record, *Beyond Military Reform*, pp. 36–37.

69. David C. Morrison, "Sharing NATO's Burden," *National Journal*, May 30, 1987, p. 1395.

70. Huntington, "Coping With the Lippmann Gap," p. 471. This applies significantly to Japan, not a NATO member.

71. If, as indicated above, America allocates between 50 and 60 percent of its defense budget to Europe, Europe's per capita cost to America in 1988 was approximately $451 (i.e., 55 percent of $820 per capita on defense). Only three NATO members—Britain (at $502 per capita), France ($529), and Norway ($529)—exceeded this; most of the others spent substantially less. See Garnham, "The United States in Decline?" p. 18.

72. *Report of the Defense Burdensharing Panel of the Committee on Armed Services, House of Representatives*, 100th Cong., 2d Sess., August 1988, p. 12.

73. Sam Nunn, "Our Allies Have to Do More," *The New York Times*, July 10, 1988, p. 31.

74. See Andy Ireland, "A Hawk Says: Pull Our Troops Out," *The New York Times*, March 7, 1989, p. 31.

75. See Record, *Beyond Military Reform*, Chapter 8, and Brzezinski, *Game Plan*, pp. 168–184. David Hendrickson disagrees: "Insofar as the United States maintains large ground forces in its arsenal . . . the majority should have a primarily European orientation." See *The Future of American Strategy* (New York: Holmes and Meier, 1987), p. 66.

76. U.S. Congress, House of Representatives, Committee on Armed Services, *Report of the Defense Burdensharing Panel*, 100th Cong., 2d Sess., August 1988, p. 12.

77. Ireland, "A Hawk Says: Pull Our Troops Out," p. 31.

78. See William G. Hyland, "Reagan-Gorbachev III," *Foreign Affairs* 66, no. 1 (Fall 1987): 15.

79. Henry Kissinger, "A Plan to Reshape NATO," *Time*, March 5, 1984.

80. The essay that touched off this debate was McGeorge Bundy et al., "Nuclear Weapons and the Atlantic Alliance," *Foreign Affairs* 60, no. 4 (Spring 1982). See especially pages 757 and 766.

81. Josef Joffe, "Nuclear Weapons, No First Use, and European Order," *Ethics* 95, no. 3 (April 1985): 615.

82. Halperin, *Nuclear Fallacy*, Chapter 5.

83. See Stanley Kober, "The Debate Over No First Use," *Foreign Affairs* 60, No. 5 (Summer 1982): 1171–1172, and General David C. Jones, Ibid., pp. 1172–1174; Joffe, "Nuclear Weapons," pp. 609, 611, 612.

84. Hendrickson, "The Future of American Strategy," pp. 48–49.

85. Josef Joffe, "Europe's American Pacifier," *Foreign Policy*, no. 54 (Spring 1984): 68.

86. See David Garnham, "Correspondence," *International Security* 10, no. 4 (Spring 1986): 207. The argument in this paragraph is similar to that made by Robert Keohane

in *After Hegemony: Cooperation and Discord in the World Political Economy* (Princeton, N.J.: Princeton University Press, 1984).

87. See Robert O. Keohane, "Hegemonic Leadership and U.S. Foreign Economic Policy in the 'Long Decade' of the 1950s," in William P. Avery and David P. Rapkin, *America in a Changing World Political Economy* (New York: Longman, 1982). The end of the "long decade" is signified partly by the Interest Equalization Tax, which indicated that the United States could no longer live within the system's rules and thus began chipping away at them—in this case, unrestricted capital exports.

88. Joseph S. Nye, "Neorealism and Neoliberalism," *World Politics* 40, no. 2 (January 1988): 233.

89. See Harry Eckstein, "Case Study and Theory in Political Science," in Fred I. Greenstein and Nelson W. Polsby, eds., *Handbook of Political Science* (Reading, Mass.: Addison-Wesley, 1975), p. 100. The case studies themselves are written from a more holistic perspective. Holism seeks to understand action from the actor's subjective perspective, and comports well with the perceptual arguments of chapters 2 and 3. For a comparison of positivistic and holistic approaches, see Jack Snyder, "Science and Sovietology: Bridging the Methods Gap in Soviet Foreign Policy Studies," *World Politics* 40, no. 2 (January 1988).

90. Calleo, "NATO's Middle Course," p. 135.

91. Ibid.

2 Hegemonic Stability and Adaptation

Much of the impetus during the 1980s for a revised American role in NATO reflected feelings that U.S. burdens were obsolescent. Various arguments to this effect were made, as discussed in Chapter 1, but all emphasized that responsibilities within the Alliance had not shifted along with relative power. In short, many observers believed that there had been little adaptation to new circumstances.

This was clearly correct in several senses. Europeans could do more even without fielding larger forces, either by offsetting some U.S. out-of-area expenses for missions from which they benefit or by filling their own meager ammunition reserves. Moreover, the U.S. contribution—whether calculated in terms of risks, deployed forces, or proportion of defense effort allocated to NATO—has changed only incrementally. Yet policy outputs do not tell the entire story; policymakers adapt internally as well as externally to constraints. The substantive implications of this distinction alone suggest practical as well as analytic payoffs from a differentiated understanding of adaptive preferences.

Students of political economy have focused on the international effects of hegemonic leadership and have largely ignored the state-level factors that produce and maintain it. Robert Keohane, who has refined and critiqued the argument that international order requires a hegemon, admits that a leadership role requires political will as well as material resources.[1] This obvious but important point has remained underdeveloped. What creates the political will to lead internationally, and what affects it as relative resources decline? These are the analytic concerns of this book.

This chapter and the next present a framework for analyzing hegemonic adaptation. Restricting the analysis to great powers suggests an indicator for the dependent variable, but also necessarily sacrifices some explanatory precision. Chapter 3 discusses this problem and a possible solution.

THE DEPENDENT VARIABLE: FOREIGN POLICY ADAPTATION

Adaptation is a set of responses to environmental change; it occurs whenever an actor cannot fully control its salient milieu. In sociology, for example, it denotes "a slow modification of individual and social activity in adjustment to cultural surroundings."[2] Adjustment to environmental constraints is the core idea. If the analysis in Chapter 1 is correct, a declining hegemon will face progressively greater opportunity costs to maintain the status quo. Internal political resistance to the price of international leadership may produce other constraints.

All purposive behavior constitutes adaptation in this general sense. Rosenau thus defines foreign policy as

all the attitudes and activities through which organized national societies seek to cope with and benefit from their international environments. . . . all nations can be viewed as adapting entities with similar problems that arise out of the need to cope with their environments.[3]

Yet this conflates mundane and significant policy change and is of little analytic use without refinement. He seems to agree, since he distinguishes "habitual," bureaucratized policymaking processes from those involving top-level officials.[4]

I therefore take policy adaptation to mean a government's nonroutine responses to environmental constraints, comprising changes either in priorities or in the means to achieve existing goals.[5] Adaptation in this sense may entail substantial adjustments in grand strategy, in other words, the calculated relation of ends and means by states.[6] It might also mean simply doing the same things more efficiently. Either way, it requires programmatic, allocative choices, not simply implementation of existing procedures. In the United States, such issues often require presidential involvement, either because they cannot be resolved below the White House level or because they impinge on central foreign-policy stakes.

From a realist perspective, foreign-policy adaptation is induced by changes in a state's international power position. Its pace and scope depend on how the changes are interpreted, the available international options, and the range of politically acceptable choices. The relationship between assessment of relative power, the specific constraints in each situation, and assessment of options is thus a key analytic issue. It is also understudied.[7] Historians have often been uninterested in generalizing about these issues, while political scientists have until the last few decades avoided perceptual approaches.

Turning first to constraints, in some classical realpolitik conceptions national leaders face inconsequential domestic impediments; the relevant environment is

Figure 2.1
Ikenberry's Typology of National Adjustment Strategies

OBJECTIVE

	Defensive	Offensive
Domestic	Protect domestic structure	Change domestic structure
LOCUS International	Remedial steps to defend current regime	Create new international regime

Source: Adapted from G. John Ikenberry, *Reasons of State* (Ithaca: Cornell University Press, 1988), p. 16.

mainly or exclusively external. For example, rising states typically stretch declining hegemons thin by challenging their geopolitical primacy. This affected Britain dramatically at the turn of the twentieth century. As Japan and the United States built modern navies, Britain lost its global command of the seas. Although the Admirality could have strengthened its Pacific and American squadrons, the naval race with Germany took priority; Britain depleted its non-European fleets to concentrate on the East Atlantic.[8]

Contemporary leaders obviously must adjust to domestic pressures. The debates discussed in Chapter 1 suggest that hegemonic decline stimulates internal questions about the costs and benefits of leadership. At its various costs mount, competitive nationalism becomes more popular.[9] U.S. leaders have successfully resisted some, and perhaps the most important, of the episodic pressures for a less ambitious world role. Since World War II British politicians have not, for the most part: personal consumption and, until the Thatcher years, social welfare spending took priority over defense commitments.[10]

Adaptation can be pursued by internal and external means as well. In comparing responses to the oil shocks of the 1970s, John Ikenberry argues that national adjustment (i.e., adaptation) varies on two dimensions, location and objective. It can be sought at home (domestic) or abroad (international) and be intended to preserve (defensive) or transform (offensive) an existing international regime, defined as "sets of explicit or implicit principles, norms, rules and decision-making procedures around which actors' expectations converge in a given area of international relations."[11] Ikenberry's formulation is depicted in Figure 2.1.

The objectives of adaptation can be classified more precisely by a continuum with three categories: capability enhancement, within-regime change, and change of regime. Regimes are defined by principles ("beliefs of fact, causation, and rectitude") and norms ("standards of behavior defined in terms of rights and

Figure 2.2
An Amended Adjustment Typology

DEGREE OF POLICY CHANGE

		Capability Enhancement	Within-Regime Change	Change of Regime
LOCUS	Internal	Unilaterally develop new capabilities to achieve existing end(s)	Redefine regime means (i.e. rules, decision-making procedures) unilaterally	Unilaterally abrogate regime ends (i.e. principles and norms)
	External	Seek help in meeting current obligation(s)/ end(s)	Renegotiate means (rules and decision-making procedures)	Renegotiate ends (principles and norms)

obligations''); various rules (''specific prescriptions or proscriptions for action'') and decision-making procedures (''prevailing practices for making and implementing collective choice'') can be consistent with the same principles and norms.[12] Rules and procedures, then, are means to some end(s) embodied in principles and norms. The degree of policy change increases as states move from (1) enhancing capabilities to achieve existing ends to (2) redefining or renegotiating regime means to (3) abrogating or renegotiating regime ends. Figure 2.2 summarizes the amended adjustment typology.

This continuum, it should be emphasized, captures only the dimension of adjustment concerning regime adherence. Another is the extent to which domestic structures such as government institutions or systems of property rights are transformed to address particular problems. This broadens the notion of capability enhancement beyond the kinds of power resources usually thought relevant in international politics, such as armed forces and industrial strength, to encompass a range of internal changes in the rules of the game. Soviet *perestroika* is a contemporary example. Internal transformation is a generic option in foreign economic policy, particularly under the precepts of liberal capitalism. At the other end of the ideological spectrum, revolutionary, mass-mobilizing regimes apparently excel at channeling popular elan into strong states able to fight protracted wars. That this changes societal rules is underscored by Theda Skocpol: ''that is no mean accomplishment in view of the fact that the prerevolutionary polities in question excluded most of the people from symbolic or practical participation in national politics.''[13]

Internal transformation is less often relevant to security policy in status quo states, although societies with deeply embedded military establishments may, due to structural inefficiencies, bear unnecessarily large extractive military burdens in relation to outputs.[14] In a more efficient U.S. procurement system, Pentagon civilians would identify the requirements for such missions as strategic nuclear deterrence and power projection and the services would compete to provide the requisite forces.[15] Substantially more competition in weapons acquisition, including significantly tighter cost controls, could eventually shrink the defense industry and entail significant industrial transformation.

The third and fourth debates discussed in Chapter 1 essentially concern future regime adherence. NATO is a security regime based on two principles: Western Europe's territories, international alignments, and (implicitly) domestic political systems should be preserved as constituted since the late 1940s; its security and North America's are indivisible in this sense. Its norms, as embodied in the North Atlantic Council's simultaneous adoption of Flexible Response (FR) and the Harmel Report in December 1967, include (1) forward defense with the option of first use, (2) political coexistence with the Soviet bloc, (3) a multi-division American troop presence on the continent, and (4) pursuit of mutual force reductions. Salient rules and decision procedures have included the following: (1) SACUER is an American; (2) NATO's Secretary-General, who runs its political apparatus, is a European; (3) Washington leads bloc-to-bloc talks on reducing theater-nuclear and conventional weapons. The fourth debate explicitly challenged the first norm, while the third debate suggested that legislators have become less committed to the third.

Precisely to stimulate Europe's collective self-reliance, Henry Kissinger recommends that the responsibilities embodied in existing rules be reversed. SACEUR should be a European, the secretary-general should be an American, and the allies should assume responsibility for reducing weapons deployed on their soil. Yet in endorsing Francois de Rose's premise that "European security should be viewed under the aspect of the defense of the West in Europe,"[16] he indicates a preference for within-regime adaptation.

Policy change seldom fits such procrustrean categories precisely, especially when the rules of a valued regime and their underlying premises are simultaneously subjected to stress. Early in his term, President Bush surprised allied leaders by "unequivocally" supporting European integration, although this eventually implied a smaller American role and less U.S. leverage. His predecessors had voiced similar sentiments but feared the consequences of more European autonomy.[17] His goal appeared to be continued partnership but more balanced responsibilities—in other words, externally induced, within-regime change in which the status quo itself would favorably evolve. The demarcation between this and a different regime, however, is unclear.

Adaptation is pervasive, but this book examines only those actors ultimately responsible for grand strategies: senior executive-branch officials and ultimately the president. If, as Gaddis argues, U.S. policymakers have alternated between "cost-minimizing" containment strategies, which take external risks to avoid spending resources, and "cost-maximizing" strategies, which spend money to play it safe, organizational responses to budgetary plenty and stringency might also be examined.[18] One could compare how different bureaucracies shift priorities, alter standard procedures, or manage uncertainties in the two kinds of budgetary environments. Logrolling—tradeoffs among groups that produce a majority coalition from minorities—might be expected among organizational subunits during periods of plenty, but not during leaner periods. A comprehensive explanation of policy adaptation requires attention to these issues, since bureaucratic repertories comprise government's capabilities. But an organizational approach obscures broader political purposes. To explain grand strategies, the motivations of responsible political leaders are more germane.

The book therefore shares the major assumptions of the contemporary "statist" foreign-policy literature. Governments have coherent *national* purposes on issues of concern to top executive-branch officials: "the limits imposed by standard operating procedures as well as the direction of policy are a function of the values of decision makers."[19] Neither bureaucratic nor societal resistance to these goals should obscure this. "Grand strategies," which give coherence to policy, are empirically elusive and analytically useless without these assumptions. In short, this study focuses on the high-level motivations for policy preferences rather than organizational task management or the eventual international consequences.

THE SPECIAL CASE OF A HEGEMON

Hegemonic states differ from others in two ways. One is the scope and impact of their structural power. Often a dominant state can change the rules rather than adapt its policies to them.[20] Even when it cannot make rules unilaterally, it can often veto new ones, as was shown by the demise of an international authority to regulate deep seabed mining, opposed by the Reagan administration. This degree of leverage provides policy options unavailable to most other states.

Powerful states, in other words, have more adaptive slack than others. Sometimes this is simply a function of aggregate capabilities. Even though the Soviet Union equaled and perhaps overtook the United States militarily during the 1970s, American leaders still had the wherewithal to deter most threats, and thus to convince the attentive public that most commitments assumed during the 1940s and 1950s could be maintained. Structural power or relatively low vulnerability also means that hegemons can often force others to adjust to self-serving policies. A key currency country can dictate, within broad limits, the value of others' reserve assets; states with large markets can export unemployment and inflation to trading partners. Security hegemons may bear greater proportional burdens than their allies, but they also take the lead in military strategy and bargaining with adversaries, sometimes to the detriment of smaller states.

Hegemons also play a distinct leadership role that involves broadly defined national interests; the term itself comes from the Greek word for leadership. Great powers typically see those interests systematically, in terms of particular kinds of world order. George Modelski identifies five "essential services" that steer the system in orderly directions: agenda formation, mobilization, decision making, administration, and innovation. Hegemons as defined here (Modelski prefers the concept "world power") perform them.[21] Agenda formation means defining problems and setting priorities. Mobilization "refers to the need to create a coalition large enough to serve as the basic infrastructure of world order," which might exclude the Soviet Union from this category. Decision making is defined, somewhat amorphously, as "making a basic decision about the political direction of the global system for a significant period ahead"; this essentially means a commitment to fight a global war in defense of the status quo if necessary, as the U.S. does in NATO. Administration refers to implementing the successful order or agenda; innovation, its antithesis, means the ability to steer into a successful future.

These roles suggest that the "American Century" was achieved through a system on which others came to depend as much as by victory in two world wars and the incapacity of other great powers. The United States was the glue within the non-Communist coalition, setting its agenda, mobilizing it to act, and administering many of its diplomatic and military instruments. In practice, the *Pax Americana* has consisted of asymmetric commitments to others, and changes in those commitments are the essence of hegemonic adaptation.

Commitments are pledges to do specific things under stipulated conditions. Obligations and circumstances can be enumerated in various ways, but some obligation is intrinsic to any commitment. Governments accept such restrictions in order to bind others and thereby reduce uncertainty. For most states, the obligations and restrictions are mutual or at least comparable. Government A thus has a security commitment to B if their relationship would incline A to use force at times or in ways that A might prefer to avoid in these circumstances,[22] and B is usually comparably obligated.

A hegemon's services have been seen as public goods. Its elites furnish (or do much to furnish) such international goods as a security umbrella for allies, a market for surplus goods, and countercyclical capital flows. It is questionable whether these goods are truly collective.[23] Even so, a hegemon's behavior often benefits others; their conformity to its agenda, in turn, creates a predictable and congenial environment from which it benefits disproportionately by virtue of size. Some scholars argue that the world economy remains stable only if one state provides such goods. Otherwise, since governments often interfere with markets for national advantage, the invisible hand yields suboptimal international results, and multilateral rule making will be fragile. This summarizes the theory of hegemonic stability.[24] For example, hegemons often prefer open economic regimes. To such ends, which require cooperation from others, they assume distinct kinds of interstate commitments.

This is illustrated by British and American behavior during their periods of economic leadership. Britain led a path to freer trade during the mid-nineteenth century by accepting less than ideal, asymmetric agreements with states, such as France, whose policies were significantly more protectionist. Britain had opened much of its market unilaterally before active trade diplomacy began in 1860; then, to move France in this direction, it accepted lower but still significant French tariffs. Once a network of states bound by unconditional Most Favored Nation clauses existed, the British bargained hard to liberalize trade within it, but they remained more open than other major states until the Great Depression. Beginning in the 1930s, America also took half an economic loaf; in return for tariff reductions, it accepted discrimination within substantial limits.[25] But there were broad political reasons to do so, and the framework for these bargains was put in place shortly after World War II, when U.S. power was at its peak. This did not prevent significant economic costs; as a result of discrimination accepted (or promoted) by the United States, the percentage of trade that took place under unconditional Most Favored Nation conditions fell from 90 percent in 1955 to 77 percent in 1977.[26] As America lost its initial postwar advantages, its trade bargains became even more lopsided.

A hegemonic role apparently requires such asymmetric commitments. In trade bargains, Britain and America effectively guaranteed nonretaliation for limited departure from reciprocal economic openness. Hegemonic systems can collapse when such costs become too great and the guarantee is withdrawn. During the 1930s, Britain failed to reconstruct the prewar economic system when its trading partners refused to dismantle wartime controls. It could not even get others to cut tariffs 25 percent in return for predominantly free trade.[27] Early versions of the theory highlight these asymmetries in arguing that only one state can provide the confidence that such systems require.

While America has struggled with relative economic decline for some time, only gradually has it made its role as leader conditional. The effects of the 1988 trade bill, which increases the executive's authority to investigate unfair foreign trade practices and initiate sanctions, could thus be profound and will depend on how aggressively presidents use it.

Security policies are also defined by interstate commitments. This is true of all states: foreign policies are commonly characterized in terms of whether alliances exist, what obligations they entail, and which partners they include. It applies particularly to great powers and security hegemons, those who protect others as a by-product of their own strategies. Britain, Russia, and the United States, for example, have had one-sided commitments in Afghanistan to the indigenous governments or rebel organizations. The largest powers have system-wide strategic interests and military obligations; the resulting commitments, as defined above, are those states' contingent responses in a variety of situations. More generally, major powers create subsystems of dependent relationships that reinforce their own positions, at least as long as their advantages over rivals are preserved. Such strategic involvements virtually define a nation's foreign policy.[28] Since World War II, U.S. strategy has fostered economic growth and political stability in Western Europe and Japan, mainly through close military alliances.

HEGEMONIC ADAPTATION

If commitments indicate the range and depth of a hegemon's role, adaptation to new constraints is signified by changes in those commitments. This section develops a framework for comparing such changes across issues and over time. Like others, hegemonic governments resist adaptation. But this inertia is even more pronounced than for smaller states; internal interests and fixed institutional routines are not the only reasons. Governmental and many private elites typically view international relations and their role in them in ways that promote expansion rather than adjustment to constraints.

Hegemonic Security Systems

International politics has traditionally been structured by the great powers. Virtually all social systems are either hierarchies or have significant hierarchical elements, and the lack of authoritative international institutions impedes redistribution from the haves to have-nots. In recent years, the international hierarchy has been softened by constraints on the use of force against socially mobilized populations in the Third World. Nevertheless, inequality simplifies the pattern of international relations. Certain issues and conflicts will be addressed, while others that challenge it too directly are kept off the agenda.[29]

Security hegemons reap these advantages by organizing subordinate states. Recent scholarship has focused on economic leadership, while recognizing that a successful economic hegemon requires sufficient military power to protect its partners from threats to their autonomy.[30] Those security arrangements are the context in which adaptation became a U.S. policy issue.

Both Cold War blocs have been hegemonic security systems, even if, in retrospect, the Soviet Union lacked the economic strength to be a long-term system leader. For much of the postwar period, the "ordering principle" of each was "boundary management"—preserving (if not expanding) the original coalition.[31] There have been obvious differences between the two coalitions, as well as between them and traditional territorial imperiums, but key similarities as well. Security hegemonies, like economic ones, are subsystemic: the international system has not been unipolar since the Roman Empire, if then, and attempts to make it so have invariably been self-defeating. For forty years, NATO has been the core of the American system.

To perform the services identified by Modelski, hegemons require abundant material advantages and a degree of deference from subordinate states. The first is discussed below; the second suggests that there must be demand for as well as a supplier of leadership. The last several centuries indicate that these services or functions are in highest demand during global wars and the systemic reconstruction that follows.[32] I assume only that elites in smaller states accept hegemonic leadership for self-interested reasons. This is consistent with their apparent preference to ride free on security supplied by someone else; no other interpretation, including neo-Marxist, is implied. Assumptions about the sources of preferences are important because noncolonial hegemonies are quasi-hierarchical systems among formally independent actors. As such, "[economic] hegemony rests on the subjective awareness by elites in secondary states that they are benefitting, as well as on the willingness of the hegemon itself to sacrifice tangible short-term benefits for intangible long-term gains."[33]

Hegemonic security systems likewise provide mutual benefits. Allies deny certain kinds of access to a hegemon's rivals and perhaps provide it greater global reach. Soviet leaders have generously supplied arms to regional clients to promote their geopolitical arms vis-à-vis the United States. This, more than specific influence over clients, has motivated Moscow's Third World policy.[34] Similar patterns seem to characterize U.S. alliances.

In return, under a hegemon's protection, its allies escape some consequences of the security dilemma, a syndrome in which adversaries can threaten each other even through measures intended as purely defensive. Generalizations across many countries are problematic, but Joffe argues that postwar Western European integration was possible only because the U.S. essentially removed security issues, historically very troublesome, from indigenous hands.[35] This is an exaggeration. While intra-European rivalries and wars were predictable in the prewar multipolar, Eurocentric system, these countries no longer posed the same threat to one another after 1945. It made more sense for them to coalesce against Moscow, the more proximate threat.[36] Nevertheless, if these arrangements facilitated European integration while memories of conflict were still fresh, America surely benefited. Moscow similarly contained internecine claims among Hungary, Romania, Poland, and East Germany for over forty years after Yalta. As often noted, both superpowers have spent proportionately more on defense than most of their allies. But this has purchased political influence and forward defense, which policymakers apparently feel more than compensates their "exploitation" by smaller partners.

Hegemony in this sense depends on beliefs that the leader is willing to pay its costs. If doubts arise, others have reason to minimize their future dependence. In mid-1989, the Japanese government apparently reached this conclusion from unpleasant U.S. policy debates about Japanese commercial practices. Earlier in the decade, Tokyo agreed to develop the FSX jet fighter with the United States, largely to mitigate trade tensions. General Dynamics, a U.S. contractor, was earmarked for about 40 percent of the project. But when the Bush administration sought to consummate the deal, it faced congressional charges that Japan planned to use the project's technology to build its commercial aerospace business. Tokyo concluded that the U.S. would begin to withhold technologies suitable for commercial use and that it should develop its own arms. Since almost all Japanese weapons have been produced under U.S. license since the 1950s, this would remove a major lever over Tokyo's strategies and defense priorities.[37]

Consistency as well as continuity is important in hegemonial relationships, and only the hegemon can ensure them. Overall, consistency benefits most members of such coalitions. For smaller states, uniform rules and practices reduce uncertainty and risk aversion. This allowed most industrialized and many developing countries to focus on growth rather than competitive power position during the heyday of Bretton Woods.[38] Ironically, perhaps, this augmented aggregate wealth but contributed to America's relative decline. Nevertheless, such consistency legitimizes the rules and order a hegemon upholds.

Examples from the postwar European blocs illustrate these points. In the Warsaw Treaty, Moscow pledged to consider any threat to another signatory as a threat to itself. The pact also institutionalized its control through various functional links:

Organizational controls addressed primarily to the membership of the East European subsystem can . . . emphasize the acceptable limits of national independence and deviation, preferred objectives for collective support, and economic preferment to those who avoid offending Soviet sensitivities. Interdependence thus becomes an institutionalized game which over time familiarizes everyone with its essential rules. Military controls are thus rendered far less necessary.[39]

These ties benefited governing elites even if they were hardly voluntary. Consistency can be unpopular and costly in particular cases. The United States refused to say which of its ships carry nuclear weapons and in 1985 reacted very strongly to New Zealand's ban on nuclear-powered or nuclear-armed ships in its ports. Washington, fearful of appearing to sanction a bad precedent, said the ban made the ANZUS pact (Australia, New Zealand, and the U.S.) unworkable and broke off regular alliance interactions.

In sum, a security hegemon organizes a coalition of subordinate states for geopolitical purposes. Imperial powers have done this for millennia. The systems of the two postwar superpowers, however, are historically unique in several respects. Both have guaranteed the integrity of formally independent regimes at great expense for a substantial period of time. Neither has needed such allies for its own protection but rather as physical and political buffers against the other. The United States, for example, had 375 major bases and hundreds of smaller installations in 35 foreign countries in 1989. In general, they provide either a "trip wire" to automatic involvement in conflicts initiated against those territories, a way to project military power abroad more generally, or the symbolism of continuing commitment. The Soviet global network is significant but considerably smaller: outside of Eastern Europe, it includes bases or special access to military facilities in nine countries. Expanding it has been a major Soviet goal, and until the late 1980s cost considerations seemed unimportant to Soviet leaders.[40]

These two examples suggest the capability requirements of a contemporary security hegemon. Hegemons must be able to provide their own physical security without allies. Others' vulnerability is a tool to be exploited in intracoalition bargaining, albeit carefully.[41] They must be willing to support proportionately large military budgets and provide others with state-of-the-art military technologies. This requires a vibrant economy attuned to innovation and perhaps no major economic rival.[42] Gorbachev's external retrenchment and internal reforms recognize this. Policing such an informal empire necessitates global reach, which in turn requires foreign installations and significant blue-water naval forces. In a nuclear age, societal invulnerability may, depending on one's assumptions about deterrence, be necessary for highly credible extended deterrence threats.

Hegemons also require a domestic political system that permits these assets to be used effectively. It must not, for instance, significantly constrain policy-makers' ability to make commitments and use force. While this obviously involves matters of degree, few would claim that post-Vietnam America could act as expeditiously abroad as before 1965.

Security hegemons are therefore necessarily great powers, but the converse is not true. In practice, the distinction between the two is one of degree; as Waltz claims,

The smaller the number of great powers, and the wider the disparities between the few most powerful states and the many others, the more likely the former are to act for the sake of the system and to participate in the management of, or interfere in the affairs of, lesser states.[43]

Yet hegemons, in order to affect the system's basic norms, must be able to mobilize, administer, and initiate agendas for a broadly based coalition. Such tasks exceeded the capacity and ambition of most traditional great powers, states that settled for local or otherwise particularistic spheres of influence.[44] Contemporary superpowers are relatively much stronger and less dependent. A security hegemon thus has a superpower's position (relative to its circumstances) and is willing to pay for wide-ranging leadership commitments.

Generalizing about hegemonic adaptation from such meager evidence may be unwise. As several scholars have noted, the theory, based at most on two cases, is of dubious scientific validity: "American [economic] hegemony, rather than being one more instance of a general phenomenon, was essentially unique in the scope and efficacy of the instruments at the disposal of a hegemonic state and the degree of success attained."[45] But this is problematic only if the British and American cases exhaust the date base. On the contrary, modern security hegemonies can be seen as sets of quasi-protectorates comparable in key ways to traditional imperial systems.

One feature common to both is the self-reinforcing expansion of great-power security systems, a familiar dynamic in international politics. Historically, great powers have found expansion cost-effective under certain political, economic, and technological conditions. Whether it takes the form of territorial conquest or economic expansion (for example, the so-called "imperialism of free trade") is less important here than the general process of expansion itself.[46] Premodern empires tended to grow until the costs of war and administration exceeded the economic surplus generated by additional territory. Although some modern states, such as Nazi Germany and Japan, have sought conquest, by the nineteenth century economic productivity had replaced territory as the major source of state power. Consequently, political influence abroad and market access have replaced territorial gains as incentives for expansion.[47]

While expansion eventually confronts diminishing returns, it can continue for long periods. In economic terms, one would expect actors to eschew the costs of expansion unless most of its benefits, often jeopardized by uneven growth, can be captured.[48] But do statesmen adjust by periodically comparing the costs and benefits of particular commitments and, if necessary, disregarding the sunk costs of past expansion? The largely voluntary decolonization of Africa and much of Asia after World War II indicates that they have. But in these cases, the colonizers had either long been minor powers (Belgium and the Netherlands), or, as with Britain and France, had become second-tier states. The question remains open for great powers and may be more complex than this rationalistic calculus would suggest. Not only do the system's largest states have substantial room to maneuver—to make mistakes, fail to adjust, and so on—but if beliefs about relative national power are like others, they change more slowly than real-world developments.[49]

Adaptation to adverse change is thus likely to lag behind it. For similar reasons, responses to increased power might be delayed, as was America's after World War I.[50] Nevertheless, hegemons typically expand more readily than they retrench.

External commitments tend to feed on each other in four ways. First, as interests expand beyond homeland defense, logistics often require new strongholds to safeguard existing ones. When President Carter declared the Persian Gulf a vital U.S. interest and formed the Rapid Development Force (later organized as the U.S. Army Central Command) to intervene there, Pentagon planners literally knocked on the door of every friendly regime in the region seeking permission to base troops. Air and naval installations in Oman were acquired, as were more limited facilities in Somalia, Kenya, Morocco and Portugal.[51]

Second, the more external interests a state acquires, the greater the number of potential threats; in countering them, states take positions and assume commitments subject to challenge by others, and a common response is further expansion.[52] Historians of European colonial expansion have called this phenomenon the "turbulent frontier." "In India, Malaya, and South Africa, British dominion implied expansion. . . . [Colonial] Governors continued to try to eliminate the disorderly frontier by annexations which in turn produced new frontier problems and further expansion."[53] British governors in the Malay Peninsula were concerned about disruptions in what were called the native (non-British) states, since this affected trade with the British Straits settlements and ultimately British revenue. As one colonial governor put it,

If these Malayan states were not immediately upon our borders, if the preservation of the peace within those states were not of vital importance to the interests of our Settlements and to the maintenance of peace and good order therein, if we had assumed no responsibility connected therewith, I might . . . advise your Lordship that the proper course to pursue would be a policy of non-interference. But . . . that policy has never been pursued, and there has always been in greater or less degree an intimate relationship between ourselves and the States in the neighborhood of these Settlements. Looking at the close relationship which we have been obliged to assume in respect to these states, especially since we have actively intervened in their affairs, I submit that the true policy to adopt . . . is to look forward to the time when the annexation of some of them will probably become a necessity.[54]

Prompted by ambitious or nervous men in the field, Britain often acted contrary to the wishes of economy-minded officials in London, and the empire, in one interpretation, grew largely ''in spite of itself.''[55]

It was usually easier to acquire such possessions than relinquish them. An analogous pattern was apparent in U.S. Central American policy during the 1980s. Pressure on the Nicaraguan regime required bases for the Contras in Honduras, whose army officers demanded substantial military aid in exchange. Similarly, Moscow became more deeply involved in the Third World during the 1970s partly because its allies often threatened to defect during crises if more extensive assistance was not forthcoming. In a crisis, Wallander argues, ''uncertainty creates incentives for incremental military intervention in the hope that further action will be unnecessary, and the fear that others will exploit inaction.''[56]

In these ways, a hegemon's power and promises become the major framework for international security. Since its commitments also reflect major rivalries, unresolved issues, and the world power structure, they can be quite resilient while those circumstances obtain. Few American leaders in the late 1940s foresaw a 40-year commitment of several hundred thousand troops in Europe. Yet until the division of Europe resolves itself, as now is occurring, some such commitment is a necessary support to the status quo.[57]

Third, great-power commitments are often buttressed by a world view that integrates or rationalizes ambitious policies. In postwar U.S. policy, while Wilsonian ''world order'' visions could be distinguished from worries about credibility or danger in remote places, the two were often closely connected in practice.[58] At least until Vietnam, there were few areas outside the Soviet bloc where nonleftist regimes and declared American security interests did *not* coincide. Moscow similarly found a world role for itself through partnership with Third World regimes opposed to Western-sponsored alliances or in conflict with Western-backed regional rivals.[59]

Fourth, certain images and beliefs often reinforce the first three factors. Two models of the process by which government officials measure power, perceive shifts in relative power, and adapt to these changes have been suggested. A ''calculative'' model implicit in some balance-of-power literature posits a routine process of counting, comparing, and adjusting to capability differentials; a ''perceptual'' model implies slower adaptation filtered through robust, symbol-laden images of self and other states. Neither, according to Friedberg, does justice to policy processes; his study of late Victorian British policy reveals a "complex mixture of calculation and belief."[60] Yet beliefs often appear to structure power assessments in ways that promote expansionist policies.

Policy debates are often couched in terms of simple capability indicators. These indicators reflect bureaucratic, academic, and perhaps public assumptions about what kinds of power are important and why; they provide a language for communication and analysis. On the other hand, the capabilities highlighted by these assumptions tend to become overly important symbolically, and analyses based on them are often misleading.[61] This in part explains why hard-line views often carry great weight in security-policy debates. Hard-liners tend to view opponents as relatively calculating and aggressive, and see conflict with them as permanent. Arsenals and military spending become pertinent indicators of resolve. Paul Nitze, a frequent hawk in postwar U.S. security policy, has been characterized as "obsessed" with the numerical aspect of the arms race.[62] In the late 1970s his concern for the vulnerability of U.S. land-based ICBMs helped bury the SALT II Treaty and build support for Reagan's rearmament program. Yet, as the Scowcroft Commission concluded, ICBMs were vulnerable only under assumptions about Soviet missile accuracies and risk-taking that struck most other specialists as extreme. Even under this worst case, the United States would hardly have been disarmed.

The common assumption that perceived resolve or staying power is indivisible also works against retreat. If decision makers believe it, reputational interests— those that involve others' inferences about one's resolve, flexibility, or reliability to clients and allies—can rival or overshadow the intrinsic stakes in a particular issue, and commitments become interdependent.[63] According to Thomas Schelling, whose work has had wide scholarly influence and some impact on U.S. policy, these ideas directly bear on policy choices. In an extended deterrence context, where a state seeks to dissuade adversaries from challenges in various places, it will be loath to relinquish voluntarily even minor stakes for fear that its resolve on others will be questioned.[64]

While there is little systematic evidence that governments make general judgments about others' resolve, statesmen believe this to be true.[65] This applies especially to great powers. Because their interests often exceed disposable resources, resolve and reputation are the currency of bargaining, and retreats that could be tolerated by a small country are thought to have more serious consequences if made by a large one.[66]

Domino beliefs—that adverse changes in the balance of power are strongly correlated with a state's resolve reputation—follow from the view that outcomes throughout the system are tightly connected. This, in turn, is strongest when adversaries are seen as monolithic. Purely geostrategic concerns may also be present: having lost one asset, losses may be likely elsewhere because the conditions for resistance have eroded. Nevertheless, in President Eisenhower's original conception and later ones, psycho-political considerations were paramount.[67]

Scholars disagree on the extent to which these beliefs result from bipolarity per se. This has been part of a broader controversy in international relations about the relative effects of system-level constraints and beliefs on behavior. According to one argument, tight bipolarity encourages domino theories because blocs are plainly demarcated. Under these conditions, since gains and losses are highly salient, adversaries and allies will infer diminished credibility in the future from today's losses.[68] Sharply defined competition between clear alternatives also makes the distribution of power fragile. Domestic as well as international disruptions can disturb it, and disturbances in one place spread easily to others. Both superpowers know the rules of the game and consequently have emphasized the prevention of defections and other defeats. Eisenhower, among others, apparently saw such connections.[69]

On the other hand, untestable and self-fulfilling assumptions apparently affect policy independently and significantly. Beliefs that are impossible or difficult to test, either because they are unfalsifiable or pertinent evidence is difficult to obtain, tend to stabilize the status quo because they are highly resistant to discrepant information.[70] Domino theories suffer both problems. They identify two sources of vulnerability: one's adversaries will respond to perceived weakness by becoming bolder or more aggressive; for similar reasons, allies or neutrals will appease potential aggressors. The first assumes that states make and act according to general adjustments about others' resolve. Since relevant data are usually unavailable, and this belief easily substitutes for detailed knowledge, it is hard to falsify.[71] The second problem, allied "bandwagoning," occurs if small states lack resolve to resist outside pressure. Hegemons hinder such resolve if they are so worried about defections that they provide constant reassurances of support. This has characterized U.S. behavior toward Europe and is discussed further in Chapters 3 through 7.

Reputation is perhaps more intrinsically important within hegemonic coalitions. Because others depend on the hegemon, its willingness and ability to keep commitments are carefully scrutinized. The importance of consistent behavior across relationships and countries was stressed earlier in this chapter. As a hegemon's capabilities erode, others' confidence declines, causing them to reduce dependence and commitment to coalition norms.[72] The FSX case illustrates what hegemonic elites usually prefer to avoid.

The unusual view of commitments often expressed by U.S. officials also recommends a perceptual approach to adaptation. Historically, pledges have most often been interpreted situationally: they are made under particular conditions, and their fulfillment depends on their utility at the time they are called due. This is the traditional realist view. In contrast, U.S. decision makers have viewed commitments nonsituationally, as signals of resolve or principle beyond the immediate circumstances. Although pledges are in fact usually context-dependent, the reasoning and rhetoric behind U.S. commitments have not been. Concerns about dominoes and credibility, as discussed above, are only part of the reason. The pattern also reflects an often moralistic approach to alignment and America's thin geopolitical tradition. The power of traditional mindsets was especially evident in the 1950s and 1960s, when U.S. officials routinely spoke about permanent partnerships and the "sanctity" of American commitments.[73] If bipolarity indeed clarified great-power interests[74] and U.S. allies understood this as well, why was such rhetoric necessary?

Domestic political processes can also actuate external expansion. The domestic determinants of policy adaptation are discussed further in chapter 3, but two interest-group arguments are pertinent here. Logrolling, first, seems conducive to ambitious or overcommitted policies. In Soviet succession struggles, rivals have typically advanced competing programs combining bold efforts in certain key sectors (defense and agriculture) with an infusion of resources into consumer-oriented sectors intended to appease the mass production. As Breslauer sees it, this leads to "very tight budgeting."[75] Snyder claims that coalition-building also explains Brezhnev's "expansionist detente": the military received an arms buildup, ideologues got an ambitious Third World policy, and technocrats got more technology from the West.[76] Similarly, U.S. policy options normally proceed to the president via bureaucratic clearances, inviting coalition formation. Domestic logrolling is less intrinsically a cause of expansion than the other factors just mentioned; it is possible because powerful states do not face sharp constraints in taking on commitments.

This hypothesis needs refinement and clear tests, and is far from a complete explanation of expansion. If, for example, the internal constituencies that profit from it have become veto groups, are their interests a product of prior expansion? The postwar U.S. "national security state" required consensual hard-line views and routinely large military budgets before the "awesome collage of money, institutions, ideology, interests, commitments, capabilities, and firepower" fully developed.[77]

Policy coalitions illuminate other patterns as well. Alan Lamborn distinguishes between two kinds of risks associated with every policy choice: policy risk is the probability that substantive goals will not be achieved, and political risk is the likelihood that policies will damage the power position of a key member of a policymaking coalition. The less coherent a coalition's policy and the more dispersed is key members' control over policy, the higher its members' level of acceptable policy risk and the lower their threshold of short-term political risk.[78] This hypothesis, applied to U.S. security policy, suggests one reason why NATO commitments have proved so resilient.

The United States has a fragmented foreign policy decision structure. Central decision makers can impose their will on the bureaucracy, but the time and political costs may be high. Congress shares authority for all policy instruments that require public funds. Consequently, stable policy coalitions usually include Congress (or a few key members) and the top uniformed military officers (who retain the right to speak their minds directly to Congress) as well as the president. The list might be longer on particular issues. Civilian defense analysts were influential during the 1960s, as were Treasury officials at a time when the exchange costs of U.S. troops in Europe made defending the dollar difficult. By Lamborn's criteria, U.S. security-policy coalitions are typically of moderate size; each key member has significant but limited control over policy. The policies themselves often balance competing ends and lack sharp coherence. Within NATO, U.S. burden-sharing policy is typically torn between competing criteria of appeasing Congress about allies' military spending and reassuring allies of continued support. Deterrence policies, as discussed below, suffer several key ambiguities. Some acceptance of policy risks as a way to avoid political risks should be expected.

These terms must be defined in context. Certain policy risks, such as allied doubts about American staying power, are unacceptable to most actors. Consequently, the risks of overextension are tolerable. Schlesinger addressed the tradeoffs squarely:

> to back away from commitments is more easily said than done. In practice, the loss in prestige may actually reduce our power more than the reduced claims on our military resources enhances that power. In that may lie the supreme irony. Closing the commitments-power gap may not be possible through reduction of commitments. The United States, as a great power, has essentially taken on the task of sustaining the international order. And any abandonment of commitments is difficult to reconcile with that imposing task. The upshot is that our commitments will remain large and that our military power will remain more modest in relation to those commitments than it has been in the past. This implies a degree of risk that we must acknowledge and accept.[79]

This view reflects the fear, common among hegemonic elites, that their resolve is the glue holding together an acceptable world order. Having committed itself broadly, the United States is locked into a hegemonic role.

It suggests that the turbulent frontier metaphor exaggerates the happenstance in hegemonic expansionism. "Turbulence" might explain individual expansionist steps, but it obscures a key underlying dynamic: security hegemons engage in clear calculations that result in knowingly overextending themselves. This seeming paradox has two major causes. Historically, as Paul Kennedy shows, states' relative economic strength tends to peak well before their military-territorial influence. Later, as others catch up, competitive pressures make security more expensive in absolute as well as opportunity-cost terms. This pattern is depicted in Figure 2.3. At time t_1 a state can afford more security commitments than it actually demands (in other words, its economic position exceeds its military position), but the situation is reversed at t_2. (The figure intends only to highlight the comparative horizontal position of the curve's peaks and does not necessarily represent their precise shapes.) Nevertheless, Kennedy's four-century survey leads him to conclude, "Great Powers in relative decline instinctively respond by spending more on 'security,' and thereby divert potential resources from 'investment' and compound their long-term dilemma."[80]

What Kennedy calls instinct refers to short-run notions of security that neglect its economic foundations. Another pattern is the tendency for security commit-

Figure 2.3
The Lag Between Economic and Military Ascendance

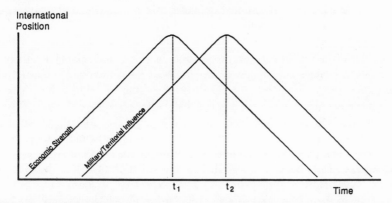

Source: Adapted from Paul Kenndy, *The Rise and Fall of the Great Powers* (New York: Random House, 1987), p. xxiii.

ments, like prices in oligopolitic markets, to be "sticky" downwards. Over-extended states find that retreating to a more sustainable defense perimeter is difficult even when warranted by the objective threats in particular circumstances. Although the Kennedy and Johnson administrations understood that Eisenhower had overstretched the country's capabilities through indiscriminate commitments, the pledges had to be kept for the reasons Schlesinger articulated later.[81] This was true despite increasing fragmentation in the Communist bloc and knowledge that the missile gap was a Soviet rather than an American problem. While one might discount these examples somewhat for nonsituational cognitive and affective biases in the U.S. policy, none of Kennedy's other great-power examples is noticeably different in this regard.

The consequences of overcommitment are tangible, serious and, within the political priorities that prevailed from the late 1940s through the 1980s, apparently irremediable. Richard Halloran sums the situation up succinctly: "the United States lacks the forces, the transport and the warmaking supplies to execute the tasks laid on the armed forces."[82] Those tasks, part of a hegemon's decision-making and military mobilization roles, are very ambitious: the United States is the first great power committed to fight different kinds of wars "in every corner of the globe."[83] Shortfalls in force units and transport are particularly worrisome with regard to contingencies outside Europe and are discussed in some detail below. Budgetary priorities exemplify the point about military readiness. The Reagan administration stipulated that stockpiles of ammunition, fuel, and other consummables should be sufficient for 180 days of combat, the time required for war production to keep pace with a durable opponent. Congressional investigators found that the Army alone needed $165 billion to meet this goal; even if it were achieved, the Navy and Air Force would remain seriously undersupplied.[84] Several SACEURs complained that this situation would force them to hold back on conventional ordnance in a war and request early authorization to use nuclear weapons.

Although NATO commanders cannot assume that they will receive authorization, the alliance's strategy and preparations have long pointed in that direction. As Western nuclear advantages over the USSR have receded, U.S. extended deterrence policy—and thus NATO doctrine—came to rely on the threat of uncontrolled nuclear escalation in ways that earlier planning did not.[85] This has probably induced caution on both sides; but as Betts has argued, no American leader has renounced the nuclear crutch and future confrontations are possible. These risks uphold U.S. commitments, and no alternative is in sight.

Congress clearly bears responsibility for this situation as well as the executive branch. Legislators routinely fight to save expensive weapons programs that bring jobs to their districts and states, preferring to nickle-and-dime readiness supplies and wartime medical care. Mushrooming weapons costs and American dependence on high-technology arms are serious problems in this regard. In *The Rise and Fall of the Great Powers*, Kennedy jokes about a time in the not-too-distant future when the entire Air Force budget will buy only a *single* aircraft. The general trend ought to worry a military establishment that has come to rely heavily on technology for a competitive edge.[86]

Executive-branch civilians, however, must balance the commitments that comprise grand strategies, and their tendency has been consistently to over-promise. The power asymmetry between a hegemon and prospective allies means that new commitments usually drain more of the leader's resources than they add in coalition strength.[87] Yet Defense Secretary Weinberger refused to set priorities: U.S. commitments simply reflected interests. In language almost identical to Kaufmann's, he asked "what risk of failure are we prepared to accept in our plans for meeting particular contingencies? How much are we prepared to pay to reduce this risk?"[88] It was not surprising, then, that Jimmy Carter's Persian Gulf Doctrine was announced without the means to meet its obligations; Richard Nixon, whose Guam Doctrine held that Asian allies would have to fight their own ground wars, likewise qualified in its ways that would still involve U.S. forces. As suggested below, this merely changed the terms of a continuing commitment and thereby lowered the nuclear threshold.[89]

The military's concerns about the risks of overcommitment have been interpreted in disparate ways. Kennedy assumes that the services worry about exposure to those risks in combat. Kaufmann is more skeptical of their motives:

As might be expected, a gap invariably exists between what the Joint Chiefs regard as required and what the president and the secretary of defense consider to be politically and fiscally feasible. One way to deal with the gap is to challenge the merits of the proposed minimum-risk force . . . and discard it as a benchmark. Another way is to use the gap as the reason for continuing to increase the defense budget. Even when this is done, however, the gap never seems to disappear.[90]

Kaufmann's Pentagon experience lends weight to these observations, but they absolve political leaders of too much responsibility. Officers complained about readiness and combat sustainability into the late 1980s, after it was clear that in leaner budgets those needs would have to come from other programs. Moreover, the services may pad their wish lists because military planners fear that political leaders invariably choose the lowest costs and highest risks they can.[91] These fears seem well founded, especially insofar as policymakers tend to make symbolic commitments without thinking through the risks or requirements. When sharp questions were raised about the Navy's rules of engagement in the 1987 deployment to the Persian Gulf, one analyst said "the question of what the ships do doesn't arise. What they do is be there and be seen to be there."[92]

Even though this book examines only American policy in detail, the preceding argument seems applicable to other hegemons. Selective perception masked the extent or effects of decline in Britain, the United States, and perhaps in the Soviet Union during the late Brezhnev years. British officials lived beyond their long-term means by relying, well into the 1960s, on colonial markets and an unsustainable parity for sterling. The Reagan administration likewise financed the largest peacetime military buildup in history on credit.

In sum, hegemons calculate that overextension is profitable and worth the risk that challenges will exceed resources. Since the vicious cycle of decline and imperial overstretch has been extensively reported and documented, some policymakers are surely aware of the long-term costs as well as the military risks. Yet when Kaufmann and Weinberger rhetorically ask how much reduced risks are worth, the evident answer is "very little." Within limits, this is an acceptable stratagem. As discussed in chapter 3, declining great powers typically have enough slack to postpone adjustment. Moreover, conventional requirements are inescapably ambiguous for a superpower that faces permanent nuclear risks.[93] Like airlines that routinely overbook flights in anticipation of "no shows," the odds are good that all commitments will never simultaneously be called due. Yet none of this denies that hegemons consciously run serious policy risks to avoid difficult choices.

Aside from losing ground to an adversary, in which case policy and political risks overlap, the major political risk for most U.S. administrations is the military's defection from a policy coalition. This does not imply that military views or interests are monolithic; it recognizes that the services are coalition players that frequently demand side-payments from civilians and might be dissatisfied enough to defect. Because senior officers can, up to a point, deal independently with Congress, keeping them on board is important to presidents, especially those perceived as dovish. The side-payments are often inconsistent with moderate security policies: the Joint Chiefs supported the Test Ban Treaty only when the Kennedy administration pledged to continue the nuclear buildup and other testing.[94] These compromises also make it difficult to adjust commitments. According to Henry Kissinger, "some in the Pentagon would rather maintain our troops in Europe . . . than return a portion to the U.S. where they are more exposed to congressional budget cutters." This was not an isolated example; troop cuts in Korea have been opposed for similar reasons.[95]

To conclude, American officials' willingness to run the risks of overextension has reinforced expansionism, mainly by impeding defense reductions and adjustment of NATO commitments. But because these risks are defined in terms of assumptions about acceptable policy consequences, they can change over time. Subsequent discussion will return to this point.

The Problem of Overdetermined Outcomes

The foregoing indicates that hegemonic expansionism is overdetermined. External missions and power-projection requirements grow along with potential capability, threats multiply, beliefs about resolve reputation make it difficult to assess commitments on their intrinsic merits, and domestic constituencies develop stakes in ambitious policies. An outcome is overdetermined when more than one independent cause suffices to produce it. Expansion is explained by both systemic and belief-system arguments: hegemons overextend themselves because they believe and to some extent see tangible evidence that their systemic role requires it. Logrolling and political-risk coalition arguments contribute to the outcome without sufficiently explaining it. Some test must be devised to rule out one of these alternative explanations, but this is difficult with only two cases (that is, accounts of conventional and nuclear commitments).

A test might proceed as follows. First, the systemic and cognitive models can be more sharply specified to generate conflicting predictions. Second, a critical case can be used to establish degrees of validity among them.

The systemic model of eroding hegemony predicts that declining hegemons will become less willing to pay for leadership commitments. Hegemons defend the status quo in their own interest, making it rational for allies to understate their demand for protection. Because their relative military power declines over time, hegemons' defense costs tend to outstrip both the "revenues" generated by external assets and their own resources. This, in turn, leaves lower shares of national product for investment, further weakening the future domestic revenue base.[96] At some point, rising opportunity costs exceed the benefits of the security supplied to others. Since capability enhancement is generally infeasible over the long run, regime responsibilities come under increasing strain.

Gilpin's framework allows us to sharpen this. He claims that the internalization of externalities creates incentives for expansion: "In the case of positive externalities, the political system seeks to increase its control over the international system in order to force the benefited party to pay revenues for the conferred benefits."[97] But this applies only to beneficiaries outside the hegemon's coalition or territory—that is, only if expansion would in fact enlarge its potential "tax base.'' If beneficiaries are already under its control or tutelage, and especially if the protection that benefits them becomes significantly more expensive to provide, a hegemon should rationally internalize those externalities by qualifying or redefining regime commitments. As explained in chapter 3, this is difficult for benefits that approximate pure public goods. The distinction between internal and external beneficiaries is important because a declining hegemon most often adjusts its role vis-à-vis existing partners.

A conflicting hypothesis can be inferred from a general cognitive argument. Chapter 3 discusses specific, shared images of Europe; this model concerns the general psychology of risk. While people usually make risk-averse choices, risk-taking is common when one must choose between, on the one hand, a sure loss and, on the other, a substantial probability of a larger loss but some probability of none. In other words, certain gains are preferred to possible, larger ones, but people will risk larger losses to avoid certain, smaller ones.[98] This explains Gilpin's empirical observation that ''when the choice ahead has appeared to be to decline or fight, statesmen have most generally fought.''[99]

Such stark choices are rare, however. Gains and losses are normally more incremental. Even declining hegemons retain relatively few certain losses. Choices about commitments are thus usually risk-averse: others are seen as incapable of assuming leadership roles. President Bush rushed largely unilaterally to protect Saudi Arabia after Iraq's invasion of Kuwait, preferring not to rely on other Arab states—depite their deep stakes in the conflict—to organize a satisfactory regional response.

A systemic-constraint model thus implies behavior quite different from the risk-aversion predicted on cognitive grounds. The former leads one to expect that costs will be most salient to a declining hegemon; consistency and reputational factors are the prime movers of policy in the latter. The overdetermined conclusion that hegemons do not retrench voluntarily can be reexamined by testing what are now two conflicting hypotheses.

A crucial case, if available, should resolve the issue. Eckstein defines such a case as one ''that *must closely fit* a theory if one is to have confidence in the theory's validity, or, conversely, *must not fit* equally well any rule contrary to that proposed.'' He later backtracks slightly to the notions of ''most-likely'' and ''least-likely'' cases. The difference is small; a most-likely case should support a theory if any will.[100] I inferred that hegemons should rationally adjust to overstretch by internalizing externalities in the only way possible, that is, by redefining commitments. For these purposes, whether costs are perceived as significant can be inferred from policy statements or the views of others who share official goals. An appropriate test case concerns the responsibilities U.S. officials preferred for themselves and other NATO members in the wake of Moscow's invasion of Afghanistan.

For two reasons, the case is a reasonably decisive way to choose between the hypotheses. First, because hegemonic decline was putatively well advanced by 1980, new obligations would have had high opportunity costs. Second, the period in question followed a major Soviet incursion and involved an issue—access to Persian Gulf resources—over which Western solidarity had broken down before. While the costs of a new commitment to protect the Gulf were high, the hegemon's concern over resolve and reputation both outside and within the coalition should have been equally significant.

The outcome appears at first to rule out the cognitive model of decline. Soon after the Carter administration committed America to defend the Gulf, it raised the issue of how Europe might help. Its motivation was twofold: the added stress on U.S. military assets, and domestic politics. Before 1968, Britain had been primarily responsible for policing the Gulf; Washington now aimed to return to that division of labor. Transport and troop depletion in Europe were the specific problems. As late as 1988, the United States could fully deploy its troops to the Gulf in the time envisioned (30 to 40 days) only by using *all* available lift capacity, and the situation was even tighter before the Reagan military buildup. Moreover, since those troops had dual assignments, a protracted engagement would have reduced by at least 20 percent (and perhaps a third) the troops available to fight in Europe. Even though hegemons are habitually overextended, it was particularly hazardous in this case because the Soviets could reinforce much more easily, and a conflict, by U.S. design, could spread. Congress thus linked funding for the Rapid Deployment Force to allied help. These pressures gave U.S. officials little choice but to raise the issue,[101] despite the fact that any substantial pressure on the allies might have been thought to risk doubts about America's own staying power.

On closer examination, the cognitive hypothesis cannot be rejected. European troop reserves, munitions stockpiles, and logistics capabilities remain inadequate to compensate for potentially diverted U.S. forces; allies promises have apparently satisfied U.S. officials concerned mainly with symbolic cooperation and congressional complaints about free-riding.[102] This makes it difficult to rule out either hypothesis, since U.S. officials *also* tried to deal substantively with their strategic problem. A key question is, therefore, how hard they pressed the allies. It is often argued that sluggish economies and a shortage of military personnel prevent the Europeans from doing more.[103] While correct, this ignores the fact that they have never met NATO's agreed force goals. America's reluctance to make its commitment conditional on more European effort suggests that the cognitive argument has some causal weight.

This case also indicates that the system hypothesis needs refinement. The Carter administration, while not unconcerned about the substantive problem of troop depletion in Europe, worried most about congressional perceptions that NATO allies were not sharing added burdens. Where precisely does this leave the hypothesis that positive externalities are redefined when a hegemon becomes more constrained? Declining hegemons apparently try to redistribute burdens, albeit cautiously. They face conflicting incentives: logistical, financial and internal political pressures signal overcommitment, while risk-aversion works the other way. A clear resolution of the resources-commitments gap would be unlikely under most such circumstances. Chapter 3 further assesses systemic theories of hegemonic decline and presents a somewhat different argument. Concluding this discussion is a further elaboration of the range of adaptive options.

Categorizing Adaptive Choices

Since expansionism is reversible, I next discuss three generic adaptive choices. This conceptualization reframes the amended adjustment typology (Figure 2.2) in terms of hegemonic commitments. As discussed above, commitments are the policy instruments through which governments adhere to regimes or other collective enterprises. Several hypotheses that sum up the argument follow this discussion.

To repeat, adaptation is a government's nonroutine response to constraints. Hegemons adapt by modifying their commitments to other states and qualifying or curtailing the "services" they perform. They can do this by adapting within the terms of an existing commitment, changing the terms of a continuing commitment, or renouncing a commitment. These are analogous, respectively, to enhancing capabilities, redefining or renegotiating regime means, and abrogating or renegotiating regime ends. These categories are not mutually exclusive, but most policies fall logically into one of them. The first nuclear-use pledge is an illustrative and ideally a representative example of the available choices.

Adaptation of First Use. Although U.S. obligations under the North Atlantic Treaty were understood to include nuclear protection, the first-use commitment was not formalized until the 1950s. In 1954 the North Atlantic Council authorized NATO military commanders to initiate use of nuclear weapons against the Warsaw Pact. The alliance's Military Committee reiterated this with directive MC 14/2 in 1957. Since British (and later French) nuclear forces were independently controlled and all nuclear weapons on the continent were then American, it was effectively a U.S. pledge. Despite strenuous U.S. efforts during the 1960s to raise the nuclear threshold to obviate first use, when NATO doctrine was revised in 1967, the result, MC 14/3, satisfied European demands and reaffirmed that possibility. Europe's preference, reflected in NATO's meager ability to sustain conventional combat, has been early use (or at least its threat) in wartime. For the United States, if not its allies, theater nuclear weapons have been a bridge between conventional defeat and intercontinental superpower conflict.

First use links U.S. territory to deterrence failures in Europe (and perhaps elsewhere); no American president wishes to execute it, and the reluctance has surely grown. But none has wished to renounce it and tempt the Soviets or, more immediately, threaten NATO's ever-fragile strategic consensus. Balancing these considerations is the aim of adjustment.

Adaptation within the terms of an existing commitment implies accepting its responsibilities and developing capabilities appropriate to new constraints. These capabilities can be developed internally, with others' help, or both. This option is generally most consistent with risk aversion within hegemonic coalitions. Under some interpretations the Kennedy administration's flexible response (FR) strategy, discussed in chapter 4, met these criteria. It held that a low nuclear threshold was dangerous and incredible. Military action would initially be conventional; nuclear weapons might be used, but in theory only after several escalatory steps. The requirements were large and mobile nonnuclear forces and flexible nuclear options. FR's deterrent rests more on where a conflict might end than on where it starts; the height of the nuclear threshold and the role of escalation are ambiguous.[104] Since Americans would rather fight a conventional (European) war than a nuclear one, FR conforms to the terms of first use only if the latter remains plausible.

U.S. planners and strategists have pursued plausible nuclear war options for thirty years. A variety of ways to escalate or indicate resolve to do so has been the thrust of these efforts: "War plans should threaten vital Soviet interests, targeting what they value most and exploiting their fears. . . . The plans must also be tailored to provide sensible options for a range of hypothetical circumstances, to allow deterrence to fail in stages, and to facilitate early termination of a war on acceptable terms."[105] Presidents, in other words, are more likely to act resolutely if they can control the interaction but still coerce the enemy. In its most demanding formulation, this requires escalation dominance, the ability to deny an adversary victory at any higher level of violence.

As discussed in chapter 6, this kind of nuclear adaptation is extremely demanding. It has four chief requirements. One, survivable nuclear forces, is shared by more modest (e.g., second-use-only) policies. A second requirement, flexible options and target assignments, was emphasized in the early 1960s and again in the 1970s and 1980s. By 1980, the Single Integrated Operational Plan (SIOP) provided various ways to attack enemy nuclear forces, conventional military forces, economic and industrial centers, and military and political leadership centers. Third, since the most critical targets are hardened, this strategy demands "hard target kill": means of destroying or threatening Moscow's most powerful, accurate weapons and its command systems. Thus, according to Ravenal, commitment to first use depends on counterforce options and the hope that they could end a war on relatively favorable terms.[106] Fourth, flexibility demands command systems capable of executing and terminating operations "for extended periods after absorbing a well-coordinated attack regardless of U.S. force and alert posture." Few if any analysts believe the last criterion can be met.[107]

Partly for these reasons, some analysts are attracted to strategies that render first use less demanding and dangerous. One of these, "countercombatant targeting," emphasizes the targeting of Soviet conventional forces, such as tank concentrations, rather than nuclear forces. The rationale is that only the former can hold territory; the latter are either invulnerable, would be used early in a conflict, or should be spared to control the war. This strategy requires more sophisticated sensor and targeting capabilities than now exist,[108] and of course does not address the problem of Soviet counterforce weapons targeted against

U.S. nuclear forces. If Moscow were to deemphasize first-strike weapons, this strategy would put fewer demands on a first-use commitment.

Changing the terms of a continuing commitment is something of a contradiction: a commitment obligates specified behavior under specified conditions, and altering either terminates it. But a promisor might alter a pledge to make its responsibilities less costly or risky, not to change fundamentally its relationships with its partner(s). It would then seek to sustain the larger framework in which the commitment is embedded. The Nixon Doctrine, as suggested above, changed the terms of continuing U.S. commitments in Asia rather than abrogate them. Allies were promised more economic and military assistance, as well as air and naval support if necessary, but not ground troops. American personnel were no longer a guaranteed part of those commitments.

Redefining commitments carries the risk that others will cut their dependence even if the hegemon remains actively involved. FR contributed to Charles de Gaulle's withdrawal from NATO's military arm, and the Association of Southeast Asian Nations (ASEAN), which Washington supports, filled a vacuum left after American withdrew from Vietnam. Some states will not have such options and devolution, a transferal of security tasks from the hegemon to its partners, can have beneficial consequences. French and British nuclear forces imply added uncertainty in wartime for Moscow. But devolution does present risks, and this is a major argument against altering commitments.

Deterrence strategies that raise the nuclear threshold without renouncing first use belong in this category. Least controversial are measures to protect nuclear weapons and command systems early in a war and reduce pressures to cross the threshold before a considered political decision can be made. Hardening command centers and aircraft shelters, moving vulnerable systems from the front lines, and eliminating particularly destabilizing weapons (e.g., nuclear artillery systems and anti-aircraft weapons, atomic demolition munitions) are steps in this direction. The last in particular would give political leaders more time to consider their options.[109]

Tighter procedures for consultation among Alliance members before nuclear weapons would be used are more controversial. The problem is that military planning has superceded detailed assurances about who would be consulted and how the fog of war might prevent it. Weapons dispersal and other decisions affecting nuclear alert levels and deployment patterns in a crisis could be made subject to political approval, even if this made the threat of first use less credible.[110]

Severely qualifying the pledge can appear to abrogate it, even if the motives are credibility and prudence. In 1988 *Discriminate Deterrence*, the report of a U.S. government advisory panel, suggested that emerging technologies portended improvements in weapons accuracies that might allow substitution of conventional for nuclear weapons in "many" potentially critical missions.[111] Insofar as this could justify further reductions in NATO's theater nuclear arsenal, it would be popular with the European public. But the proposal reinforced

Figure 2.4
Adjusting Foreign Policy Commitments

DEGREE OF POLICY CHANGE

	Adapt Within Terms of Existing Commitment	Change Terms of a Continuing Commitment	Renounce Commitment
Internal	Create capabilities unilaterally or transform domestic structures (e.g. build one's own options to maintain first-use pledge)	Change terms (specific obligations) unilaterally (e.g. raise nuclear threshold unilaterally but retain first-use)	Relinquish unilaterally the purposes of the commitment (e.g. abrogate first-use without allied acquiescence)
LOCUS			
External	Ask others' help in maintaining commitment (e.g. ask others to build up conventional forces)	Renegotiate terms (e.g. negotiate with Allies a new military doctrine that raises threshold but retains first-use)	Negotiate devolution of commitment to Allies (e.g. seek a substitute for existing deterrence regime)

concerns among European leaders and defense specialists that the U.S. nuclear commitment was weakening: such a goal undermined the shared nuclear risks that underlie first use and separate America's security from Europe's.[112]

Admittedly, redefining a commitment can be a hair's breadth from renouncing it. But the distinction can be meaningful. An explicit NFU policy exemplifies renunciation: the four former officials who revived the idea in 1982 were transparently disingenuous in calling it a "redefinition." They emphasized that nuclear guarantees of "some sort" are essential in Europe, that only America could at present provide them, and that the United States should continue to pledge nuclear retaliation for any nuclear attack.[113] But for most Europeans, first use has signified America's willingness to take unprecedented risks to deter *any* major conflict on their territories. NFU, in short, qualifies this pledge so fundamentally as to abrogate it. Figure 2.4 summarizes the three adaptive options in terms of commitments.

Many have argued that first use is patently incredible and was abrogated de facto years ago. Even if this is true, it is significant that NATO's political leaders have never officially sanctioned such a change. NFU is a form of devolution; while this usually implies troop cuts, it applies equally to a drastic reduction in nuclear protection. It amounts to a gamble that Europeans would assume those responsibilities relinquished by the United States. To those who believe that postwar Europeans have never defined their security in terms of territorial defense, this is a major risk.[114]

It is important to remember that a hegemon's role encourages risk-acceptant behavior by its partners. A much higher nuclear threshold could catalyze a stronger West European defense role. Dependencies, though, can work in both directions: the strong often depend on the order provided by their ties to the weak.

Adaptive Preferences: Some Hypotheses. The argument thus far can be summarized by two hypotheses. The research design precludes rigorous tests; my purpose is rather to make the argument as explicit as possible and examine the historical materials systematically.

Hypothesis 1: Hegemons postpone adaptation to decline by knowingly overextending themselves.

This is a rational course of action if it is assumed that all commitments will not be called due simultaneously. Great powers typically take these risks, and not only in decline; America's foreign commitments have consistently exceeded its means to honor them since the early 1950s.[115] But because opportunity costs mount and policymakers find it difficult to adjust to tight resources, the problem is especially serious for declining hegemons. This hypothesis indicates only that overextension is conscious; it does not suggest the extent to which the process accelerates as power erodes.

Hypothesis 2: In decline, hegemons face conflicting cues and incentives. Consequently, governments will adjust to environmental constraints by first trying to adapt within the terms of existing commitments and then by changing the terms of a continuing commitment. Renunciation will be rejected unless it is the only available option.

This hypothesis clarifies the above point somewhat. Declining hegemons will try to maintain allies' confidence by adjusting commitments as little as possible. This does not tell us whether adjustment, if necessary, will be sought at home or abroad. Ikenberry argues that policymakers look for the proper fit between policy instruments and the problem at hand, suggesting no a priori preference.[116] All else equal, risk aversion would suggest defensive internal adjustment. The Persian Gulf case indicates that legislative pressures affect the policy instruments with which executive-branch officials have to work and thus the locus of adaptation. This point raises the issues of issue-area and state capacity, both of which are discussed in Chapter 3.

CONCLUSIONS

For reasons recognized since antiquity, great powers tend to expand their territorial and political reach. Where territorial control over others is precluded, a hegemon's role is structured by commitments to legally independent but politically dependent states. Such commitments encourage its partners to accept the risks of vulnerability, and give it substantial capacity to organize international affairs.

Policy adaptation necessarily occurs through redefining and qualifying these commitments. Overextension is a notable result in both instances: hegemons engage in clear calculations that involve knowingly overcommitting themselves.

Such states prefer the risks of overextension to the loss of order associated with control.

Because overcommitment is preferred to devolution, hegemons find themselves in a vicious cycle. Resolve reputation is valuable because it reinforces deterrence and because hegemons are routinely overextended. If, as Schlesinger put it, a state aims to sustain the world order, reputational concerns make it difficult to discriminate among commitments. Overextension seems an intrinsic part of the hegemonic role itself.

These patterns became more costly and their effects become more controversial as American power declined in the 1970s and 1980s and the Cold War eased in the late 1980s. While both trends produced pressures for adjustment, it was not easy to achieve politically. President Bush appeared to be adjusting to new geopolitical conditions at the end of the 1980s, aided by benign Soviet behavior and renewed emphasis in Europe on political and military integration. Nevertheless, the consensus around which U.S. grand strategy was built in the 1950s was durable, in part because clear alternatives were lacking. At the end of the 1980s, although the two American commitments to NATO appeared intact for the time being, both were being subjected to internal and external stress. Chapter 3 discusses the kinds of pressures that induce policy adjustment.

NOTES

1. Robert O. Keohane, *After Hegemony: Cooperation and Discord in the World Political Economy* (Princeton: Princeton University Press, 1984), pp. 33–34.

2. *The Random House College Dictionary*, rev. ed. (New York: Random House, 1984), p. 15.

3. James N. Rosenau, "Foreign Policy as Adaptive Behavior: Some Preliminary Notes for a Theoretical Model," *Comparative Politics* 2, no. 3 (April 1970): 366.

4. Ibid., p. 379.

5. Kjell Goldmann usefully distinguishes between "adaptation" and "learning" as sources of policy change. Adaptation occurs when policies shift in response to environmental circumstances; for example, America's normalization of relations with Beijing in the 1970s was prompted, belatedly, by the Sino-Soviet split. Learning results when policies are revised due to negative feedback; "a typical case would be the abandonment of a conciliatory policy because the response had been nonconciliatory." See Goldmann, *Change and Stability in Foreign Policy: The Problems and Possibilities of Detente* (Princeton, N.J.: Princeton University Press, 1988), p. 6. In U.S. NATO policy, adaptation has been exemplified by long-term efforts to raise the nuclear threshold. Learning occurred when subsequent defense secretaries gave up Robert McNamara's attempts to convince Europeans that a full conventional defense of the continent was desirable and feasible. Policymakers, however, frequently respond both to environmental pressures and negative feedback about existing policies. In these cases, adaptation seems the dominant process. For this reason, and because the study focuses on hegemonic decline, I use adaptation generically to connote both possibilities.

6. This is the definition offered by John Lewis Gaddis in "Containment and the Logic of Strategy," *The National Interest* no. 10 (Winter 1987–88), p. 29.

7. Aaron L. Friedberg, *The Weary Titan: Britain and the Experience of Relative Decline, 1895–1905* (Princeton, N.J.: Princeton University Press, 1988), p. 3.

8. Harold and Margaret Sprout, "The Dilemma of Rising Demands and Insufficient Resources," *World Politics* 20, no. 4 (July 1968): 670.

9. Robert O. Keohane and Joseph S. Nye, Jr., *Power and Interdependence: World Politics in Transition* (Boston: Little, Brown, 1977), pp. 45–46.

10. Harold and Margaret Sprout, "The Dilemma of Rising Demands and Insufficient Resources," passim.

11. G. John Ikenberry, *Reasons of State: Oil Politics and the Capacities of American Government* (Ithaca, N.Y.: Cornell University Press, 1988), pp. 16–19. The quoted passage is from Stephen D. Krasner, "Structural Causes and Regime Consequences: Regimes as Intervening Variables," *International Organization* 36, no. 2 (Spring 1982): 186.

12. The language is Krasner's in Ibid., pp. 186–187.

13. Theda Skocpol, "Social Revolutions and Mass Military Mobilization," *World Politics* 40, no. 2 (January 1988): 150.

14. The distinction between "extractive" and "performance" defense burdens is developed in Daniel N. Nelson and Joseph Lepgold, "Alliances and Burden-Sharing: A NATO-Warsaw Pact Comparison," *Defense Analysis* 2, no. 3 (1986).

15. Huntington, "Coping With the Lippmann Gap," *Foreign Affairs* 66, no. 3, pp. 469–470.

16. Quoted in Kissinger, "A Plan to Reshape NATO," *Time*, March 5, 1984, p. 23.

17. James M. Markham, "A New Europe," *New York Times*, July 20, 1989, p. 4.

18. For a good brief discussion, see Gaddis, "Containment and the Logic of Strategy." His major work on these issues is *Strategies of Containment: A Critical Appraisal of Postwar American National Security Policy* (New York: Oxford University Press, 1982).

19. Stephen D. Krasner, "Are Bureaucracies Important?" in G. John Ikenberry, ed., *American Foreign Policy: Theoretical Essays* (Glenview, Ill.: Scott, Foresman, 1989), p. 426. Krasner's theoretical position is further developed in *Defending the National Interest: Raw Materials Investments and U.S. Foreign Policy* (Princeton, N.J.: Princeton University Press, 1978). Ikenberry's work on American oil policy (note 8) explicitly belongs to this school.

20. Keohane and Nye, *Power and Interdependence*, p. 44.

21. George Modelski, *Long Cycles in World Politics* (Seattle: University of Washington Press, 1987), pp. 14–15.

22. This is adapted from the discussion in Roland Paul, *American Military Commitments Abroad* (New Brunswick, N.J.: Rutgers University Press, 1973), p. 6.

23. This issue is complex and depends in part on how the relevant group is defined. Stein and Keohane argue that countries can be excluded from international regimes or the benefits they provide (e.g. Most Favored Nation status). (Stein also claims that all international economic orders have been subsystemic. If so, and strong regimes prevail, consistency requirements would make it would be hard to discriminate within the relevant group.) See Arthur A. Stein, "The Hegemon's Dilemma: Great Britain, the United States, and the International Economic Order," *International Organization* 38, no. 2 (Spring 1984): 359; Robert O. Keohane, "The Theory of Hegemonic Stability and Changes in International Economic Regimes, 1967–1977," in Ole R. Holsti, Randolph M. Siverson,

and Alexander L. George, eds., *Change in the International System* (Boulder, Colo.: Westview, 1980), p. 158, n. 10.

24. This school has developed a vast literature. The most influential works have been Stephen D. Krasner, "State Power and the Structure of International Trade," *World Politics* 28, No. 3 (April 1976); Charles P. Kindleberger, "Systems of International Economic Organization," in David P. Calleo, ed., *Money and the Coming World Order* (New York: New York University Press, 1976); Robert Gilpin, *U.S. Power and the Multinational Corporation: The Political Economy of Direct Foreign Investment* (New York: Basic Books, 1975); Keohane, "The Theory of Hegemonic Stability."

25. Stein, "The Hegemon's Dilemma," passim.

26. Stephen D. Krasner, "American Policy and Global Economic Stability," in William P. Avery and David P. Rapkin, eds., *America in a Changing World Political Economy* (New York: Longman, 1982), pp. 33–34.

27. Stein, "The Hegemon's Dilemma," p. 375.

28. Earl C. Ravenal, *Defining Defense: The 1985 Military Budget* (Washington, D.C.: Cato Institute, 1984), pp. 15, 22.

29. Hedley Bull, *The Anarchical Society: A Study of Order in World Politics* (New York: Columbia University Press, 1977), p. 206.

30. Keohane, *After Hegemony*, pp. 136–137.

31. The term "ordering principle" is Modelski's and refers to all global systems under a "world power." See *Long Cycles in World Politics*, p. 217. The notion of boundary management comes from Manfred Halpern, "A Redefinition of the Revolutionary Situation," *Journal of International Affairs* (January 1969).

32. Modelski, *Long Cycles in World Politics*, pp. 15–16.

33. Keohane, *After Hegemony*, p. 45.

34. Alvin Z. Rubinstein, "The Changing Strategic Balance and Soviet Third World Risk-Taking," *Naval War College Review* 38, no. 2 (March–April 1985): 6.

35. Josef Joffe, "Europe's American Pacifier," *Foreign Policy* 54 (Spring 1984).

36. David Garnham, "Correspondence," *International Security* 10, no. 4 (Spring 1986): 205–207.

37. "Tokyo, Unsure of U.S., Talks of Developing Its Own Arms," *New York Times*, June 28, 1989, pp. 1, 7.

38. Robert O. Keohane, "Externalities and Risk in International Policy Coordination: Some Tentative Thoughts," Stanford University, mimeo, July 1978, pp. 5–6; Keohane, *After Hegemony*, pp. 137–138.

39. Nish Jamgotch, Jr., "Alliance Management in Eastern Europe," *World Politics* 27, no. 3 (April 1975): 417.

40. *The Defense Monitor*, 18, no. 3 (1989): 1; Rubinstein, "The Changing Strategic Balance," p. 6.

41. In practical terms this means their territories are relatively impervious to conquest. Modelski's criterion is "oceanic insularity," and this may have been true before World War II. But the contemporary Soviet Union fits my more general stipulation, which seems to make it preferable here. See *Long Cycles in World Politics*, pp. 221–222.

42. See Keohane, *After Hegemony*, p. 33; Modelski, *Long Cycles in World Politics*, pp. 223–224.

43. Kenneth Waltz, *Theory of International Politics* (Reading, Mass.: Addison-Wesley, 1979), p. 198.

44. Bull, *The Anarchical Society*, pp. 92–93. Napoleon's France is an exception to this generalization.

45. Keohane, *After Hegemony*, p. 37.

46. Most of this paragraph and the next draw on Robert Gilpin, *War and Change in World Politics* (Cambridge: Cambridge University Press, 1981), chap. 3.

47. Ibid., pp. 132, 138. This has been less true of Soviet than British or American policy, so the generalization is tentative. Gilpin avoids the comparison by characterizing Britain and America, but not the USSR, as hegemons. Although this assumption is common in the political economy literature, it downplays the security dimension emphasized in this book.

48. Ibid., pp. 149, 152.

49. Friedberg, *The Weary Titan*, p. 17.

50. Ibid.

51. Due to sensitivity about U.S. support for Israel and pressure from Islamic fundamentalists, most of these airstrips and ports are not U.S. bases, but instead are available under specific prearranged conditions, such as exercises or a regional conflict. See *Christian Science Monitor*, January 19, 1988, p. 1.

52. Robert Jervis, "Cooperation Under the Security Dilemma," *World Politics* 30, no. 2 (January 1978): 169.

53. John S. Galbraith, "The 'Turbulent Frontier' as a Factor in British Expansion," *Comparative Studies in Society and History* 2 (1959–60): 168; see also Ibid., p. 185.

54. Communication from W. F. Jervois, governor of Malaya, to Carnarvon, the British Colonial Secretary, February 10, 1876, in Galbraith, "The 'Turbulent Frontier,' " p. 162.

55. Galbraith, "The 'Turbulent Frontier,' " p. 168.

56. Celeste A. Wallander, "Opportunity, Incrementalism, and Learning in the Extension and Retraction of Soviet Global Commitments," paper prepared for delivery at the 1989 annual meeting of the American Political Science Association, Atlanta, Georgia. The quoted passage is on page 12.

57. Paul Seabury, "The Revolt Against Obligation," in Paul Seabury and Aaron Wildavsky, eds., *U.S. Foreign Policy: Perspectives and Proposals for the 1970s*, (New York: McGraw-Hill, 1969), p. 6.

58. Waltz, *Theory of International Politics*, p. 200.

59. Rubinstein, "The Changing Strategic Balance," p. 8.

60. Friedberg, *The Weary Titan*, p. 282.

61. Ibid., pp. 282–284.

62. Lord Solly Zuckerman, "The Silver Fox," *The New York Review of Books*, January 19, 1989, p. 23.

63. Glenn H. Snyder and Paul Diesing, *Conflict Among Nations: Bargaining, Decision Making, and System Structure in International Crises* (Princeton, N.J.: Princeton University Press, 1978), p. 183.

64. Thomas C. Schelling, *Arms and Influence* (New Haven, Conn.: Yale University Press, 1966), pp. 55–59.

65. Snyder and Diesing, *Conflict Among Nations*, p. 187. "Seamless web" arguments assume that the credibility of all commitments, even the most vital, depend on adversaries' perceptions of a state's *general* resolve. But there is no adequate theoretical or empirical basis for claiming that potential aggressors perceive all commitments as equally credible regardless of context. On this point, see Robert Jervis, "Deterrence and

Perception," *International Security* 7, no. 3 (Winter 1982/1983): 9–10. But these arguments are powerful if policymakers assume that their adversaries are driven by coherent, aggressive purposes, and are thus commonly made by hard-liners.

66. Jervis, "Cooperation Under the Security Dilemma," p. 169.

67. Gaddis, *Strategies of Containment*, p. 144. Assistant Secretary of Defense John McNaughton told Secretary Robert McNamara that 70 percent of the rationale for U.S. military involvement in Vietnam was "to avoid a humiliating U.S. defeat (to our reputation as a guarantor)." See "McNaughton Draft for McNamara on 'Proposed Course of Action,' " in Neil Sheehan et al., *The Pentagon Papers* (Toronto: Bantam, 1971), p. 432. I thank David Garnham for reminding me that there can also be a significant geostrategic dimension to domino beliefs.

68. John Spanier, *Games Nations Play*, 5th ed. (New York: Holt, Rinehart and Winston, 1984), p. 105.

69. In January 1955, Eisenhower approved a National Security Council paper stating that

As the lines between the Communist bloc and the Western coalition have come to be more clearly drawn over the last few years, a situation has arisen in which any further Communist territorial gain would have an unfavorable impact within the free world that might be out of all proportion to the strategic or economic significance of the territory lost.

NSC 5501, "Basic National Security Policy," January 7, 1955, cited in Gaddis, *Strategies of Containment*, p. 131.

70. Robert Jervis, *Perception and Misperception in International Politics* (Princeton, N.J.: Princeton University Press, 1976), pp. 310–315; Goldmann, *Change and Stability in Foreign Policy*, pp. 38–39.

71. Jervis, "Deterrence and Perception," pp. 9–10.

72. Robert O. Keohane, "Externalities and Risk in International Policy Coordination," p. 5.

73. Much of this paragraph draws on Franklin B. Weinstein, "The Concept of a Commitment in International Relations," *Journal of Conflict Resolution* 13, no. 1 (March 1969).

74. This view was expressed by Henry Kissinger in "Coalition Diplomacy in a Nuclear Age," *Foreign Affairs* 42, no. 4 (July 1964): 529–530.

75. George W. Breslauer, *Khruschev and Brezhnev as Leaders: Building Authority in Soviet Politics* (London: Allen and Unwin, 1982), p. 286.

76. Jack Snyder, "Science and Sovietology: Bridging the Methods Gap in Soviet Foreign Policy Studies," *World Politics* 40, no. 2 (January 1988): 178.

77. Daniel Yergin, *Shattered Peace: The Origins of the Cold War and the National Security State* (Boston: Houghton Mifflin, 1978), p. 408.

78. Alan C. Lamborn, "Risk and Foreign Policy Choice," *International Studies Quarterly* 29, no. 4 (December 1985): 387, 389.

79. "Excerpts from Senate Testimony by Schlesinger on Foreign Policy," *New York Times*, February 7, 1985, p. A–14.

80. Kennedy, *The Rise and Fall of the Great Powers* (New York: Random House, 1987), p. xxiii.

81. Gaddis, *Strategies of Containment*, pp. 212–213.

82. Halloran, *To Arm a Nation*, p. 241.

83. Eliot A. Cohen, "When Policy Outstrips Power—American Strategy and State-craft," *The Public Interest* no. 75 (Spring 1984): 11.

84. Halloran, *To Arm a Nation*, pp. 230–232.

85. Smoke, "Extended Deterrence," pp. 41–48.

86. See Cohen, "When Policy Outstrips Power," p. 12.

87. Ibid., p. 17.

88. Caspar W. Weinberger, "U.S. Defense Strategy," *Foreign Affairs* 64, no. 4 (Spring 1986): 678.

89. Earl C. Ravenal, "The Nixon Doctrine and Our Asian Commitments," *Foreign Affairs* 49, no. 2 (January 1971): pp. 209, 216; Henry Brandon, *The Retreat of American Power* (New York: Doubleday, 1973), p. 214.

90. Kaufmann, *The 1986 Defense Budget*, p. 2.

91. Ibid., p. 4.

92. "Showing the Flag," *The New York Times*, May 22, 1987, p. 4.

93. Richard K. Betts, "Conventional Strategy: New Critics, Old Choices," *International Security* 7, no. 4 (Spring 1983): 153.

. 94. Arthur M. Schlesinger, Jr., *A Thousand Days: John F. Kennedy in the White House* (New York: Fawcett, 1965), p. 833.

95. Henry Kissinger, "A Plan to Reshape NATO," p. 23; Richard Halloran, "U.S. Considers the Once Unthinkable on Korea," *The New York Times*, July 13, 1989, p. 8.

96. Gilpin, *War and Change in World Politics*, pp. 158, 169.

97. Ibid., p. 70. This terminology is a bit loose. In *Modern Political Economy* (New York: McGraw-Hill, 1978), p. 345, McKenzie and Tullock define externalities as "the positive or negative effects which exchanges have on people not participating in the market." There is no "market" as such for defense protection, although states do register different preferences and demand different amounts. The European members of NATO, of course, *are* autonomous participants, even though they also benefit from protection America provides as a by-product of its rivalry with Moscow. "Positive externalities" usefully describe America's nuclear and conventional commitments if one assumes that European real estate would be protected regardless of who inhabited it, that a socially more efficient arrangement could be achieved if the allies were somehow forced to purchase their true preference for protection, and that this amount is higher than what they now provide for themselves. One also suspects that states reap fewer gains from colonial expansion than territorial accretion, since administrative costs are higher and direct economic benefits probably lower. On the other hand, the sunk costs of annexation are much greater, so that even if its costs outweigh benefits, the option of devolution is at least improbable if not foreclosed.

98. Daniel Kahneman and Amos Tversky, "The Psychology of Preferences," *Scientific American* 246, no. 1 (January 1982).

99. Gilpin, *War and Change in World Politics*, p. 191.

100. Eckstein, "Case Study and Theory in Political Science," p. 118, emphasis in original.

101. This draws on Charles Kupchan, *The Persian Gulf and the West: The Dilemma of Security* (Boston: Allen and Unwin, 1987), Chap. 8 and page 117, note 39.

102. Kupchan, *The Persian Gulf and the West*, pp. 187, 191–192; see also Charles Kupchan, "NATO and the Persian Gulf: Examining Intra-Alliance Behavior," *International Organization* 42, no. 2 (Spring 1988): 337–338, 345.

103. Kupchan, "NATO and the Persian Gulf," pp. 343–344.

104. Smoke, "Extended Deterrence," p. 43.

105. Bruce G. Blair, *Strategic Command and Control: Redefining the Nuclear Threat* (Washington, D.C.: Brookings Institution, 1985), p. 40.

106. Ravenal, "Counterforce and Alliance," p. 34.

107. Blair, *Strategic Command and Control*, p. 43. He quotes Lt. Gen. Hillman Dickinson, who directed strategic command and control in the Carter administration.

108. Jan Lodal, "An Arms Control Agenda," *Foreign Policy* no. 72 (Fall 1988), p. 170; "US Conferees See Diminishing Role for Nuclear Weapons," *Christian Science Monitor*, June 28, 1989, p. 7.

109. Daniel Charles, *Nuclear Planning in NATO: Pitfalls of First Use* (Cambridge, Mass.: Ballinger, 1987), p. 159. The tactical portion of the U.S. arsenal has steadily decreased over the past several years, and this should continue as more warheads are retired than replaced. Some missions, such as air defense, are scheduled to be performed by conventional weapons. See *Bulletin of the Atomic Scientists*, June 1989, p. 49.

110. Charles, *Nuclear Planning in NATO*, chap. 8.

111. Fred C. Ikle and Albert Wohlstetter, *Discriminate Deterrence* (Washington, D.C.: U.S. Government Printing Office, 1988), pp. 8, 50.

112. Hunter, "Will the United States Remain a European Power?" p. 213.

113. Bundy et al., "Nuclear Weapons and the Atlantic Alliance," pp. 758–759.

114. Colin S. Gray, "NATO: Time to Call It a Day?" *The National Interest* 10 (1987/88): 16–17.

115. See David Garnham and Joseph Lepgold, "Toward a Sustainable Containment Strategy," *Coexistence* 25 (1988), and the literature cited in note 1.

116. Ikenberry, *Reasons of State*, p. 204.

3 Explaining Hegemonic Adaptation

Few individuals, organizations, or governments adjust established behavior unless pressed to do so. This is especially true of declining hegemons. Yet commitments assumed under favorable circumstances may become unsustainable and adaptation may be unavoidable. Chapter 2 argued that hegemons under these circumstances have consistent adjustment preferences across three jointly exhaustive classes of options. That argument provides baseline expectations in relation to which anomalies can be identified and explained.

Even so, this only begins to explain how governments respond to decline. It indicates neither the kinds of environmental changes that make adaptation probable nor, as the last chapter suggested, the precise levels at which they become politically salient. Friedberg shows that British policy under comparable conditions reflected the internal pattern of capability assessments and the division of domestic political power.[1] A theoretical argument about hegemonic adjustment must come to terms with both. In this chapter, I attempt to show that the international relations literature contains interesting but implicit arguments about governments' priorities as they assess their relative positions. These patterns, while rather general, contain various specific behavioral implications. I also show that cognitive arguments pinpoint other factors relevant to inter-alliance policy. The division of domestic political power is important because, as might be expected, the executive is often hard-pressed to implement its preferences in a decentralized democracy. Those problems, however, vary from issue to issue in important and regular ways.

The chapter begins with a brief discussion of policy change and the difficulties of coming to grips with it. I then discuss arguments at the international, decision-making group, and state levels that seem most useful in understanding hegemonic adaptation. The chapter concludes with a summary and several additional hypotheses.

PROBLEMS IN EXPLAINING POLICY CHANGE

Systematic attempts to explain foreign-policy behavior invariably confront complex levels-of-analysis issues. Are the sources of state action found mainly at the international, national, or individual level? Realists typically have one answer, organizational and cognitive theorists look in other directions, and conceptual integration seems elusive. Two problems make a grand theory satisfactory to most social scientists unlikely. First, since most patterns are produced by multiple causes at different levels, cutting into the chain of causation becomes difficult and often arbitrary. Second, different research problems send analysts in different directions; even "policy" is defined and operationalized differently by various researchers. The most fruitful level of analysis may depend on the kind of policy issue involved, the stage of a decision under scrutiny, or the degree of detail one seeks.[2] Both problems sharpen inevitable tensions between explanatory breadth and precision.

One response is to change the research problem—for example, to scrutinize policy continuity rather than change. In Kjell Goldmann's framework, the "conditions" for a policy are those environmental features to which it is a goal-directed response. A change in objectively relevant conditions implies pressure for adaptation. But negative feedback from existing policy has the same effect, as do "residual factors." Since residual factors cannot be incorporated into a theory, Goldmann argues, theories about the pressures for policy change are necessarily incomplete. His solution is to focus on various "stabilizers" of policy rather than its sources.[3] This rationale is intellectually candid and could be broadened. Most important policies are stabilized over time; as discussed in chapter 2, multiple factors have that effect. Analysts who focus on explaining stability would capture most important policy patterns. Yet this circumvents critical questions: students of foreign policy also want to understand why and how it changes. Defining the problem away is not a satisfactory long-term solution.

My objective is to understand policy adaptation; mindful of the problems that Goldmann identifies, I deal with some of them by limiting the study's scope. What follows is a mid-range theoretical argument that accounts for one important kind of adjustment under constraint. Restricting the analysis to hegemonic security commitments allows me to identify the environmental constraints that make it difficult for a declining hegemon to provide the "services" identified in chapter 2. Because these functions have been defined broadly, it is also useful to examine how specific consequences of decline affect a hegemon's leadership requirements. Since hegemons have wider margins in which to adjust than other states, and pressures for change can originate internationally or within a polity, the framework that follows is necessarily somewhat eclectic.

SYSTEMIC ARGUMENTS

Foreign policy is interpreted systemically as responses to external constraints, disturbances, or opportunities. Systemic arguments make two assumptions: (1) governments must contend with external pressures that affect their goals but over which, at most, they have partial control; and (2) these are the principal determinants of policy preference. External factors can be categorized as environmental and system-structural. Salient environmental variables include the costs of transport and communication, extant military technologies, and such economic factors as the prevalence of economies of scale, the ability to internalize externalities, and problems of diminishing returns.[4] Pertinent elements of structure include the number of great powers, the degree of status of power hierarchy and discrepancy, and a state's position in the relevant hierarchy. These factors are "structural" insofar as they affect the form, substance, and effects of interactions.[5] Systemic arguments are often indiscriminately called structural in the literature discussed in this section, but the distinction between ordering mechanisms and environmental effects is useful and should be preserved.

In systemic arguments, policy change is explained either by changes in external conditions or a state's relative ability to manage their effects, not by internal developments. Since hegemonic decline is a structural or positional shift, it should affect the state's leverage over others and its vulnerability to them. Systemic arguments might therefore identify the external context for adaptation.

Structural Realism, Collective Goods, and Hegemonic Stability

Much of the literature on hegemonic stability and decline accepts Realist assumptions that foreign policy behavior "is primarily determined by the distribution of power in the global system and the place of a particular state in that system."[6] A hegemon's role is more comprehensible in terms of broad systemic rewards than narrowly defined security or material goals, although those rewards are usually assumed to vary directly with size. In general, realist approaches focus on states' relative international wealth and power.

Some, however, are more analytically explicit and rigorous than others. Classical Realism—the tradition of Thucydides, Machiavelli, and Morgenthau—focused on the sources, uses, and effects of state power in international relations. Aside from these insights, Classical Realism left few sharp hypotheses or carefully worked-out causal relationships among variables. Conceptual progress demands that independent and dependent variables be clearly specified and that arguments be placed carefully at appropriate levels of analysis. These have been the aims of a contemporary reformulation, Structural Realism. In the words of Kenneth Waltz, a seminal contributor to this literature, "A theory of international politics bears on the foreign policies of nations while claiming to explain only certain aspects of them . . . to claim to be following a systems approach or to be constructing a systems theory requires one to show how system and unit levels can be distinctly defined."[7]

What light does this shed on a hegemon's interests or strategies? The answer requires appreciation of what structural theories can and cannot explain. To Waltz, the system is a "constraining and disposing force" on the constituent states: "to say that 'structure selects' means simply that those who conform to accepted and successful practices more often rise to the top and are likelier to stay there." Structural theories can specify the pressures on states, that is, the obstacles to success, but not precise responses. Bipolarity, for example, demands that the two great powers deal with each other on most issues affecting global security. This tends to reinforce each side's competitive stakes. On the other hand, because neither can eliminate the other, moderate behavior is rewarded.[8] The structural constraints on smaller states change as the distribution of power among actors shifts. Regional powers, for instance, would find quite different alignment opportunities in a system of three rather than two major powers.

I have shown that ascending hegemons' commitments reinforce each other in various ways, some of them systemic. Aside from the specific dynamics discussed in Chapter 2, "units having a large enough stake in the system will act for its sake, even though they pay unduly in doing so. . . . The likelihood that great powers will try to manage the system is greatest when their number reduces to two. With many great powers, the concerns of some of them are regional, not global."[9] Since the actual number has either been two or at least five, this leaves unclear when a declining hegemon should cease to have the requisite global stakes.

Robert Gilpin explicitly addresses the dynamic processes omitted in Waltz's theory. His work, like Modelski's, examines recurring cycles of hegemonic expansion, war, and decline. Hegemonic wars determine the system's prestige hierarchy and essential norms; they recur because power continually diffuses, and challengers are motivated to contest the regnant hegemon's order. On the upside of the cycle aspirants try to alter the rules in their favor until doing so becomes unprofitable. Five internal changes undermine a hegemon's power: technological innovation is exhausted; military costs rise and civil society increasingly resists them; private and public consumption tend to grow faster than national wealth as affluence increases; there is a collective "psychological shift" from production and innovation to consumption. Externally, power shifts as military technology diffuses outward.[10] It is assumed that the hegemon's strategies reflect these changes, though precisely how is not discussed.

Structural Realist theories provide a coherent, parsimonious research program: system-structure explanations for behavior should be ruled out before investigating decision processes in detail. But more conceptual links between system and unit-level theories are needed, since Realism cannot fully account for either the sources of decline or hegemons' reactions to it. Although Gilpin carefully examines the external antecedents of decline, his argument also falls back on internal processes.[11] By itself this hardly vitiates Realism, which has not claimed that states react *only* to external circumstances. Yet Realists do contend that states act rationally to maximize expected utility on the basis of their international situation. This is often incomplete, for it fails to indicate conditions under which structural incentives produce certain kinds of policies: Otto von Bismarck, Kaiser Wilhelm, and Adolf Hitler had different answers to the same geopolitical problem.[12] A major reason is that Structural Realism says little about how decision makers perceive power or external necessity, assuming this to be self-evident.[13]

The theory of hegemonic stability is narrower in scope. It claims that hegemons are able and willing to maintain strong regimes; as their power declines, so do the regimes. While worldwide security regimes (e.g., collective security systems) have been drawn up and subsystemic regimes have been the institutional framework for NATO and the Warsaw Pact, recent literature has focused on economic, social, and technical regimes. The theory, though, is not intrinsically limited to them. Theorists have often accepted the collective goods assumption that benefits, usually operationalized as regime strength, are roughly proportional to a hegemon's size. Within this framework, hegemonic decline is difficult to reconcile with the persistence of postwar economic and especially security arrangements long past the era of American primacy. Either international order does not always require a hegemon, or power is imperfectly correlated with leadership commitments.

Since the first possibility deals with systemic phenomena, implications for national policy must be teased out. As discussed in chapter 2, hegemons maintain consistency for their coalitions through comparable behavior toward each of their partners. Transactions costs and uncertainty are thereby reduced; smaller states become linked to a leader in numerous, overlapping ways. Although decline may preclude a hegemon from continuing to maintain such relationships unilaterally, Keohane argues that multilateral regimes perform analogous functions. They provide governments with otherwise unobtainable information about one another and extend their time horizons by linking issues. By increasing the transparency of states' policies, making reputation a factor in bargaining over many issues, and limiting governments' legitimate strategies, regimes furnish some of the certainty formerly provided by the hegemon.[14] Declining hegemons can apparently learn to cooperate differently, as one of several parties influencing the rules rather an undisputed agenda setter. This suggests that institutionalization, learning, and changes in commitments are related, although *After Hegemony* does not explore the last two in detail.

It does, however, thoughtfully discuss the effect of hegemonic decline on U. S. adaptation. While America became less able and willing to maintain earlier obligations as its economic position declined, the patterns differed somewhat in the oil, exchange-rate, and trade regimes. In oil, when an earlier regime dominated by the major international firms collapsed, the United States took the lead in promoting the International Energy Agency, an "insurance" arrangement to share supplies and costs in emergencies. This substituted a multilateral mechanism for the unilateral guarantees of the 1950s. On exchange-rate issues, the

United States refused to return to the par-value system or modify the domestic policies that had shattered confidence in the gold-exchange rule. An important difference was that support for the liberal principles of Bretton Woods remained widespread even after key rules disintegrated, whereas oil politics had no such foundation: "The United States consequently had to make a substantial commitment of its own to create a new consumers' regime. In the absence of ongoing institutions, . . . [it] had to take on new . . . obligations . . . in order to reassure its allies."[15] Those commitments, though, would only be activated in a severe shortage. In trade, the United States began to reject disproportionate burdens of liberalization, as hegemonic theories predict. But this was due more to domestic pressures than reduced international position in the issue area.[16] In each case, a declining hegemon continued to cooperate as long as the domestic costs were low or improbable.

External position, then, does not sufficiently explain a hegemon's willingness to make and retain asymmetric leadership commitments. Simple power models are often wrong, while more refined versions that include other variables do not make precise predictions and become "interpretive frameworks."[17] The institutionalization argument is interesting but could be developed further, since a hegemon may decline amidst nascent regimes or where leadership costs continue to be high. On what basis does it behave under those conditions? The importance of domestic costs is a reminder that no systemic theory can explain the proximate conditions for policy.

In seeking parsimony, theorists have frequently failed to distinguish carefully among various dimensions of a hegemon's size and incentives. Duncan Snidal argues that hegemonic leadership takes two forms, "benevolent" and "coercive." In the benevolent (public goods) model, a hegemon provides leadership in proportion to its absolute size. Olson and Zeckhauser, whose formulation influenced some of the later work in this group, in fact define the "larger" state in a two-state model as one that places the higher absolute value on the good.[18] This strand of the theory is identified with Keohane and especially Charles Kindleberger (see note 24, chapter 2). Coercive leadership, in which a hegemon creates a more explicitly hierarchical system, makes relative capability critical. Hegemons in this case structure the broader international order, not just market relationships. Gilpin emphasizes this pattern.[19] While coalition leadership involves elements of both, the distinction is a useful way to discriminate among various kinds of capabilities, interests, and leadership goods.

For reasons discussed later in this chapter, the U.S. nuclear umbrella is effectively nonexcludable and nonrival within NATO, meaning that no nation can be denied protection and that one's protection does not reduce that available to others. The benevolent model should account for its provision. Conventional deterrence, by contrast, is rival to a greater degree and control over exclusion is possible. If a substantially rival good becomes more costly, a hegemon's relative size and relative returns become pertinent criteria in assessing commitments.[20] Extractive Military Burdens—a state's aggregate economic and social costs—are then assessed in light of allied economic capabilities. The second and third debates discussed in Chapter 1 become more intelligible in this light. While the United States cannot force Europeans to share conventional burdens more equally, some would like to use its troops as a lever to that end; commitments of rival goods *can* be adjusted in varying increments. America's general reluctance to bargain harder on burden-sharing thus highlights the importance of beliefs about European resolve discussed later in this chapter.

Since a declining hegemon remains interested in systemic order, its adaptive preferences depend partly on which coalitions might form to share its burdens. But the nature of the good involved also turns out to be quite significant. Snidal uses a game-theory model to derive solutions in which, under one distribution of capabilities, the United States is large enough to supply unilaterally a three-country group, although cooperation among the three for higher payoffs is problematic. If U.S. hegemony erodes, it will neither provide the (unspecified) good by itself, nor will a two-country coalition replace it, but three-way cooperation among it, West Germany, and Japan is likely.[21] These results contradict the theory's prediction that decline inevitably produces regime decay, and suggest a plausible scenario for the devolution predicted in Hypothesis 2. It depends, however, on the assumption that the benefits that hegemons derive from their commitments are proportional to absolute size. This is too restrictive for an a priori assumption; many of the goods provided by hegemons are partially rival and excludable.

Systemic theorists have also deduced more differentiated interests or strategies from states' external positions. Several formulations place states within an international economic structure. Stephen Krasner argues that preferences for open trade depend on how it affects four interests: aggregate national income, social stability, political power, and economic growth. The effects depend on economic size and level of development. For example, large, developed states are more self-sufficient than smaller ones and better able to bear the costs of closure; they prefer openness. Predictions based on these preferences and systemic power distributions were largely confirmed for nineteenth- and twentieth-century trading structures.[22] David Lake maintains that all nations' trade preferences can be predicted on the basis of relative economic size, defined as percentage of world trade, and relative labor productivity. Hegemonic Leaders (large and productive countries) have a dominant free-trade strategy. "Spoilers" and "Protectionist Free Riders" (relatively unproductive and middle or small, respectively) have dominant strategies of protectionism. "Opportunists" and "Liberal Free Riders" (medium and small but productive countries) have mixed strategies. In a case study of U.S. policy, systemic position predicts the executive's preferences, although not always the final policy position.[23]

A comparable formulation predicting states' propensity to expand is conceivable. It is based on systemic position, as are the works just discussed. Self-help makes states' relative size, geographic exposure to threat, and economic vulnerability salient dimensions of geopolitical structure.

Relative size is a gross but reasonably reliable predictor of expansion and, less reliably, the international roles states play in the process. All else being equal, it correlates positively with external interests and commitments. While size has economic and military components, it is conceived here only in economic terms. National product captures both extant economic power and military potential, as indicated especially by charges of free-riding directed at Japan. Also, insofar as military size is a response to perceived threat, it is more behavioral than structural.

Geographic exposure to threat explains expansion through what Arthur Stinchcombe calls "environmental effects." This kind of argument specifies variables characterizing the salient environment and an entity's relation to it. States are exposed to their environments in varying degrees, measured by "mapping variables" which "translate environmental variables into causal forces acting on behavior associated with that element."[24] The number, location, and power of a state's enemies at a given time "map" exposure to threat. All but the largest states need help from allies in responding to threats. Hegemons are territorially secure but protect states that are not; their allies' exposure is an impetus for more or deeper commitments.[25] More specific environmental and mapping variables are enumerated in various geopolitical arguments.

A second environmental variable, economic vulnerability, "maps" onto states in various ways, some not entirely distinct from threats created by geographic exposure. Should trade stop, a state's economic vulnerability consists of the length and costs of adjustment as well as distinct income losses.[26] Stoppages take the form of boycotts or embargoes. States earning high shares of GNP through exports, those whose exports are heavily concentrated in a few products or markets, and those with relatively immobile factors of production are most vulnerable to boycotts. Embargoes will be costly insofar as the opportunity costs of replacement are high and suppliers are few. Vulnerability is more precise and easily operationalized than threats to world "access," although the latter can appear disastrous to statesmen.[27]

Turning to measurement, states can be categorized as large, medium, or small based on shares of world product. The cutoff points might be determined inductively, that is, at levels corresponding approximately to states of agreed-upon size. For example, America's 1983 share of world product in constant 1982 dollars was 24.9 percent and the Soviet Union's was 13.9 percent. France and West Germany, both middle powers, had respective shares of 4.3 percent and 5.3 percent. The lower threshold for "large" size might therefore be set at 10 percent. Mainland China's share was just over 3 percent, while India's was 1.4 percent. Since India is commonly considered a medium-size country, the lower cutoff point for that category might be 1 percent. Most of the system is small by these criteria.[28]

For reasons of parsimony, and because borders correlate strongly with war participation, the number of borders a state shares with others might be used to "map" threat. The more borders a state has, the greater its risks, opportunities, and uncertainty regarding core values.[29] These are geographic givens for most states. Yet insofar as their borders reflect past expansion, great powers have more discretion. External possessions and defense pacts with noncontiguous allies effectively multiply the number of borders and threats, as exemplified by the "turbulent frontier" discussed in chapter 2.

Vulnerability in the sense used here means that states with high export/GNP ratios that nevertheless have numerous customers, diversified export sectors, and relatively mobile labor forces are dependent by choice rather than systemic position. The distinction is crucial in a structurally based typology. Although sensitive to the world market, their long-run strategies are less constrained than those of states with one or two raw materials to sell or those heavily dependent either on foreign capital or imports obtainable from a limited number of suppliers. Where imports are irreplaceable or substitutes are very expensive, trade is more valuable than if volume alone is high and markets are merely sensitive to one another. Trade is always "high politics" in the first case.[30] Vulnerability therefore often drives the security dilemma:

Countries that are not self-sufficient must try to assure that the necessary supplies will continue to flow in wartime. This was part of the explanation for Japan's drive into China and Southeast Asia before War War II. If there were an international authority that could guarantee access, this motive for control would disappear. But since there is not, even a state that would prefer the status quo to increasing its area of control may pursue the latter policy.[31]

Because these threats occur only if governments hostile to a state control markets, access routes, or goods it needs, economic vulnerability can coincide with other dangers exacerbated by geography. This was true of Cuba vis-à-vis the United States in the early 1960s and of oil consumers vis-à-vis some Persian Gulf governments in the 1970s and 1980s. But there is a key difference: while geography exposes states to threats in some proportion to proximity, economic threats arise from the inherent risks and uncertainties of market activity as well as predatory behavior by foreign sovereigns.[32] The two are analytically if not always empirically distinct.

The typology and a few illustrative examples are depicted in Figure 3.1. Since America's geopolitical position has changed considerably in the last two hundred years and the case study concerns U.S. policy, the United States is shown at various historical points. Placement on these dimensions, especially economic vulnerability, is tentative and only intended here as heuristic; rigorous measures of adjustment costs would be needed for precise placement on the vulnerability dimension.

The polar cases are easily interpretable. Countries near point A (bottom left front) will be most likely to expand, while those near point M (top right back) will be least likely to do so. Correspondingly, the former will be system leaders, the latter peripheral actors. Other cases are less straightforward. Countries near

Figure 3.1
Geopolitical Determinants of State Expansionism

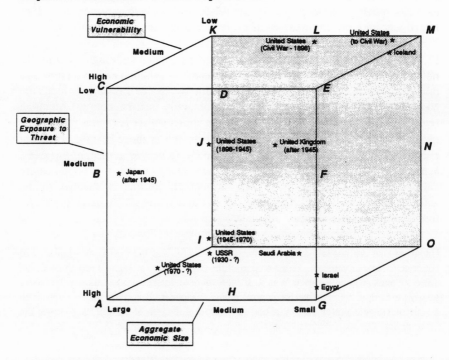

the center of the cube will tend to be free-riders—exposed or vulnerable enough to consume protection, but too small to carry proportionate burdens themselves. A useful, although hardly precise distinction might be made between significant and unimportant free-riders. While those near the mid-right side of the cube might be allowed to ride free, countries near the mid-left side are too large and have too great a stake in regime norms for this. Coalition leaders have incentives to make the latter reveal their preferences as fully as possible.

This kind of analysis is appealing but seriously limited. Most important, geographic exposure to threat may be too crude an environmental effect for any but the most general behavioral predictions. For one thing, incentives to expand are stronger if offensive military technologies overwhelm or are difficult to distinguish from defensive ones.[33] Second, while more differentiated geographic dimensions might better predict states' behavior, a richer typology would be theoretically problematic. Adding more variables would sacrifice the parsimony that makes such schema attractive in the first place. In any case, strategists have continued for nearly a century the debate begun between Alfred Thayer Mahan and Halford Mackinder. Mahan saw control of the seas as the key to world dominance; Mackinder identified control of the Eurasian-African landmass as critical. There is no definitive basis for settling the issue: British and American primacy lend credence to Mahan's view, but the Russian Empire, which won the crucial land battle in World War II and was threatening enough to induce a counter-coalition afterwards, does not. If sea and land power are both highly important, the cruder dimension of proximity would have to suffice.

Strategy, moreover, is particularly open-ended for nuclear powers. In Aaron Friedberg's apt characterization, the Soviet Union's deployment of intercontinental nuclear forces in the late 1950's "seemed to push the burden of deterrence downward onto the conventional forces of the United States and its allies."[34] Yet the debate over the nuclear threshold suggests that nuclear risks and the constraints they pose depend only partly on the balance of military forces. The risks also depend on the extent of a hegemon's overcommitment, its adversaries, their incentives to expand, and the balance of resolve between them. The last especially is inexplicable in purely geopolitical terms.

Finally, expansion need not manifest itself in particular leadership roles. Whether great powers lead "benevolently" or "coercively" is partly a subjective judgment, but allies' autonomy can also be assessed more objectively by examining in some detail their options and constraints. It is usually cheaper to lead by invitation; especially in the late twentieth century, ideologies with wide and deep popular appear are important power resources. Further discussion of this issue is beyond the scope of this book, but a broader comparison of security hegemonies might incorporate ideological cohesion as a resource available to coalition leaders or a constraint on adjustment.

Limitations of Systemic Arguments

Given these problems, it is easy to see why spare geopolitical frameworks have not successfully explained grand strategies. Theories about trade strategy explain less, but do so more precisely and use better-grounded independent variables. Pinning down the causes of expansion and retrenchment is more difficult. And restricting the domain of the argument to hegemonic security adaptation is only a partial solution, since broader analytical issues are involved.

Systemic approaches to foreign policy have provoked a stimulating discussion in recent literature. In identifying incentives and constraints, they pinpoint a range of necessary (but not sufficient) conditions for state behavior. This is often adequate if the dependent variable is an international outcome, but might not explain policy choice. On the one hand, Realists argue that policy is predictable to the extent that options are limited by the system. Individuals' beliefs and motivations, for instance, are significant only within the constraints of relative power.[35] One need not examine cognitions to explain why people would flee a burning building; situational pressures suffice.[36] Only discrepant behavior requires decision-making analysis. The security imperatives facing European rulers during the early modern period of state building provide a more realistic example. They had little or no slack under these circumstances; those who failed to heed external cues were swallowed up.[37]

On the other hand, an overheated house better analogizes much of international politics. External compulsion is minimal; opportunities and dangers are key variables, and responses depend on "varying individual predispositions."[38] Under these conditions, considerably weaker systemic arguments that do not depend on highly restrictive assumptions about situational determinism are appropriate.

Distinguishing between "single" and "multiple-exit" situations helps clarify the different explanatory logics. In the former, situational constraints alone prescribe a course of action to rational actors. The environment is more permissive in the latter. Spiro Latsis suggests these as alternative research programs in economics. Each such program contain hypotheses, scope conditions, characteristic axioms, and a "positive heuristic" that shapes a cumulative research process. The heuristic of single-exit approaches makes their appeal obvious:

Look at the situational constraints and preferences of the actor in question. Look at the institutional, technological, or structural obstacles, given his goal. Given that the actor correctly perceives all these, they will uniquely determine his course of action. Then, using the rationality principle as the trivial animating law, you will be led to an explanatory argument which suggests the the actor in question did x rather than not x.[39]

Multiple-exit explanations, in contrast, demand considerable information about actors' dispositions and decision processes—so much, according to Latsis, that some work on imperfect competition has assumed away complications with which deterministic theories of monopoly and perfect competition need not contend. A heuristic for a multiple-exit research program would be much more complex, and Latsis does not offer one.

This is not to argue that Structural Realists have misapplied their research program. By taking systemic arguments as far as possible, they have clarified levels-of-analysis issues and suggested further research. But since systemic constraints vary inversely with aggregate power, standard structural arguments have little to say about hegemonic adaptation. Countries of this size usually have multiple exits. For example, U.S. hostility to Third World radicalism cannot be understood in terms of material interests alone. Liberal ideology motivated U.S. policy toward Fidel Castro's Cuba before the regime became a significant Soviet base, as well as in Vietnam, Chile, Guatemala, and the Dominican Republic. Core values were not even remotely threatened in the other four cases. Only a state powerful enough to be unconcerned about them could afford to pursue such ideological goals, some quite costly.[40] Policymakers' beliefs constrained U.S. Third World options more than systemic position during much of the postwar period.

In sum, if actors' environments underspecify their utility functions in multiple-exit situations, and states usually have more than one option, systemic theories cannot explain most policy patterns. They contain no conception of *how* external forces produce government choices; the final behavior alone is important. As Lake put it, "the way nation-states arrive at policy is an unanswerable and unimportant question."[41] While this position is defensible if power-structure arguments produce satisfactory explanations, no simple geopolitical theory answers the questions addressed in this book. One needs instead to examine how problems are framed and which kinds of policymaking coalitions are essential on which issues.

Theories about systemic constraints pose two specific problems in explaining policy. One involves the intensity of preferences. System-level arguments can rarely specify governments' cardinal utilities. The more exits they face, and the more that decisions require value integration or trade-offs, the more serious this limitation will be. Hegemonic adjustment may thus be incomprehensible without knowing how much certain kinds of outcomes are preferred or disfavored. Costs substantial enough to put pressure on some commitments may be tolerable with respect to more highly valued goals. Taking this seriously will sacrifice parsimony; if motivation becomes a key variable and varies independently of international position, a systemic theory becomes a decision-making one.[42]

Another difficulty, discussed extensively in the literature on foreign economic policy, is that central decision makers may be unable to implement their preferences. Even if they are sensitive to external cues, other domestic actors might have different views and veto power over all or certain decisions. If so, systemic theories will not reliably explain final policy position.

These problems make parsimonious and concrete explanations of behavior problematic. What follows, therefore, is necessarily more eclectic than the work discussed thus far.

A Probabilistic Adaptive Space Framework

Multiple exits are rarely, if ever, infinite in number. Available conceptual tools can narrow the range of predictive indeterminacy. Richard Herrmann's critique of Realism thus goes too far. In his view, system-level approaches cannot even identify important constraints; impediments imputed to the system are instead products of great-power policy and motivation.[43] But if hegemonic decline is a systemic change—a change "in the international distribution of power, the hierarchy of prestige, and the rules and rights embodied in the system"[44]—a declining hegemon's opportunity costs would increase however others behaved. Structural transformations are qualitatively different from changes in behavior alone, and the resulting constraints on behavior can be at least generally specified. We can, indeed, go beyond this. The next step in the argument shows how likely exits can be identified.

One approach, "environmental possibilism," identifies the capabilities that affect the outcome or feasibility of a given decision or goal.[45] Possibilism deals with exits, not preferences. Deborah Larson makes an analogous argument about the postwar superpower relationship. While structural theories would predict rivalry under the conditions prevailing in 1945, it could have taken various forms: a gentleman's agreement to create two spheres of influence, competition for alliance with a unified Germany, an American return to isolation and Soviet domination of Western Europe, a mixed relationship of cooperation and conflict on different issues, or war. These possibilities were filtered by domestic U.S. politics and decision makers' beliefs, which account for the Cold War.[46] In general, a hegemon's systemic position at any time opens certain doors while closing others. One could catalog the possibilities and move to lower levels of analysis for a more precise prediction or explanation.

One problem in specifying exits, however, is that the number increases as a hegemon's power declines. Some options will be closed, but others, such as partial devolution, may open. All else being equal, the number of potential exits varies directly with the complexity of an actor's goals and that of its environment, and inversely with the amount of information it possesses about its environment.[47] A declining hegemon will want to adjust with as much consistency and continuity as possible across its various relationships. Yet decline stimulates challenges to its leadership abroad and resistance to hegemonic burdens at home. These complexities open up possible exits and make it difficult to formulate a predictive theory of interests or strategies. At most, a loose set of policy parameters can be specified.

An alternative formulation focuses on priorities rather than possibilities. It necessarily uses a probabilistic approach, which posits that some choices are likelier than others. "Environmental probabilism," according to Harold and Margaret Sprout, "draw[s] inferences on the basis of the individual's probable conformity to some hypothetical norm. This amounts to reasoning from a 'model' of typical, or normally expectable behavior." Such models include assumptions about three decision-making variables: (1) actors' motivation, (2) the quantity and quality of environmental knowledge, and (3) actors' methods of using knowledge in defining alternatives and making decisions.[48]

A probabilistic framework is preferable to one that simply identifies viable exits because it provides a theoretical basis for reducing explanatory indeterminacy. The one suggested here assumes that goal-seeking actors will monitor negative feedback vis-à-vis key policies above some random-noise level—in short, that policymakers pay attention to things they care about. This seems common sensical, but whether the argument is compelling also depends on the adequacy of its other assumptions.

One concerns decision makers' motivations; the extensive discussion in chapter 2 requires only a brief review. As external capabilities grow, hegemonic elites define interests in system-wide terms and acquire capabilities to act on that scale. Expansion feeds on itself; the importance of consistency, resolve, and reputation make it difficult to modify commitments. If adjustment is unavoidable, hegemons will try to stretch existing resources or develop new ones. It is no coincidence that postwar U.S. policy (and the literature about it) has often been preoccupied with "alliance management" and "crisis management."

A second assumption, concerning decision makers' situational knowledge, requires more discussion. The case study does *not* explicitly scrutinize this variable: I explain general patterns within broadly defined issue areas over a twenty-year period, making it impossible to examine discrete decisions at that level of detail. But this is not necessary, because theoretically useful *and* plausible assumptions follow from more general patterns. I assume that decision makers monitor those variables that could impede the hegemonic roles discussed in Chapter 2. For any ongoing policy, administrative guidelines emerge about what to watch in monitoring the environment. Goldmann calls these "critical variables."[49] They can be defined as the external or internal conditions that could affect policy consistency or the provision of hegemonic services. For reasons already discussed, bureaucrats as well as political leaders have incentives to monitor such conditions, and the case study bears this out.

This presumption of adequate knowledge is strong and should not be misunderstood. I obviously do not claim that policymakers typically possess perfect information; I do assume that in noncrisis situations they most often have information adequate to their purposes. More information is not always cost-effective. Even for business firms, the requirements depend on individual motivation and market characteristics.[50] Surely international hegemons have enough at stake to monitor carefully the conditions that could impede their performance.

A third assumption, concerning the use of information in defining alternatives and making decisions, relates to broader criteria for acceptable policies. Decision makers are assumed here to be rational, meaning simply that they believe purposively—that they choose more rather than less preferred alternatives across consistently ordered preference sets. Some such assumption is necessary to infer behavior patterns from international conditions; without it, there is no reason to expect hegemonic decline to affect policy decisions systematically. Rather than complete information or consideration of all alternatives, rationality here implies only that actors seek their objectives purposefully within whatever cognitive or other internal limits apply.[51]

A brief summary of the argument is useful at this point. As a first cut, certain adaptive exits can be ruled out by analyzing systemic position in specific issue areas. But even a declining hegemon faces relatively few locked doors. Assumptions about a hegemon's priorities imply that decision makers will carefully monitor constraints that could impede performance of commitments. Hypothesis 2 predicts how they will adjust within these impediments. In other words, Structural Realism is interpreted here as a theory of constraints rather than a deterministic theory of interests. By itself, it is only possibilistic. A probabilistic approach to priorities, which suggests what decision makers will monitor, along with Hypotheses 1 and 2 of chapter 2, which predict how political leaders adjust to constraints, permit inferences about the kinds of choices made by declining hegemons.

It is useful to indicate the kinds of constraints that matter and why. From chapter 2, it follows that hegemons will be concerned about impediments to shaping agendas, mobilizing a sizable coalition, making global decisions, administering the coalition, or planning for the future. One need not agree with

Modelski that these are functionally essential services; I assume only that policymakers see them as highly useful means of leadership. The impediments encountered by a declining hegemon may be environmental, structural, or both.

Insufficient resources relative to tasks is the most general problem. In many cases, specific capabilities-commitments ratios are more relevant than absolute size. From 1960 to 1971, U.S. officials worried about the "gold drain" and consequently about the exchange costs of troops in Europe. But this was problematic only under the extant gold-exchange rules, and concerns were considerably broader by the late 1980s. By the early months of the Bush administration, budget deficits had weakened U.S. influence abroad by reducing resources for global projects, such as aid to Eastern Europe, and by making American economic advice less credible than otherwise.[52] Mikhail Gorbachev's far-reaching foreign policy changes of 1989—withdrawal from Afghanistan, sizable proposed force reductions in Europe, and reductions in military and economic aid to Cuba— have been ascribed to huge budget deficits and an attendant inflation that finally became too large to ignore.[53] Fiscal constraints often have more immediate impact than military ones: deterrence commitments are generally not subject to continuous market-like pressures, and huge deficits make the costs of international leadership obvious and politically vulnerable. Profound resource shortfalls can indicate a change in system structure. Even less serious gaps can affect agenda formation, mobilization, and administration.

Policymakers are often ambivalent about the balance between resources and responsibilities. On the one hand, as discussed in chapter 2, hegemons tend to overextend themselves and many policymakers willingly accept the general risks that follow from this. On the other hand, military planners and civilians with clear strategic priorities tend to find this disquieting. This ambivalence means that serious doubts about the implications of overextension are often raised, although rarely resolved, within the policy machinery.[54]

Eroding technological superiority makes others less dependent on a hegemon, threatening its ability to control key agendas or plan for the future. In the summer of 1989, a Japanese politician observed that neither American nor Japanese had yet grasped the implications of changes in their relative positions. If Japan decided to sell computer chips to Moscow instead of Washington, he said, "that would instantly change the balance of military power."[55] Not every technology has military applications, but many of the most advanced ones do. If technological prowess is an element of the international structure, major shifts can indicate change between rather than within systems.

Two constraints arise from the diffusion of weaponry. First, the influence that great powers derive from supplying weapons will gradually decline. This diffusion, evident in Indian ballistic missile deployments and China's emergence as a major arms exporter, will also make Soviet and American intervention in regional wars riskier. Over twenty Third World countries were buying or developing ballistic missiles at the end of the 1980s.[56] Both superpowers will try to control this process and hedge against it, perhaps by giving "preference to more mobile and versatile forces—forces that can . . . respond rapidly and discriminately to a wide range of attacks."[57] Nuclear proliferation and growing popular revulsion toward provocative nuclear strategies will complicate life for the superpowers, especially the United States, which has relied more on extended deterrence. Assuming that security coalitions of some kind survive in Europe, the disutility of nuclear threats and proliferation of weapons will over time erode power hierarchies within NATO and other such groups.[58] But until another security hegemon emerges, Waltz, at least, would argue that the international structure remains unchanged and this constitutes an environmental effect.

These problems, especially the demise of nuclear hegemony, affect mobilization, agenda formation, and decision making. *Discriminate Deterrence*, the report cited in Chapter 2, can be interpreted as recommendations for adjustment within the terms of existing commitments.

Credible extended deterrence depends on relative power projection capabilities, and a hegemon's leaders will monitor them closely. Chapter 6 discusses the importance this issue assumed during the 1970s. Mobilization and decision making could be jeopardized unless allies believe a leader can help them in a crunch. In recent years, deteriorating U.S. access to foreign bases and the growth of Soviet airlift and sealift forces have greatly concerned American officials.

Finally, bloc cohesion can be an important resource for the leading state. Europeans dread a recrudescence of superpower hostility less because it threatens them physically than because it undercuts their room to maneuver. Correspondingly, when George Kennan suggested superpower military disengagement from Europe in 1957, Acheson was vehemently opposed; NATO, in his view, could be used to control internal politics as well as military strategies. From an American perspective, diminished conflict, manifested in looser blocs, presents clear dangers as well as opportunities.[59] While Waltz defines system structure in terms only of national capabilities, very fluid blocs or the disappearance of the postwar coalitions would strike most observers as a structural change.

Each of the next three chapters begins with an overview that applies this framework. For each time period, highly problematic exits are first ruled out on the basis of issue-specific capabilities. I then discuss environmental variables that were critical during that period and suggest the kind of adaptation predictable from the hypotheses of Chapter 2. This part of the argument is systemic because it specifies likely exits and strategies on the basis of external position alone. Circularity is avoided by showing how these inferences follow from the arguments of chapters 2 and 3.

SUBSYSTEMIC ARGUMENTS

In single-exit situations, behavior can be predicted simply from an actor's aims and relevant environmental conditions. Foreign policy analysis would be much easier if this were typically true. Since it is not, behavior can often be understood only with knowledge of an actor's "inner structure and organization.''[60] This should not be used as an excuse to add explanatory variables at will; not all state or individual-level variables are pertinent. Appending them indiscriminately to a rather spare system-level argument would defeat my purpose.

Chapter 2 and the first part of this chapter argue that a hegemon's systemic position inclines its leaders toward expansionism, especially during its ascendancy. Unfortunately, this neither allows for motivational variations based on strong beliefs and images nor accounts for exits that are closed by the domestic policymaking system. Cognitive arguments fill out expectations about a hegemon's interests, while certain domestic-process arguments help explain what emerges from the policy process.

Cognitive Arguments: Shared Images of Europe

Actors' motivation depends at least partly on how they perceive their circumstances. In multiple-exit situations, expectations about others' behavior heavily affect one's own.[61] Unless system structure strongly determines behavior, such expectations can have significant, independent causal impact. Waltz's structural theory exemplifies some of these gaps. It predicts that the great powers in a bipolar system will be largely self-sufficient. While true of homeland defense, this leaves the resources and attention both superpowers devote to such "unnecessary" alliances unexplained.[62]

An argument about shared images of Europe helps account for this anomaly. Decision makers' beliefs, images, and assumptions are seen here as an important source of their goals. The beliefs at issue depict Europe as pussilanimous and in need of constant bolstering. Decision makers have feared that it will be "Finlandized," or find its autonomy vis-à-vis a potential aggressor(s) circumscribed in key ways. Finlandization implies that a weaker state is internally free but has lost some or all external independence. A related possibility is that small states will "bandwagon," or actually align with the source of the threat. Romania and Bulgaria did so with Nazi Germany. In both cases, appeasement results from fear of the stronger power and contradicts the predictions of balance-of-power theory.

U.S. policymakers commonly express these fears publicly. When they tried to refute arguments for unilateral troop cuts during the 1960s and early 1970s, European confidence in American pledges was described as very fragile. A Europe less visibly tied to the U.S. would inevitably become "politically penetrated" by Moscow; force withdrawals would "require Western Europe to tune antennae toward Moscow."[63] Finlandization or bandwagoning was the only acknowledged alternative to the status quo.

A cognitive explanation of policy adaptation will work only under two conditions. Since cognitions pertain to individuals, beliefs explain long-term patterns only insofar as they are widely shared among policymakers.[64] The units of analysis in the case study are successive groups of central decision makers with similar assumptions and beliefs. A persuasive case must also be made that these cognitions are not simply epiphenomenal.

Analytic Assumptions. Too many treatments of cognitions simply assume that they are autonomous and causally powerful. Since the beliefs discussed here were used to justify policy, it is difficult to show that they did not simply rationalize other motivations. It seems clear, however, that policymakers' professed reasoning was the only way they could have reached their original conclusion that Europe needed protection. Their motivation was reflected in NAT's unprecedented scope and the fact that it had to be sold to Congress. It should also be remembered that from Washington, the main threat to Europe in the early years of the Cold War was psychological, not military. The troop deployment did provide a lever on the allies and thus a vested interest in keeping forces in Europe. But this does not explain steadfast resistance to adjusting the commitment in light of changed circumstances, especially when there were fairly strong incentives to do so.

Because U.S. officials have been so concerned with Europe's resolve, a psychological factor, neither the specific foundations for these images nor the evidence to support them are always clear. Both need to be explicated as clearly as possible. Much of the U.S.-European relationship is based on symbols, and the dominant American image of its allies encourages self-fulfilling tendencies. Moreover, the policies analyzed in this book had multiple causes.

I address these problems in two ways. One uses a weak form of what George calls the "congruence procedure" for assessing the impact of beliefs on choice. This involves deducing policy implications from general images or beliefs, establishing the degree of congruence with behavior, and trying to rule out other causal factors.[65] For reasons explained above, this cannot be done in detail. The case study shows that these images are inconsistent with other imaginable policies and that a range of alternative exits existed for both commitments. The argument also rests on evidence that predictive biases were employed in assessing hypothetical scenarios, that those who valued the status quo were particularly susceptible, and that this overcame strong contrary incentives. Before proceeding, some discussion of the origins and consequences of these beliefs is useful.

The Origins and Consequences of Shared Images. Observers have noted that Americans tend to generalize in their approach to the world; examples include isolationism, strong preferences for democracies and free trade, and sharply ideological anti-communism. U.S. presidents have often maintained, not simply for public consumption, that important values and interests are indivisible.[66] A nonsituational approach to commitments fits comfortably into this cultural milieu. These inclinations were strongly reinforced by the Munich lessons that potential aggressors should never be appeased. An implication was that smaller, exposed states needed to be bolstered firmly when confronting possible aggression.

Between 1946 and 1949, a compelling image of Europe was formed and appended to these general views. Americans had correctly seen themselves as rescuers of the Old World in both world wars; now they saw the Western half endangered again. Britain's desperate financial position in early 1947 forced it to give up responsibilities for Greek and Turkish security. Athens's situation seemed even worse; its government would soon be forced by economic collapse to cede a civil war to Communist guerrillas, leading to political disintegration and a pro-Soviet government. Dean Acheson saw only one exit: American assumption of all British responsibilities for the two countries.[67]

Something more fundamental had also happened; Europe seemed off track psychologically as well over a year after the war ended. Acheson remembered that in early 1947 "only in Britain and Russia did people have any confidence in government, or social or economic organization, or currencies."[68] His view was shared by other key figures, including Lucius Clay and John McCloy, both of whom were High Commissioners in occupied Germany. Europeans were frightened of Moscow and unsure of their own system; to some, even Labour's electoral victory in Britain seemed to portend an ominous shift further left.[69]

This conclusion was unsurprising, for it comported with traditional American beliefs that Europe is weak-willed and decadent. In this view, an inner sickness, produced by the Old World's social divisions and corrupt values, was the deeper cause. Societies so cynical, so lacking in what Americans consider meaningful purpose, could be expedient enough to accept Finlandization. This indictment may have been emotionally necessary to justify America's secession from and later leadership of Europe. It fits Friedberg's perceptual model of adaptation and suggests deep roots for Finlandization beliefs.[70]

The terrible winter of 1947 crystallized the new image for many Americans. Factories virtually shut down in Britain; French and Italian farmers reverted to subsistence production, starving the cities. A State Department official later observed that "the underfed, freezing people were reaching a point where they would accept any system that fed them and kept them warm." This created a "profound impression" within the government and among the attentive public, making restoration of European self-confidence critical.[71]

Initially, European and American leaders differed on what would be necessary. The dominant U.S. view in 1946 and 1947 was that economic assistance would suffice, but the Europeans also wanted a military guarantee. NAT at first constituted little more than a written pledge; aside from the atomic bomb, U.S. forces had been stripped to the bone. Although a consensus emerged in 1948 that only a stronger military posture could reassure Europe, pre-Korean defense budgets precluded it.

As discussed in chapter 1, the Korean War neutralized domestic opposition to large defense budgets and a U.S. troop presence in Europe. It also appeared to validate the domino theory, in which every potential trouble spot became a test of U.S. resolve. This dovetailed neatly with the emerging view that Europe's resolve had to be bolstered by American steadfastness. Since NATO had been organized to reassure Europe at least as much as to deter the Soviet Union, the allies had to be continually convinced of America's staying power. The image of Europe's helplessness made this seem necessary, but the belief that the allies would bandwagon at the slightest shift of the wind made it difficult. In 1954, the American ambassador to Italy told columnist C. L. Sulzberger that "the Italians were great bandwagon riders. As soon as they thought communism going to win or Russia was going to win, they all jumped on the Soviet bandwagon."[72]

For obvious reasons, analysts often doubt whether such statements reflect private beliefs and motives. Official and private beliefs are likely to overlap, although to what degree is usually unknown.[73] Because sovereignty ultimately undermines purely verbal assurances, consistent behavior must reinforce them.[74]

Verbal reassurances remain important, however, since governments also develop expectations from them. And since U.S. officials have been strongly motivated to prevent a possible outcome, their words have been chosen with very precise messages in mind. Words, in turn, have been scrutinized carefully, in part because consistency often has entailed inaction and language is the only evidence of intentions available. Further, since the situation has been assumed to be very sensitive—Europe will move toward neutrality if American resolve is in the slightest doubt—stable allied expectations have been especially important.

Reassurances are intended to reinforce credibility; within NATO, they have signified virtually unqualified U.S. support.[75] One kind of reassurance is military: the allies are shown and told that America can continue to protect them. This has made the viability of extended deterrence a continuing concern in Washington. Another involves repeated promises that Europe will not be abandoned. Whatever the current policy issue, officials are urged, often by fellow Americans, that they should "promptly reassure our allies that, except for defense of America's homeland, they stand first in our interests."[76] While the allies have often demanded such reassurances, these patterns appear to be overkill. Fears about European irresolution seem a better explanation. They appear to intensify during periods when established policy is under pressure, suggesting the risk aversion one would expect of a declining hegemon.

Patrick Morgan argues that America's preoccupation with resolve and staying power masks considerable insecurity. In effect, he claims, we have been reassuring ourselves. Geographic distance makes pledges problematic, especially when it was once used as a buffer for isolationism.[77] If so, U.S. fears of European bandwagoning or Finlandization have been exaggerated and may constitute projection.

Stable beliefs have been largely responsible for the continuity of U.S. NATO policy. American officials have been reluctant to find out if the allies can stand more on their own feet. Beliefs supporting a policy will be stable if they are consistent, central, and untestable.[78] Each of these applies to fears of bandwagoning and the felt need for reassurances.

Consistency means that a policy is believed to produce an objective(s) without negative side effects. Reassurances have seemed necessary and largely cost-free to most U.S. officials since the late 1940s. The case study shows that only rarely has an administration predicated the troop deployment on higher European military spending, and then only implicitly. A few officials have criticized the dependency this reinforces; in a memorandum to President Johnson arguing that Bonn should fully compensate the exchange costs incurred by U.S. forces, McGeorge Bundy said, "our troop levels in Germany are justified finally more by the psychological needs of the Germans than by strategic necessity. If the Germans will not pay for psychological comfort, why should we?"[79] Few others, though, saw the policy as counterproductive.

Chapter 2 discussed centrality and testability in connection with domino theories; I argued that these beliefs are connected to many others and difficult to falsify. The same applies to more specific beliefs about Europe. Harlan Cleveland, U.S. ambassador to NATO during the 1960s, maintains that NATO is a continuing forum for allied consultation, not simply an alliance. If so, reassurances about U.S. interest and staying power must transcend immediate threats. Consultation will be necessary as long as there is a Soviet Union, even a less threatening one. Cleveland put it this way:

If both alliances were abolished, what difference would it make? An enormous difference—a change in the balance of power profoundly to the advantage of the Soviet Union. The Russians would remain in charge of East European armies, and could keep their troops in Europe under existing bilateral agreements. But without NATO or something very much like it, the basis for a U.S., British, and Canadian presence on the Continent would be destroyed, along with the basis for the arrangements with Germany that make German military strength acceptable to its Western neighbors. Each European country, in isolation from its friends, would have to make its bilateral security arrangements with the USSR, and its political antenna and internal political alignments would shift accordingly.... [European politicians and journalists] have come to see that even if the Warsaw Pact were to abolish itself... we would still need a Western solidarity organization. We would need it for defense. We would need it to induce the Soviets to bargain realistically about European security and the German question. We would need it to keep honest whatever East-West bargains can be struck in Europe.[80]

In one sense, this simply exemplifies the argument about regime persistence in *After Hegemony*: NATO will endure because adapting it is cheaper than starting from scratch. Yet the felt need for an instrument to maintain solidarity goes far beyond the purposes and mechanics of consultation. Balance-of-power theory predicts that Europeans will coalesce as needed with or without a mechanism such as Cleveland describes. Its necessity is driven largely by Finlandization beliefs.

Finally, testability depends on the extent to which beliefs can, in principle, be falsified and the amount of evidence actually available.[81] Finlandization scenarios can be tested, but decision makers have been reluctant to do so. More benign Soviet behavior and tight budgetary constraints make it virtually certain that some U.S. troops will be withdrawn during the 1990s. For two generations, though, the beliefs have been largely invulnerable.

Causal Impact. The preceding arguments have much less import if beliefs about allied resolve lack independent causal weight. This would be true if they rationalized behavior preferred on other grounds or simply reflected external reality. Have fears of Finlandization induced stronger or more rigid support for Europe than would otherwise have been the case? Are they reasonable in light of ambiguous evidence?

The first issue is critical in evaluating cognitive explanations of foreign policy, but difficult because the analyst cannot know what policymakers truly believed. Unfortunately, this is a weak case that will not help resolve longstanding disputes about the theoretical importance of cognitive variables. An indirect argument for causal weight must therefore suffice.

First, contrary systemic cues are available. Anarchy makes bandwagoning risky because it requires trust that a dominant power will remain benevolent. "Balancing"—aligning against threats—is more prudent and in fact more common. This has two important implications. In general, if balancing is the norm, security is easily achieved for status quo powers because aggressors will face numerous opponents.[82] Finlandization or bandwagoning beliefs impose much stiffer requirements on bloc leaders than are necessary. Specifically, power-balancing arguments dominate the international relations literature and are generally endorsed by U.S. statesmen; a calmer view of threats and obligations would have substantial intellectual support. Strong beliefs would be needed to reach different conclusions.

Second, one might consider a counterfactual possibility: why weren't more troops withdrawn from Europe during eight years of congressional battles over the Mansfield Amendments? Doing so would have removed a major irritant in congressional-legislative relations. One knowledgeable observer attributed resistance to fears about the psychological effects of withdrawals.[83] In the absence of the beliefs discussed here, it is plausible, albeit not certain, that substantial cuts would have been made despite European protests.

Third, several decisional "heuristics" have probably contributed to these images and beliefs. Cognitive psychologists have shown that people frequently cope with uncertainty through such devices. Although Western Europe differs greatly from Finland in size and location, policymakers might easily err in judging the probability of outcomes for which there is little relevant historical experience.[84] Not only has Finland's experience been rather exceptional, but Americans have no experience with allies who became more self-sufficient after some devolution of security responsibilities.

One such heuristic is an "availability" bias, in which the likelihood of an outcome is judged by the relative prominence of examples of occurrence and non-occurrence. This is strengthened by tendencies toward "creeping determinism" in retrospective inferences: the inevitability of known outcomes is systematically overestimated.[85] Since Finlandization had occurred once, these inference patterns inclined policymakers to predict it if U.S. commitments weakened or appeared to weaken.

Although these are examples of non-affect-driven bias, preferences do influence predispositions and information processing in another way. While Finlandization has been strongly undesired, critics of U.S. policy outside the executive branch have been less wedded to the status quo. Critics like Senator Mansfield were more inclined to notice

the changes which had taken place in Western Europe—and which, he argued—had transformed it beyond all recognition from the continent of the late 1940s and early 1950s, when it had been "hurt beyond help, threatened by revolutionary upheaval from within and aggression from without." . . . American policy, however, was still based on an image of a ravaged, weak, and insecure Europe.[86]

Each side, in part, saw what it wanted and expected to see. Since the evidence was ambiguous—Europe had progressed, but remained dependent in key ways—and the effects of troop cuts were uncertain, a judgment that serious cognitive distortion occurred in the executive branch is too severe. But cognitive processes such as these seem to have played a diagnostic role for both groups.

The causal importance of cognitions becomes greatest if the operational environment is highly incongruous. This gap seems to have widened since the early postwar years. As Europe recovered economically and postwar regimes legitimated themselves through higher living standards and social stability, self-confidence has returned as well. To be sure, "a long-range strategy of trying to coax the Soviet Union and the rest of Eastern Europe into an interdependent relationship of benefits and restraints that would make war unprofitable and promote internal evolution of the Eastern regimes"[87] can look like Finlandization. Truly mutual interdependence, moreover, may make sense for countries that share a continent with the Soviets. Instead of appeasement as pejoratively defined since the 1930s, it may reflect genuinely two-sided accommodation and the maturation of Europe. Any such judgment is subjective, but James Goldsborough has carefully described an emerging assertiveness in Western Europe, one that contradicts old assumptions.[88] This is discussed further in Chapter 7.

Organizational Arguments

Organizations adjust because their environments signal that it is necessary. Adjustment here means (1) different organizational priorities, or (2) generation of different options to accomplish the same ends. In either case, new standard procedures will be required; new priorities also implicate different critical variables. Organizational adjustment is clearly part of policy adaptation as discussed here, and may have to be considered in detail under some circumstances.

It does not, however, in this study. Decisions about the substance of key commitments or ways to perform them involve political, not administrative issues. Only after policies are stabilized for geopolitical, cognitive, or sociopolitical reasons do bureaucracies develop stakes in them.[89] The issues discussed in the next three chapters received presidential attention and were carefully monitored by cabinet and subcabinet officials whose ultimate constituency was the White House. This is to be expected of issues relating to hegemonic commitments. While bureaucracies can manipulate somewhat the options presented to political leaders, the latter have more fundamental control of the decision-making process. Bureaucratic autonomy ultimately depends on presidential inattention. In this sense, "neither organizational necessity nor bureaucratic interests are the fundamental determinants of policy," especially in explaining states' final policy positions.[90]

Issue Area and State Structure

To conclude, issue area and state structure are discussed together because they interact closely. A state's external constraints and foreign policymakers' perception of risk or opportunity reliably indicate only the executive's adjustment preferences. Its ability to implement them depends on whether it controls the necessary policy instruments. This is a function of the issue involved as well as a state's general institutional structure: The connection between them is spelled out after brief discussion of each.

Issue Area. There are nearly as many conceptualizations of foreign-policy issue dimensions as interested researchers, making it difficult to integrate disparate frameworks. Issue areas are defined independently of changes in power configurations or environmental effects, so I discuss them at the subsystemic level of analysis.

They are usually delineated in terms of process variables or substantive content. Rosenau assumes that "issues which are resolved in the same way also tap similar motives and activate similar roles." To Keohane and Nye, issue areas are problems seen and dealt with as interdependent.[91] Process-oriented typologies are better developed theoretically, but harder to operationalize; circularity arises if issue types delineated by process characteristics are used to explain policy-making variations. William Potter thus suggests that substantive issue areas be identified and linked to types of policy processes or outcomes.[92]

This approach is used here. Truly public defense goods need to be distinguished from those that have important private characteristics. Public goods have two characteristics: (1) jointness of supply (nonrivalness), meaning that for a given level of physical production, consumption by one more person does not diminish the supply available to others; and (2) noncontrol over exclusion.[93] All else being equal, a hegemon's absolute size determines its willingness to supply a good only if the state follows a strictly egoistic decision criterion, one intended to maximize only its individual (rather than relative) returns. This decision rule makes sense only if the good is either purely private or necessarily available to everyone in the group once a hegemon supplies it at all. Contrariwise, for goods that are either partially rival in consumption or for which exclusion is feasible, a hegemon may choose to consider the relative gains from various levels of supply. In these cases, its relative size may determine its contribution.

Extended nuclear deterrence approximates a public good within NATO. As Defense Secretary McNamara put it in presenting FR to his fellow defense ministers in 1962,

in a major nuclear war there are no theaters, or rather, the theater is world-wide. . . . We are convinced that a general nuclear war target system is indivisible and if nuclear war should occur, our best hope lies in conducting a centrally controlled campaign against all of the enemy's vital nuclear capabilities.[94]

McNamara's major purposes in these remarks were to justify Washington's opposition to other national nuclear forces within NATO and argue for a unitary nuclear command structure. But there is other evidence that he believed this assertion. He apparently assumed that once nuclear deterrence failed, all allied assets were vulnerable and all Soviet launch points thus had to be covered by American nuclear weapons. In the same meeting, he also said,

SACEUR schedules sorties against [deleted] or more targets with his own forces, but the assurance that he will be able to destroy them is not enough to warrant reliance on his attacks alone. Therefore, with respect to these [deleted] targets additional sorties are assigned to forces external to his theater. The entire threat list is covered and approximately [deleted] of it is scheduled for attack by external forces.[95]

Secretary of State Dean Rusk later emphasized that the nuclear umbrella was considered a public good. In replying to McNamara's contention that the "assured destruction" deterrence criterion could be met with 200 fewer Minuteman missiles than had been originally programmed, he said,

What is not entirely clear from your memorandum is the effect which such a reduction would have upon damage limitation in Western Europe. I can readily imagine that the result would be negligible; nevertheless, having repeatedly assured the Europeans that US forces cover targets threatening Western Europe with the same priority as those which threaten the US, we have assumed the obligation to demonstrate that we have in fact considered their interests.[96]

Rusk was insisting that the principle of indivisible security among all NATO members be maintained in U.S. operational planning.

A good is nonrival only if the marginal cost of extension (the cost of extending consumption of a given unit to an additional person) is zero. Extended deterrence is not strictly joint, since weapons threatening Europe may need to be targeted by more or other American weapons than those needed only to protect U.S. assets. Nevertheless, Rusk intended that America would regard this cost as zero in its procurement and targeting plans. He claimed, in effect, that the United States had given up control over exclusion from its nuclear umbrella within NATO. If so, extended deterrence satisfies the key requisite of a public good, noncontrol over exclusion.[97] The French, in fact, might have defied Washington as much as they did in the early 1960s because they knew it could not partially remove the nuclear umbrella.[98] Of importance here is that U.S. officials do not assess extended deterrence commitments as if the good were rival, that is, by comparing their risks, extractive burdens or economic position to the allies.

Conventional forces are viewed quite differently. Insofar as they are designed to take and hold territory, they are subject to thinning effects and spatial rivalry. This problem is well recognized in NATO. Senior U.S. military officers were reluctant to admit Italy, since that drained existing military assets; when the United States stationed an extra brigade in Germany in 1976, the Dutch, who directly benefited from it, agreed to help support its cost.[99] Out-of-area problems, as discussed in Chapter 2, exacerbate the problem. Because Central Command (Rapid Deployment Force, or RDF) units have various other responsibilities, they cannot concentrate on training for Persian Gulf contingencies.[100]

Rivalness does entail flexibility: land units can be reassigned down to the company level, provided equipment and training are suitable for more than one theater; fleets or air wings can be split into squadrons. Escalation in Vietnam sent individual specialists there from Europe. Provision of nonrival, nonexcludable goods, such as nuclear protection, is more difficult to control. Rivalness and excludability make it possible to change the terms of existing commitments in a variety of ways, but harder to adapt existing capabilities to a wider group or more demanding environmental conditions.

This distinction can be linked to three other issue-area attributes: (1) the extent to which strategies and commitments are tied to force size or other physical characteristics of the arsenal; (2) whether a good is provided collectively within a coalition or unilaterally by a hegemon; and (3) specifically in the U.S. case, the degree to which Congress can affect strategies and commitments.

Rivalness means that conventional strategies are more constrained by force size than nuclear strategies. As Richard Betts put it,

The overall size of U.S. forces (that is, their comparative smallness) is more the source of difficulties than is their structure or doctrine. . . . Geography makes the U.S. homeland more secure than the USSR, but reverses the advantage where defense of allies and conflict in crucial third areas is concerned. Washington must inevitably sacrifice combat power to logistics more than Moscow, so combat force levels are limited by support force structure. Political, social and economic constraints further inhibit overall force size by limiting military manpower, which reinforces the orientation to qualitative solutions by technological substitution.[101]

Other constraints compound the problem. Even though protection of allies imposes huge mobility requirements, the U.S. strategic reserve has never been up to the task, chiefly because the strategic mobility program has been unpopular in Congress. It first encountered resistance because of cost overruns and the threat some saw to rival commercial carriers. Even when conventional forces were rebuilt after Vietnam, lift capabilities were still assigned lower priority, seriously reducing war-fighting flexibility.[102]

Nuclear strategies are not so constrained. "Pencil-and-paper" strategists, most of them civilians, derive notions such as "limited nuclear options" innocent of operational experience. As I argue in Chapter 6, these concepts tend to be taken beyond the limits of existing capabilities. Yet because deterrence has not failed, their advocates cannot be proven wrong.

In large part, nuclear flexibility results from a process in which doctrine has often followed and rationalized a growing force structure. In a detailed account, David Rosenberg shows a loose fit between the early stockpile and how it could be used. Although a 1959 study, designed to hold down the size of the bomber force, was based on the premise that "there was no logical link between the target selection and deterrence, since deterrence depended on Soviet perceptions, and the Soviets were not privy to U.S. target lists," the first SIOP (and presumably subsequent ones) remained a "capabilities plan" rather than an "objectives plan," one that institutionalized "nuclear overkill."[103] Since capabilities were generated independently of any single strategy, they could be used in various ways.

There are two major reasons for this. The nuclear arsenal has continued to grow in sophistication and, until recently, size. New weapons are often procured because the technology is available or for symbolic reasons; only later is a strategic rationale developed. As the arsenal becomes more sophisticated, there are more ways to use it: the first Submarine-Launched Ballistic Missiles (SLBMs) were very inaccurate and suitable only for countervalue attacks, but by the 1980s the Trident II guidance systems allowed pinpoint attacks. The arsenal has long been so large and diverse that even were it reduced substantially, a wide variety of retaliatory options would remain.

Second, deterrence itself allows some disjunction between threats and their execution. This applies more to nuclear than conventional threats, although some exceptions should be noted. It is less true of battlefield nuclear weapons, which could have a significant role in territorial defense, and would not apply to a "pure" warfighting posture or a defense-dominant one. Yet within "flexible response," which relies heavily on the potential for escalation, there is enough discretion to accommodate different mixes and numbers of weapons.

Both of these issue-specific properties work against American leverage in NATO. Given the size of the U.S. nuclear arsenal and the rate of warhead production, nuclear deterrence can be "extended" at what appears to be little extra cost. Europe has thus relied on U.S. protection; even British and France, the other nuclear members, have "minimum" forces sufficient only for homeland protection, and America has paid for 97 percent of NATO's nuclear capabilities. Conventional rivalness, however, makes it logical for a hegemon to provide only a portion of the local garrison, and Europe provides 90 percent of NATO's ground forces, 80 percent of its tanks and combat aircraft, and 90 percent of its peacetime armored divisions.[104] So U.S. leverage as chief provider of nuclear deterrence is undercut by inability to divide a nonrival good, and the leverage afforded by rival conventional forces is undercut by collective provision.

As a result, modern hegemonic expansionism is limited more on the conventional than the nuclear side. Conventional forces are much more expensive, visible, and socially disruptive. The executive may prefer to stretch forces thinly rather than pay for adequate capabilities, but Congress is highly sensitive to relative extractive burdens and outside analysts are quick to point out that in conventional planning, prudence demands realistic preparations for operational use.[105]

On the other hand, after the Iranian Revolution and Moscow's invasion of Afghanistan, Pentagon officials suggested using tactical nuclear weapons to stop an otherwise successful Soviet move into the Persian Gulf. The idea was rightly criticized for failing to show how a tactical nuclear war could be fought or controlled. Waltz, who made the critique, suggested an "asset-seizing deterrent strategy" for the RDF. He acknowledges that "to rely on a tripwire force makes people uneasy," yet asks

Who will risk all by attacking a nuclear power's vital interests? . . . The Soviet Union is likelier to test an American defensive force than to test a deterrent force. . . . an American deterrent strategy would be highly credible [because] . . . We would be protecting a prize of undoubted value. In protecting it, we would not be able to fight to a very high level. If Russian forces challenged us directly, and if their forces were about to overcome ours and take control of the oil fields, leaders of the Soviet Union would have to believe that in response, we might do something highly damaging to them. The Soviets do not have to believe that the United States will, but they do have to believe that it might—all the more so because if we pass, we lessen the credibility of American deterrence worldwide.[106]

What is this if not a prescription for a tripwire? Why should American nuclear commitments credibly cover the Gulf, of vital interest mainly to Europe and Japan, when there is doubt that first-use credibly protects those assets directly? For obvious but nevertheless disheartening reasons, nuclear pledges can be threatened even more casually than the risks of conventional overcommitment.

State Structure and Legislative Impact. A third issue-area characteristic, the degree to which Congress can affect strategies and commitments, depends on the nature of the goods involved and legislative capacity. The latter, in turn, depends largely on state structure. Some discussion of one important dimension, that state's internal strength, is necessary before preceding with the argument.

Analytically, the "state" can be distinguished from civil society and from nonstate governmental institutions. The state in this sense is a set of roles and institutions insulated from specific societal pressures and charged with furthering the general collective good. Entities meeting these criteria can be located within every polity. In the United States, for foreign affairs, the White House and State Department constitute the state.[107] On non-procurement issues, the Pentagon is included. The strength of central state institutions depends on capacity to implement preferences over domestic resistance, including, in this conception, other parts of the government.

By world standards, the American state lacks authority and autonomy. Even those parts of the executive branch charged with defining security interests can find it difficult to implement them. Oliver North's schemes to finance the Contras would have been unnecessary even in many other democracies. Europeans, for instance, accept a security apparatus outside the contestable realm of politics "that represents and defends the continuing interests of the community and the state irrespective of the ideologies that may from one time to another dominate its politics."[108]

In a weak state, the executive may be unable to implement its priorities. On issues of national strategy, central decision makers are motivated mainly by *realpolitik* criteria that may not be shared by other parts of the government or mobilized societal groups. This means that the executive takes systemic position seriously in making policy; it does not imply that the state's interests can be objectively defined in multiple-exit situations. Lake thus distinguishes between the "foreign policy executive" and the representative element of government. The former corresponds to the central state and is chiefly responsible for furthering the nation's international interests, while legislators represent specific segments of society and are evaluated accordingly by their constituents.[109]

Lest this distinction appear less applicable to security policy than economic policy, recall that even in the traditional military-diplomatic sphere the house is rarely on fire. Hegemons deal with various security issues unrelated to core values. Institutional outlooks differ in most systems with popularly chosen legislatures, with the executive typically taking a broader geopolitical view.

The executive can implement its priorities easily only if it, rather than the legislature, controls the necessary resources. Although a "weak" state can mean a relatively weak executive, and the U.S. Constitution clearly does invite struggle over much of foreign policy, actual control typically varies significantly by issue area. Executive authority and autonomy are enhanced if problems appear to have single exits and reduced if issues have clear, concentrated distributive effects. In the latter case, affected groups will mobilize support in the legislature. Extended deterrence and conventional forces in Europe fall between these extremes. The arena in which such issues are resolved depends both on their inherent nature and on the way they are defined.[110] The burden-sharing and nuclear-threshold debates discussed in chapter 1 indicate that extractive burdens are more salient politically than shared risks. Here I emphasize the intrinsic characteristics that cause issues to be resolved in particular fora.

Congress's impact on policy depends upon legislators' interest and institutional capacity. Congressional willingness to question presidential priorities has ebbed and peaked cyclically. During the Civil War, the early years of the Great Depression, and from 1950 to the late 1960s, legislators gave the president what amounted to emergency authority. This was the institutional basis for the Cold War consensus. At some point, though, the rationale for crisis has typically worn thin and Congress has moved to regain lost prerogatives. A period of readjustment eventually restores a rough equilibrium between the branches.[111]

The recent penchant for activism, however, has been exercised in traditional ways. Their electoral constituencies give most legislators a fairly narrow range of concerns. Large representative bodies find it difficult to take coherent positions, especially over extended periods. In recent years, overspecialization and increasingly fragmented power within both houses have made congressional representatives even less capable of taking broad approaches to foreign policy. Congress therefore often reacts somewhat spasmodically to the executive—cutting appropriations for specific programs, adding them to others, denying trade concessions, and attaching conditions to treaties.

These institutional characteristics and the issue-area ones already noted give Congress greater impact on conventional policy than extended deterrence. Although state structure rarely determines policy, it sets internal bargaining parameters.[112] An important parameter is the budgetary veto, Congress's ultimate policymaking tool. It is an effective way to shape conventional strategies and commitments, which depend closely on the size and composition of the arsenal. In 1985, for example, Congress came under pressure to reduce budget deficits, which squeezed military spending for the first time in several years. Cuts in the range being discussed would have reduced conventional capabilities by one-fourth to one-third. Depending on service and White House priorities, a smaller force structure or diminished readiness at existing levels would result. Nuclear weapons modernization would also suffer, but it consumed a relatively small share of Pentagon dollars and the effect would be small.[113]

Legislators have specific incentives to micro-manage conventional expenditures. Since defense has in recent years made up almost 75 percent of controllable federal spending, Congress has gradually become more involved with the Pentagon budget than with federal spending as a whole. Certain manipulable budget categories are scrutinized particularly closely. The reason is that only a fraction of budget authority is spent during the fiscal year it is appropriated. That percentage is higher for the Operations and Maintenance and Personnel accounts than, for instance, Procurement or Research, Development, Testing and Evaluation. So when congressional representatives want to cut near-term outlays, they logically trim the former, which affects the readiness and size of conventional forces.[114]

In sum, the budget process gives Congress a direct means of affecting conventional strategies and commitments. Its capabilities are much blunter for nuclear strategy. It would have to act much more consistently over a number of years to have a comparable effect. As seen in chapter 6, the loose link between nuclear capabilities and employment policy allowed Schlesinger to announce changes in the latter without guarantees that Congress would upgrade the arsenal. By contrast, the Army in the early 1970s was highly uncertain about how many troops Congress would leave in Europe, making operational planning difficult.[115]

Planners have some flexibility with conventional forces, which are partly

Figure 3.2
International Goods and Hegemonic Control

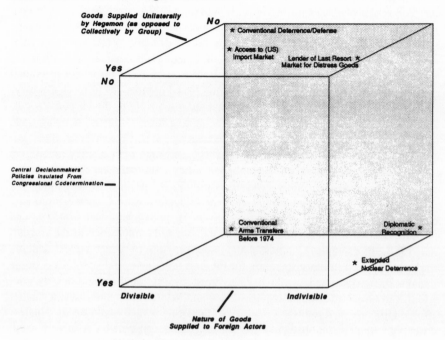

Hegemon has most adaptive control over goods near
lower left front of cube, least over those near upper back right.
Leverage over those in or near center is mixed.

fungible. But nuclear weapons are more so, and scenarios in which relative force size matters are more plausible on the conventional side.[116] Moreover, given the size and sophistication of the contemporary U.S. nuclear arsenal, U.S. allies are fairly indifferent to its composition. What matters to them is how it would be used in a crisis and whether their interests would be taken into account. In these respects, Congress's ability to influence operational policy is slight.

Figure 3.2 presents a typology depicting the two issue-area characteristics and the degree of congressional impact. A hegemon has most adaptive control over goods near the lower left front of the cube and least over those near the upper back right.

Myopic and Sophisticated Incrementalism. The last step in the argument links these issue and institutional differences to two policy patterns. Each is a form of incrementalism, which differs from so-called ''synoptic'' decision-making methods in three ways. First, instead of trying to optimize, decision makers compare a number of modest experiments. Marginal rather than dramatic improvements are sought. Second, no attempt is made to compare all policy alternatives. Only a prominent or convenient few are considered. Third, ends are not chosen independently of means. A satisfactory policy may simply "work" better than known alternatives, even if nonoptimal.[117] As should be evident, American NATO policies have been incremental in each sense.

Conventional and nuclear policies however, have differed in a key respect. Alexander George's distinction between myopic incrementalism and a more sophisticated version captures it. Short-sighted strategies attack symptoms rather than causes and lack a planning context for individual decisions. Alternatively, decisions can be embedded in a more comprehensive design. Large problems are broken down; policymakers try to sequence decisions so as to use information and other resources best.[118] This strategy of sequential decision making requires that the executive control the resources necessary to implement policy.

Extended deterrence and specific nuclear employment policies have allowed this. Change in both areas has been incremental. Until the early 1990s, the nuclear umbrella covered most of the same countries as in 1960; the basic categories of SIOP targets, their priorities, procedures for allocating weapons to targets, and the target planning process also remained much the same during that time. The executive branch has also controlled the pace and scope of change. SIOP targets have been increasingly packaged in varying sizes and types, continually augmenting the National Command Authority's (NCA) flexibility.[119] Jimmy Carter was the first president to subject himself to detailed SIOP briefings, so it is hardly surprising that Congress has remained aloof. Even had it chosen differently, legislating target selection would, at the least, be awkward. Even when the Nixon administration changed U.S. "centralization" policy and began advising France on warhead design, it needed no legislative authorization.

The executive has much less leverage over conventional-forces policies. Planning depends on what Congress is willing to fund, frequently giving decision makers a short time horizon. This was most evident when domestic constraints were strongest, between 1966 and 1974. Congressional pressures put the White House, State Department, and Pentagon on the defensive, encouraging stop-gap measures such as foreign-exchange offset. It also made it difficult to settle upon long-term security priorities after Vietnam, although the Pentagon tried hard to increase the efficiency of combat forces in the mid–1970s. A similar pattern was evident during the late 1980s. Budgetary pressures made the 46,000 troops in Korea an inviting target. The Pentagon tried to plan for a withdrawal through a regional redeployment strategy, but its success, in one official's words, "depends on the time we've got."[120]

George's distinction is borne out by deductive reasoning about the relative utility of myopic strategies and the evidence in chapters 5 and 6.[121] Different policy processes have had important substantive consequences. Nuclear deterrence adaptation has been unhindered by the representative part of government and has consistently reflected the executive's preferences. Neither has been true of conventional planning and commitments.

SUMMARY AND CONCLUSIONS

The arguments in this chapter suggest three additional hypotheses:

Hypothesis 3: Central decision makers will monitor critical variables that could affect policy consistency or the provision of key commitments and services. This specifically includes resources relative to tasks, the margin and scope of technological advantage, diffusion of nuclear and conventional weapons, relative power projection capabilities, and the degree of bloc cohesion.

Hypothesis 4: Conventional-forces commitments are more vulnerable to hegemonic decline than is first-nuclear use.

Although Hypothesis 3 seems to contradict Hypothesis 1, a penchant for overextension implies tolerance of some policy risks, not indifference to the balance between capabilities and commitments. Many policymakers are ambivalent about this problem and object to overstretch only when it threatens commitments they consider most important, such as Europe.[122]

Hypothesis 4 follows from two arguments: because conventional forces are rival in consumption, troop commitments are easier to adjust at the margins; their explicit connection to extractive defense burdens makes them an attractive target. The executive will be generally loath to alter any commitments, but conventional cuts can help ease overburdened economies in ways that redefined nuclear commitments cannot. Particularly in a weak state, the executive also has less leverage over conventional-forces levels and policies.

Hypothesis 5: Central decision makers will prefer defensive (versus offensive) and internal (versus external) adaptive options if they can use sophisticated incremental policymaking procedures.

Declining hegemons are generally risk averse, and risk aversion implies a preference for defensive, internal adaptation. All else being equal, this is how the executive should adjust if it controls the necessary policy instruments.

Chapters 2 and 3 presented a framework for understanding hegemonic security expansion and adaptation. Declining hegemons will be pressed by their environments to shed commitments, while a heightened fear of policy risks works against this. A "probabilistic" systemic argument identifies priorities and therefore suggests the areas in which adaptation should take place. Although the specific cognitive argument discussed in this chapter applies only to the United States, it indicates the kind of images and beliefs which form the context for risk assessment. Depending upon the kind of commitment and the executive's overall level of foreign affairs autonomy, the executive may or may not control the policy instruments it needs to adapt as preferred. So long as "interests" refer only to the preferences of central decision makers, domestic-process variables per se are not necessary to explain them.

The Theory of Hegemonic Stability does not reveal much about foreign-policy adaptation. Its most specific prediction is that a declining hegemon will try to internalize the external benefits it provides to its partners. The theory itself cannot tell us whether this overrides contradictory incentives toward risk aversion. Instead, the theory's implications had to be teased out in another way. The last two chapters have essentially worked backward from a hegemon's interest in system stability to the type of leadership and commitments that provide it. The kinds of constraints that could affect these commitments are "critical variables," and I argue that decision makers will focus their efforts and resources on the problems they identify. But adaptation also depends on whether the executive controls the necessary policy instruments. Some commitments, for issue-specific reasons, are more vulnerable than others. The executive can be presumed to understand this and adjust preemptively if necessary. Issue-area arguments do not necessarily conflict with Hegemonic Theory, since there is no reason to expect all regimes or commitments to erode uniformly. But they do suggest that the theory's emphasis on power needs to complemented with analysis of how issues are defined by domestic actors other than the executive.

This is not necessarily a setback for structural realism. Even its proponents concede that policy cannot be explained if one black-boxes the state. Doing so is possible only in single-exit situations or those where the representative element of government can be excluded for other reasons. As this implies, much of the controversy over NATO policy and pressure on central decision makers has occurred in areas where Congress has a significant role and a variety of options appear feasible to those outside the executive branch. In the next three chapters, considerable attention is thus given to domestic and congressional politics, but only insofar as it affected executive-branch strategies.

NOTES

1. Friedberg, *The Weary Titan* (Princeton: Princeton University Press, 1988), Chap. 2–6 passim.

2. Jervis, *Perception and Misperception in International Politics* (Princeton: Princeton University Press, 1976), pp. 16–18.

3. Goldmann, *Change and Stability in Foreign Policy* (Princeton: Princeton University Press, 1988), pp. 13–15.

4. This distinction is made by Gilpin in *War and Change in World Politics* (Cambridge: Cambridge University Press, 1981), Chap. 2.

5. Arthur L. Stinchcombe, *Constructing Social Theories* (Chicago: University of Chicago Press, 1987), p. 149.

6. Stephen D. Krasner, *Structural Conflict: The Third World Against Global Liberalism* (Berkeley: University of California Press, 1985), p. 306.

7. Waltz, *Theory of International Politics*, p. 78. On the limitations of Classical Realism, see Robert O. Keohane, "Theory of World Politics: Structural Realism and Beyond," in Ada Finifter, ed., *Political Science: The State of the Discipline* (Washington, D.C.: American Political Science Association, 1983), pp. 510–511, and Michael Mas-

tanduno, David A. Lake, and G. John Ikenberry, "Toward a Realist Theory of State Action," *International Studies Quarterly* 33, no. 4 (December 1989).

   8. Ibid., pp. 71, 92, 174.

   9. Ibid., p. 198.

   10. Gilpin, *War and Change in World Politics*, pp. 95, 159–168, 177.

   11. Keohane, "Theory of World Politics," p. 519; Joseph Nye, "Neorealism and Neoliberalism," *World Politics* 40, no. 2 (January 1988), p. 245.

   12. Nye, "Neorealism and Neoliberalism," p. 238.

   13. Friedberg, *The Weary Titan*, pp. 4–8.

   14. See Keohane, *After Hegemony* (Princeton: Princeton University Press, 1984), pp. 100–103, 183, 184, 195.

   15. Ibid., p. 210; see also Chap. 9, passim.

   16. Ibid., pp. 210–214. Keohane evidently wishes to argue that domestic politics affected the *response* to hegemonic decline, which is certainly true. But in doing so he makes the theory seem weaker than it is. For example, on pages 210 and 211, he says that U.S. power resources as measured by shares of world trade declined relative to those of American trading partners, partly because the EEC became a coherent trading bloc between the mid–1960s and early 1980s. He also alludes on pages 212 and 213 to the pressures of international competition. Why these are not changes in effective market power, at least under the regime rules, is not made clear.

   17. Ibid., p. 195.

   18. Mancur Olson, Jr., and Richard Zeckhauser, "An Economic Theory of Alliances," in Bruce M. Russett, ed., *Economic Theories of International Politics* (Chicago: Markham, 1968), p. 30.

   19. Duncan Snidal, "The Limits of Hegemonic Stability Theory," *International Organization* 39, no. 4 (Autumn 1985): 588–589; David A. Lake, *Power, Protection, and Free Trade: International Sources of U.S. Commercial Strategy, 1887–1939* (Ithaca, N.Y.: Cornell University Press, 1988), pp. 9–10.

   20. See Duncan Snidal, "Limits of Hegemonic Stability Theory," *International Organization* 39, no. 4 (Autumn 1985), p. 589, and note 21.

   21. Ibid., pp. 604–612.

   22. Stephen D. Krasner, "State Power and the Structure of International Trade," *World Politics* 28, no. 3 (April 1976): 319–321.

   23. David Lake, *Power, Protection, and Free Trade* (Ithaca: Cornell University Press, 1988), Chap. 1.

   24. Stinchcombe, *Constructing Social Theories*, p. 231 and Chap. 5, passim.

   25. The distinction between "internal" and "external" means of balancing power of adversaries is found in Kenneth Waltz, *Theory of International Politics* (Reading: Addison-Wesley, 1979), p. 168.

   26. Albert O. Hirschman, *National Power and the Structure of Foreign Trade* (Berkeley: University of California Press, 1980), pp. 14–29.

   27. According to John Gaddis, "Eisenhower and Dulles could agree that the chief American interest in the word was access to the world, and that in turn required a world of at least minimal congeniality." See John Lewis Gaddis, *Strategies of Containment* (New York: Oxford University Press, 1982), p. 132.

   28. United States Arms Control and Disarmament Agency, *World Military Expenditures and Arms Transfers, 1985* (Washington: ACDA Publication 123, 1985), pp. 47–130.

29. Randolph M. Siverson and Harvey Starr, "Opportunity, Willingness and the Diffusion of War, 1815–1965," *The American Political Science Review* 84, no. 1, March 1990. For an earlier discussion, see James Paul Wesley, "Frequency of Wars and Geographical Opportunity," *Journal of Conflict Resolution* Vol. 6, No. 4 (December 1962).

30. Waltz, *Theory of International Politics*, p. 142.

31. Jervis, "Cooperation Under the Security Dilemma," *World Politics* 30, no. 2 (January 1978), p. 168.

32. Barry Buzan, *People, States and Fear: the National Security Problem in International Relations* (Chapel Hill: The University of North Carolina Press, 1983), pp. 79–83.

33. Jervis, "Cooperation Under the Security Dilemma," pp. 187–210.

34. Friedberg, "The Political Economy of American Strategy," *World Politics* 41, no. 3 (April 1989), p. 383.

35. Waltz, *Theory of International Politics*; Krasner, *Structural Conflict*, p. 306.

36. Arnold Wolfers, "The Actors in International Politics," in Wolfers, ed. *Discord and Collaboration: Essays on International Politics* (Baltimore, Md.: The Johns Hopkins University Press, 1962), p. 13.

37. I thank Robert Keohane for pointing this out to me.

38. Wolfers, "Actors in International Politics," pp. 14, 15.

39. Spiro J. Latsis, "A Research Programme in Economics," in Latsis, ed., *Method and Appraisal in Economics* (Cambridge: Cambridge University Press, 1976), p. 21.

40. Krasner, *Defending the National Interest* (Princeton: Princeton University Press, 1978), pp. 35, 333–347.

41. Lake, *Power, Protection, and Free Trade*, p. 13.

42. Keohane, "Theory of World Politics," p. 524.

43. Richard Herrmann, "The Empirical Challenge of the Cognitive Revolution," *International Studies Quarterly* 32, no. 2 (June 1988): 178.

44. Gilpin, *War and Change in World Politics*, p. 42.

45. See Harold and Margaret Sprout, *The Ecological Perspective on Human Affairs* (Princeton, N.J.: Princeton University Press, 1965), Chap. 5; Harold and Margaret Sprout, "Environmental Factors in the Study of International Politics," in James N. Rosenau, ed., *International Politics and Foreign Policy* (New York: Free Press, 1969).

46. Deborah Welch Larson, *The Origins of Containment: A Psychological Explanation* (Princeton, N.J.: Princeton University Press, 1985), pp. 18–23, 328–329.

47. Spiro J. Latsis, "The Limitations of Single-Exit Models: A Reply to Machlup," *The British Journal for the Philosophy of Science* 27 (1976): 59.

48. Harold and Margaret Sprout, *The Ecological Perspective*, Chap. 6. The quoted passage is from pp. 100–101.

49. Goldmann, *Change and Stability in Foreign Policy*, pp. 59–60.

50. Latsis, "The Limitations of Single-Exit Models," p. 55.

51. This paragraph draws on Keohane, "Theory of World Politics," p. 529, and Simon, "Human Nature in Politics."

52. "Diplomatic Deftness Wins Applause," *The Christian Science Monitor*, July 26, 1989, p. 8.

53. Celeste Wallander, "Opportunity, Incrementalism, and Learning in the Extension and Retraction of Soviet Global Commitments," paper prepared for delivery at the 1989 meeting of the American Political Science Association, Atlanta, Georgia, pp. 15–17.

54. During his last year in office, Lyndon Johnson was confronted by a military

request for 200,000 additional men. These were not all needed at the time for Vietnam: the Joint Chiefs wanted Johnson to clarify his priorities and stop trying to fight the war without a general mobilization. Nitze, then a Deputy Secretary of Defense, told the new secretary, Clark Clifford, that the war could not be won, that it was straining relations with NATO allies, and that it was shortchanging U.S. forces elsewhere. Nitze was a dove on Vietnam precisely because he was a hawk in Europe: the war in Asia was distracting attention from the Soviet buildup. See Walter Isaacson and Evan Thomas, *The Wise Men* (New York: Simon and Schuster, 1986), pp. 670, 689.

55. "Seeing a Dependent and Declining U.S., More Japanese Adopt a Nationalistic Spirit," *The New York Times*, August 4, 1989, p. 6.

56. *The Economist*, September 23, 1989, p. 16.

57. Fred C. Ikle and Albert Wohlstetter, *Discriminate Deterrence* (Washington, D.C.: U.S. Government Printing Office, 1988), p. 11.

58. Bruce Russett, "The Real Decline in Nuclear Hegemony," in Ernst-Otto Czempiel and James N. Rosenau, eds., *Global Changes and Theoretical Challenges: Approaches to World Politics for the 1990s* (Lexington, Mass.: Lexington Books, 1989), p. 177.

59. Walter LaFeber, *America, Russia, and the Cold War, 1945–1984* (New York: Knopf, 1985), p. 203; "A New Europe," *The New York Times*, July 20, 1989, p. 4.

60. Latsis, "The Limitations of Single-Exit Models," p. 58.

61. Keohane, *After Hegemony*, p. 28.

62. Nye, "Neorealism and Neoliberalism," p. 244.

63. See statement of Martin Hillenbrand, Assistant Secretary of State for European Affairs, in U.S. Congress, Senate, Committee on Foreign Relations, *United States Forces in Europe, Hearings Before the Subcommittee on United States Security Agreements and Commitments Abroad*, 91st Cong., 2nd sess., pp. 2199, 2211, 2213–2214; interview with Harlan Cleveland, U.S. Ambassador to NATO, 1965–1969, October 27, 1984.

64. Goldmann, *Change and Stability in Foreign Policy*, p. 35.

65. See Alexander L. George, "The Causal Nexus Between Cognitive Beliefs and Decision-Making Behavior: The 'Operational Code' Belief System," in Lawrence S. Falkowski, ed., *Psychological Models in International Politics* (Boulder: Westview, 1979), p. 103.

66. Morton Halperin lists "peace is indivisible" as one of the general images shared by U.S. leaders and the public. See *Bureaucratic Politics and Foreign Policy* (Washington, D.C.: Brookings Institution, 1974), p. 12. George Kennan objected to the Truman Doctrine on these grounds; see *Memoirs: 1925–1950* (Boston: Little, Brown, 1967), pp. 322–324. For evidence that presidents reflect this tendency and do not use it simply as a public rationalization, see Steven L. Spiegel, *The Other Arab-Israeli Conflict: Making America's Middle East Policy, from Truman to Reagan* (Chicago: University of Chicago Press, 1985), pp. 121, 169–170.

67. Dean Acheson, *Present at the Creation: My Years in the State Department* (New York: W. W. Norton, 1969), p. 218; see also Hanson Baldwin, "World Role for U.S.," *The New York Times*, March 2, 1947, p. 4L.

68. Acheson, *Present at the Creation*, p. 212.

69. I thank David Healy for pointing this out to me. Deborah Larson claims that "instead of deducing policy from a Weltanschauung, decisionmakers match current events to what is familiar, concrete, and close to home." See *The Origins of Containment*, p. 326. While the second part of the assertion is surely true, more than the lessons of

Munich seems to have been operating here. Europe's internal resolve was seen as very low and its propensity to bandwagon high; both suggest a general view of the world or at least of these matters.

70. William Pfaff, "Reflections: Finlandization," *The New Yorker*, September 1, 1980, p. 33; Friedberg, *The Weary Titan*, p. 282.

71. Joseph M. Jones, *The Fifteen Weeks* (New York: Viking Press, 1955), pp. 83, 85.

72. C. L. Sulzberger, *A Long Row of Candles: Memoirs and Diaries, 1934–1954* (Toronto: Macmillan, 1969), p. 976. Sulzberger notes the political motivations for this remark, but does not dispute its accuracy.

73. Goldmann, *Change and Stability in Foreign Policy*, p. 35.

74. Paul A. Anderson, "Justifications and Precedents as Constraints in Foreign Policy Decision-Making," *American Journal of Political Science* 25 (November 1981): 740–742.

75. See Raymond Cohen, *International Politics: The Rules of the Game* (New York: Longman, 1981), pp. 44–46, for a discussion of measures governments take to enhance credibility and demonstrate political support.

76. Robert E. Hunter, "Now, Reassure Our Allies on the Treaty," *The New York Times*, December 10, 1987, p. 31.

77. Patrick Morgan, "Saving Face for the Sake of Deterrence," in *Psychology and Deterrence*, Robert Jervis et al., eds. (Baltimore, Md.: The Johns Hopkins University Press, 1985), p. 142.

78. Goldmann, *Change and Stability in Foreign Policy*, pp. 35–39.

79. Memorandum for the President re Erhard Briefing Papers, June 11, 1964, National Security File: Aides Files, Memos for the President 6/64–2/65, Box 2, Lyndon B. Johnson Library.

80. Harlan Cleveland, *NATO: The Transatlantic Bargain* (New York: Harper and Row, 1970), pp. 183–184.

81. Goldmann, *Change and Stability in Foreign Policy*, p. 38.

82. Stephen M. Walt, "Testing Theories of Alliance Formation: The Case of Southwest Asia," *International Organization* 42, no. 2 (Spring 1988): 277–279.

83. Henry Brandon, *The Retreat of American Power* (New York: Doubleday, 1973), p. 214; see also Morton H. Halperin, "Why Bureaucrats Play Games," *Foreign Policy*, no. 2 (Spring 1971): 72–73.

84. Alexander L. George, *Presidential Decisionmaking in Foreign Policy: The Effective Use of Information and Advice* (Boulder, Colo.: Westview, 1980), p. 61.

85. Baruch Fischoff, "Hindsight ≠ Foresight: The Effect of Outcome Knowledge on Judgment Under Uncertainty," *Journal of Experimental Psychology: Human Perception and Performance* 1, no. 3 (1975).

86. Phil Williams, *The Senate and U.S. Troops in Europe* (New York: St. Martin's, 1985), p. 131.

87. David P. Calleo, "NATO's Middle Course," *Foreign Policy* no. 69 (Winter 1987–88), p. 140.

88. James O. Goldsborough, "Europe Cashes in On Carter's Cold War," *New York Times Magazine*, April 27, 1980; Goldsborough, *Rebel Europe: How America Can Live with a Changing Continent* (New York: Macmillan, 1982).

89. Goldmann, *Change and Stability in Foreign Policy*, pp. 54, 70–71, 76.

90. Stephen D. Krasner, "Are Bureaucracies Important?" *Foreign Policy* no. 7 (Summer 1972), p. 426.

91. James N. Rosenau, "Foreign Policy as an Issue-Area," in Rosenau, ed., *Domestic Sources of Foreign Policy* (New York: Free Press, 1967), p. 17; Keohane and Nye, *Power and Interdependence*, p. 65.

92. William C. Potter, "Issue-Area and Foreign Policy Analysis," *International Organization* 34, no. 3 (Summer 1980): 421, 424, 426.

93. This definition is taken from Duncan Snidal, "Public Goods, Property Rights, and Political Organizations," *International Studies Quarterly* 23, no. 4 (December 1979): 533–534.

94. David N. Schwartz, *NATO's Nuclear Dilemmas* (Washington, D.C.: Brookings Institution, 1983), p. 159.

95. Ibid., p. 158.

96. Rusk to McNamara, National Security File re Defense Budget FY 1966, Lyndon B. Johnson Library.

97. Snidal, "Public Goods, Property Rights, and Political Organizations," p. 542.

98. Bernard Brodie, "What Price Conventional Capabilities in Europe?" *The Reporter*, May 23, 1963, p. 27.

99. Acheson, *Present at the Creation*, p. 279; "NATO Views Rise in Power of East," *The New York Times*, June 12, 1976.

100. Eliot A. Cohen, "When Policy Outstrips Power," *The Public Interest*, no. 75 (Spring 1984), p. 16.

101. Richard K. Betts, "Conventional Strategy: New Critics, Old Choices," *International Security* 7, no. 4 (Spring 1983): 162.

102. William W. Kaufmann, *Planning Conventional Forces 1950–1980* (Washington, D.C.: Brookings Institution, 1982), pp. 16–19.

103. David Alan Rosenberg, "The Origins of Overkill: Nuclear Weapons and American Strategy, 1945–1960," *International Security* 7, no. 4 (Spring 1983): 56, 65, 69.

104. David Garnham, *The Politics of European Defense Cooperation: Germany, France, Britain and America* (Cambridge, Mass.: Ballinger, 1988), p. 11.

105. Cohen, "When Policy Outstrips Power," p. 11.

106. Kenneth N. Waltz, "A Strategy for the Rapid Deployment Force," *International Security* 5, no. 4 (Spring 1981): 66, 70–71.

107. Krasner, *Defending the National Interest*, pp. 10–11.

108. Ibid., p. 61. The quote is from Samuel P. Huntington, *American Politics: The Promise of Disharmony*, p. 237.

109. Lake, *Power, Protection and Free Trade*, pp. 67–74.

110. Krasner, *Defending the National Interest*, p. 89.

111. This paragraph and part of the next draw on Hrach Gregorian, "Assessing Congressional Involvement in Foreign Policy: Lessons of the Post-Vietnam Period," *The Review of Politics* 46, no. 1 (January 1984): 96–97, 101, 104.

112. Lake, *Power, Protection and Free Trade*, p. 73.

113. "Effect of Limiting Military Budget Is Gauged," *The New York Times*, December 9, 1985.

114. Fen Osler Hampson, *Unguided Missiles: How America Buys Its Weapons* (New York: Norton, 1989), Chap. 4.

115. Brandon, *The Retreat of American Power*, p. 215.

116. For this argument, see Robert Jervis, "Why Nuclear Superiority Doesn't Matter," *Political Science Quarterly* 94, no. 4 (Winter 1979–1980).

117. See Charles E. Lindblom, "The Science of 'Muddling Through,' " *Public Administration Review* 19, no. 2 (Spring 1959).

118. George, *Presidential Decisionmaking in Foreign Policy*, pp. 40–41.

119. Desmond Ball, "The Development of the SIOP, 1960–1983," in Desmond Ball and Jeffrey Richelson, eds., *Strategic Nuclear Targeting* (Ithaca, N.Y.: Cornell University Press, 1986), pp. 82–83.

120. Richard Halloran, "U.S. Considers the Once Unthinkable on Korea," p. 8.

121. See Ian Lustick, "Explaining the Variable Utility of Disjointed Incrementalism," *American Political Science Review* 74, no. 2 (June 1980). Two of the four conditions under which myopic strategies must be discounted that are explicated in this article fit nuclear deterrence, indicating that the more sophisticated version is indeed functional (in light of official goals) as well as convenient for the executive branch.

122. See the example about Nitze and Vietnam in Isaacson and Thomas, *The Wise Men*, p. 689.

4 The United States and European Defense, 1961–1965

OVERVIEW AND BACKGROUND

More than is often recognized, the Kennedy and early Johnson administrations were ambivalent about America's world position. Their public faces were optimistic, ambitious, and confident. Others, worn largely in private, reflected doubts about the costs of U.S. commitments and viability of a hegemonic leadership role.

On the positive side, Secretary McNamara was soon able to announce that fears of an intercontinental ballistic missile gap were unfounded. Although the Soviets had test flown an ICBM before the United States, they produced only a few of these early, technologically inferior models. Technical problems with the second-generation versions apparently precluded production in quantity until the mid–1960s, and Soviet development of submarine launched ballistic missiles (SLBMs) lagged even further behind Washington's. Moscow's bomber force was also much smaller and less sophisticated. Some policymakers thus believed that nuclear superiority could be maintained for a time, as Nitze, then an Assistant Secretary of Defense, said in late 1961.[1] In two respects, Kennedy's military buildup did prolong overall U.S. military superiority for at least a half-decade: it restored confidence in at least a robust second-strike capability for much of the 1960s and provided an unprecedented range of conventional forces and power-projection options.

Whether Washington's quantitative and qualitative nuclear advantage could have been preserved longer than it ultimately was is debatable; Kennedy was convinced after a year in office that a superpower nuclear stalemate was inevitable.[2] Others were more optimistic. Averell Harriman, who negotiated the Atmospheric Test Ban Treaty in 1963, had originally wanted a complete ban but accepted the partial one when Moscow would go no further. He later speculated that he should have tried harder: "When you stop to think what the advantages were to us of stopping all testing in the early 1960s when we were still ahead of the Soviets, it's really appalling to realize what an opportunity we missed."[3] Kennedy and McNamara, it should also be recalled, requested 1,000 Minutemen missiles from Congress because this was the lowest politically acceptable number, not because they believed them militarily necessary.

In other respects the picture was more pessimistic. Before assured destruction applied to both superpower homelands, the Soviets countered a potential U.S. nuclear strike by threatening to destroy Western Europe. In strategic jargon, this was the ability to hold it "hostage." It was first achieved by large conventional forces in close proximity. Moscow quickly built up its European-theater nuclear forces, first with aircraft and then, after 1961, by deploying medium and intermediate-range missiles. Figure 1.1 indicates the extent and composition of the Soviet theater buildup. It removed America's ability to dominate the escalation ladder in a European conflict and was one impetus for the conventional emphasis in the new U.S. FR strategy.

Raising the nuclear thereshold was a major policy change and is discussed extensively in this chapter. NATO's original force goal was thirty-six divisions by 1955. This was increased substantially after the North Korean attack; in February 1952 the North Atlantic Council set a target of ninety-six divisions to be available in Europe within thirty days of the order to mobilize (in military terminology, M + 30). It reflected a risk-averse preference for a force that could hold off an attacker two or three times as large without nuclear weapons.[4] After the uncertainty about immediate Soviet intentions in Europe dissipated in 1951 and 1952, European governments became much less enthusiastic about fielding such large forces. They were soon let off the hook; in December 1953, Secretary of State John Foster Dulles publicly justified NATO's abandonment of the Lisbon force goals by noting the reduced threat to Europe.[5] Despite Washington's continued prodding after 1961, they would never again commit themselves to an adequate non-nuclear defense.

Their refusal was significant because if the first-use commitment was originally based on the invulnerability of the American homeland, its foundation had eroded by 1961. In 1957 Moscow ended the era of U.S. nuclear invulnerability by deploying intercontinental bombers and flight-testing an ICBM. Since a first nuclear strike was essential to Eisenhower's massive retaliation policy and remained implicit in FR, U.S. strategy thereafter was based on a potentially suicidal threat. This could have been paralyzing in conflicts such as Berlin where a first nuclear move would probably have been Washington's. The absolute level of damage a country might suffer in a nuclear exchange should be distinguished from the quantitative balance of forces, which continued in Washington's favor through the 1960s. Even the forces deployed during the Kennedy buildup would have been useful mainly in a counterforce strike against unready Soviet forces;

in any other contingency, they could have done little to avert devastating population losses.[6]

The other component of the nuclear stalemate was mutually secure second-strike forces. U.S. planners assumed (and some hoped) that Moscow would place its ICBMs in dispersed, hardened silos to disincline preemption in a crisis. This took some time, but the pace of Soviet deployments deprived the United States of a confident first-strike capability after the mid–1960s.

Another concern was the U.S. balance-of-payments position. One source of the problem were the commitments Washington had assumed in order to implement the Bretton Woods regime. The regime had established adjustable par rates with the dollar as "key" currency, which tied it officially to gold and to other convertible currencies. Aside from its value as a vehicle currency, heightened during the 1950s and 1960s by steadily growing international trade, foreigners' willingness to hold dollars depended upon confidence in Washington's pledge to sell gold, the "real" reserve asset, for $35 per ounce. The ultimate issue was not the size of U.S. gold reserves (clearly insufficient to settle all claims), but confidence that the dollar would retain its gold value and that a run on the bank was unnecessary.

Under these rules, external financial means of adjustment were ruled out. Yet, as Robert Triffin showed, the dollar's liquidity and reserve asset functions were incompatible: while increasingly more dollars would be needed for international transactions, the resulting glut would make it difficult to defend its parity. In the end, Triffin's dilemma proved inescapable; even the new source of liquidity created in 1967, Special Drawing Rights, could not save the gold-dollar link.

The Kennedy administration soon understood the outlines of this problem. It recognized a long-term tension among domestic expansion, liberal internationalism, and America's relative position within the Atlantic Community. Nevertheless, as David Calleo argues, the administration was unwilling to establish clear priorities among these objectives. Although U.S. short-term external obligations exceeded monetary reserves as early as 1958, the first year of full currency convertibility under Bretton Woods, foreign aid increased by more than one-half over the next decade.[7] Neither Kennedy nor Johnson was willing to cut substantially the military and aid expenditures that helped pile up dollars abroad, although Kennedy seriously considered it and Johnson ultimately took some small steps.

The payments problem, which put pressure on both the gold-exchange and troop commitments, was also largely a product of the foreign exchange costs of six divisions in Europe. It was apparently unanticipated in 1951; Europe was severely short of dollars, and providing more through a military channel was consistent with other U.S. policies at the time. Rusk thought that the failure to secure an agreement at the outset to neutralize American exchange costs had been an error.[8] Kennedy became preoccupied with the limitations imposed by recurring payments deficits; in January 1962 he told his advisers that U.S.

commitments required a continued export surplus: "We must either do a good job selling abroad or pull back."[9]

The administration's doubts, then, were reflected in the fact that virtually its entire European policy was crafted with an eye on the eroding U.S. position.[10] Kennedy saw a clear link between liberalized trade with Europe, the payments deficit, and the troop commitment. U.S. economic and military power were still overwhelming, but a long-range view suggested that the extraordinary advantages of the first postwar decade would not survive the 1960s. Nevertheless, Kennedy's grand strategy involved "bolstering... American hegemony, both by a reassertion of power abroad and by a renewal of strength and commitment at home."[11] The Cold War and the administration's fashionable style made commitment at home fairly easy at least until Vietnam. But its "Grand Design" depended partly on European cooperation, and only some was forthcoming.

Only a few exits were closed in 1961. Restoring physical invulnerability was impossible, as was recapturing the early postwar share of world production (50 percent). Kennedy's desire to sell the United States out of its balance-of-payments bind would also prove infeasible. In general, however, Kennedy and Johnson faced fewer problems and more exits than their successors.[12]

Two key balances became critical variables during the early 1960s. The superpower nuclear balance was the foundation for the first-use pledge; under prevailing monetary obligations, the balance of payments constrained U.S. expenditures abroad. Since neither NATO commitment was under serious strain at the beginning of the 1960s, Hypotheses 1 and 2 would predict incremental adjustment within the terms of those obligations.

REVISIONS IN MILITARY STRATEGY: FLEXIBLE RESPONSE

Although McNamara lacked experience in military matters, he was given wide authority to revise policies that many critics of the preceding administration believed lacked credibility and coherence. Rather than continuing to allow the services to set priorities, civilians would henceforth assess them according to more coherent programmatic criteria. Substantively, the new administration emphasized control of risks rather than costs. This was the strategic philosophy of NSC-68, what Gaddis calls "symmetric" containment: options at each level of potential conflict would avoid either needless escalation or capitulation. This would be costly, although economically prudent if military spending were used to stimulate the civilian sector.[13]

FR acknowledged the loss of an all-purpose nuclear deterrent and in that sense was a response to declining hegemony. The objective was more "firebreaks" or escalatory steps below as well as above the nuclear threshold. No administration since 1961 has reversed the basic emphasis.

Raising the Nuclear Threshold

Eisenhower's military strategy, based on a low nuclear threshold, had been attacked on two general grounds. First, as anticipated in NSC–68, irremediable mutual vulnerability was simply a matter of time once Moscow obtained the bomb. Threatening nuclear war over anything less than a major threat to the most vital interests would then be incredible. William Kaufmann, among the civilian strategists who began to make this argument in the late 1950s, later claimed that no president since the second Eisenhower administration had the slightest intention of starting a nuclear war.[14] Massive retaliation by this account was pure bluff.

Nuclear stalemate explicitly was recognized in mid–1964, at a time when Washington had a four-to-one advantage in ICBMs. According to a paper prepared at the Board of National Estimates (an interagency intelligence community panel charged with signing off on National Intelligence Estimates before they were sent to the National Security Council),

In this age of mobile striking forces and hardened missile sites, it does not appear possible to build a military force capable of destroying an enemy's capabilities and simultaneously protecting oneself from unacceptable damage. . . . Thus while strategic military power has become substantial on both sides, it has not been particularly useful in the achievement of objectives beyond that of maintaining the strategic balance itself.[15]

It followed, second, that the very implausibility of most nuclear threats encouraged conflict at lower levels. This was the "stability-instability" paradox worked out independently by several people during the late 1950s: "to the extent that all-out war is unthinkable, states have greater opportunities to push as hard as they can."[16] It meant that Eisenhower's efforts to stretch the nuclear deterrent across the spectrum of violence had been plausible only because of a temporary American superiority. Once that advantage disappeared, different kinds of challenges would have to be deterred at specifically appropriate levels of military force.[17] Robert Jervis credits these insights with much of the force of FR.[18] Accordingly, where nuclear weapons mainly deter their use by an adversary, status quo powers should expect multiple challenges below that level of violence.

Detailed attention was paid to the size and composition of Soviet missile deployments, as implied by Hypothesis 3. McNamara told Congress that since U.S. procurement programs had to be projected ahead at least five years, estimates of Soviet forces needed to be extrapolated at least that far as well. Partly because research and production leadtimes were shorter in the USSR, Washington overbuilt in the early 1960s and underbuilt a few years later. But McNamara did correctly anticipate that Moscow could catch up in numbers of ICBMs by 1970. When production of its SS–11 missile peaked a few years later, it alone outnumbered the U.S. Minuteman arsenal.[19]

The term "flexible response" first appeared in a book by General Maxwell

D. Taylor, a former Army Chief of Staff who had been frustrated by Eisenhower's emphasis on strategic air power. Taylor's argument for forces that could be used in most, if not all, situations short of total war obviously reflected the Army's interests and perspective. But it also impressed the new administration, and Taylor became an influential chairman of the Joint Chiefs of Staff. As summarized by Bernard Brodie, dean of American civilian strategists and by then unsympathetic, FR meant that "although we will not voluntarily relinquish the nuclear ascendancy now enjoyed by the United States, prudent anticipation of the coming nuclear stalemate requires us to return to conventional forces for the tactical defense even of Europe."[20] It also meant that battlefield nuclear weapons would be used, if at all, in a highly controlled way.

As these arguments were fleshed out during the early 1960s, a coherent rationale emerged for a higher nuclear threshold. One factor was the belief that viable conventional options would simply be more believable to the Soviets and NATO allies. Advocates of FR worried that a reluctance to risk nuclear war could embolden adversaries to probe Western resolve. The common view that Communists were relentless opportunists contributed to this, as did the belief that nuclear stalemate precluded all-out war. It should be remembered that most people were extremely hawkish about Soviet intentions during the early 1960s, the period of Berlin and the Cuban Missile Crisis. Deterrent credibility was perhaps the main motivation for the new strategy.

A second motivation was the realization that in as crowded a region as Central Europe, tactical nuclear weapons would destroy what they were meant to defend. This should have been obvious from the beginning, but Eisenhower and Dulles had spent eight years essentially telling the allies to ignore the problem: U.S. nuclear weapons would provide cheap security. It was a comforting message; only later did war games within NATO's Nuclear Planning Group convince the Germans that a tactical nuclear war would devastate their territory most of all.[21]

A third was skepticism that a tactical nuclear war would remain limited. If nuclear *deterrence* within Europe was an indivisible good, this assumption was the opposite side of that coin. It implied that *any* use of nuclear weapons could expose the U.S. homeland to destruction. Most official statements avoided the conclusion that crossing the nuclear threshold necessarily meant total war, as this would vitiate the entire point of controlled response as well as theater nuclear weapons. But the dominant feeling was that no control could be assumed once the threshold was crossed, and that this eventuality should not be forced on NATO for lack of strong conventional forces.[22] In official doctrine, the nuclear threshold became the most salient "firebreak" in a series of potential escalatory steps.

A fourth factor resulted from a reexamination of the European conventional balance. While a low threshold did not require such scrutiny, FR as described by Brodie did. The Pentagon realized that European skepticism about a higher nuclear threshold was based partly on an assumption that no feasible conventional improvements would matter; it had long been believed that NATO's twenty-four divisions were hopelessly outmatched by the Warsaw Pact's 175. But careful analysis of the size, structure, and equipment of a typical Soviet division revealed that it was only about one-third the size of its American counterpart. Moscow apparently had no more than sixty U.S.-size divisions on NATO's central front, a force that could likely be held off by NATO's longtime goal of thirty active and thirty reserve divisions. McNamara thus argued that a viable conventional capability was possible. This assertion was made with increasing confidence after 1962, and was used to justify the major effort Washington expected from the allies.[23]

A fifth factor was a fear that continued reliance on nuclear weapons might lead more nations to acquire them.[24] This primarily meant West Germany, as President Johnson observed a few years later. Washington's fear on this point led to some enthusiasm in the Kennedy and Johnson administrations for the Multilateral Force, a fleet of strategic missile submarines (SSBNs) staffed by crews of at least three nationalities. The proposal died later in the decade, as discussed below.

Washington's determination to raise the threshold led to persistent pressure for stronger allied conventional forces. Shortly after he took office, Kennedy chose Acheson to chair a task force on NATO strategy. The sponsor of NSC–68 not surprisingly recommended

an attainable increase in non-nuclear capabilities . . . [that] would give NATO flexibility to meet a wide range of Soviet aggressions without recklessness, since it would provide a non-nuclear capability to impose a pause in the event of quite large attacks by Soviet non-nuclear ready forces, i.e. by the bulk of the Soviet forces in the satellites reinforced by such forces as the Soviets could quickly deploy to the central front.

The report also urged the United States to "press strongly for NATO execution of this program, as a matter of the highest priority."[25] The advice was taken with a vengeance from the president on down. With a certitude that aroused resentment in the Pentagon as well as abroad, McNamara's civilian associates believed that the Europeans would accept the requirements of FR if they were "educated" about nuclear war. Quantitative force improvements were asked of France and Germany, qualitative improvements in staffing levels and supplies of the others. The message was repeated over and over again.

Bonn felt much of the pressure, especially after the 1961 Berlin Crisis. The Germans were asked to bring their active-duty personnel up to full strength and add six combat brigades.[26] McNamara had originally thought that additional regular troops were unnecessary—that FR's major requirements would be at the level of unconventional warfare. Berlin suggested otherwise. It showed how reluctant everyone was to contemplate nuclear war and made clear that inadequate nonnuclear capabilities severely limited NATO's other options. Few thought that war over access to the divided city was likely, but Kennedy believed his actions in calling up the reserves and sending additional troops had prevented Khrushchev from bargaining with the West from a militarily advantageous position.[27]

To be sure, the United States was ready to put some of its own money where its words were. Although the extra troops in Europe were only temporary, sustained conventional improvements were made in the arsenal. Between 1961 and mid-decade the number of combat-ready Army divisions increased from eleven to sixteen, the infantry divisions in Europe were mechanized, tactical Air Force fighter wings were increased from sixteen to twenty-three, and their supplies of conventional ordnance were substantially augmented.[28]

Nevertheless, U.S. pressure on the allies seems to contradict Hypothesis 5, according to which a declining hegemon should choose defensive, internal methods of adjustment where possible. Of course, no major improvement in NATO's conventional forces was possible without cooperation, mainly from Bonn. But was such a barrage necessary? Brodie assessed it this way:

In providing protection for ourselves, we have created what in large measure protects also our European allies. It is a mistake to assume that we can now induce them to compensate us by raising additional forces which they feel they do not need and which in the French case would be at the expense of forces they insist on having.[29]

Morton Halperin, an associate of McNamara, was equally disparaging. He later averred that "telling American allies that they should increase their conventional capability so that the United States can reduce its reliance on nuclear weapons is like telling young children that if they eat their vegetables they will *not* be given any dessert."[30] No subsequent administration, whatever its private thoughts on the matter, would be so insistent on this point.

The Kennedy and Johnson administrations stand out in the way high officials tried to raise the threshold at a discernible diplomatic cost. Resentment toward Washington over the issue was significant during the early 1960s. How can this behavior be explained? One possibility is the strong beliefs about the dangers of nuclear war held by Kennedy, McNamara, and Rusk. By 1964, the United States considered cooperating with Moscow against the emerging Chinese nuclear capability, including "preventive military action." Nuclear war had apparently become as salient a threat as most of the challenges that might have led to it.[31]

Pushing the allies did *not*, then, constitute defensive, internal adaptation. But U.S. behavior in its entirety during this period presents a more complex picture. Washington did not declare a NFU policy, although it seemed very close to one at times. McNamara told Johnson in January 1964 that "despite my confidence in the feasibility and desirability of a major nonnuclear option, we cannot exclude the possibility that, under heavy pressure, NATO's nonnuclear defenses might begin to crumble."[32] This caution was understandable: Soviet conventional forces were still much larger than NATO's, and the allies were unenthusiastic about major efforts to redress the imbalance. Yet deploying many more tactical nuclear weapons at a time when Washington was continually warning of their dangers and deprecating their practicality was less coherent.

Despite McNamara's disavowal, Washington's de facto policy during the early 1960s may have been *undeclared* NFU. A "pause" before tactical nuclear weapons (TNWs) would be used was not a new idea, but a capability to ride out "quite large attacks" was. In a 1983 article, McNamara admitted recommending to Kennedy and Johnson that they never initiate nuclear use.[33] His goal at the time was to improve conventional forces enough so that NFU would be possible in practice, whatever American declaratory policy.[34] Alain Enthoven, a deputy assistant secretary of defense who was very close to his boss, put it most bluntly in public: there was "no sensible alternative to building up our conventional forces to the point at which they could safely resist all forms of non-nuclear aggression."[35]

But this was only a goal, and McNamara refused to specify the circumstances under which the threshold might be crossed.[36] Moreover, tactical nuclear deployments in Europe were then growing quickly. So long as policymakers were prepared to use them rather than "lose" Europe—and this was reiterated many times—it is arguable that their goals represented adjustment within a continuing first-use pledge (Hypothesis 2). Kennedy was apparently prepared to begin a nuclear war over Berlin if the Soviets forced a confrontation.[37] So despite sentiment in that direction, NFU was never declared government policy. Kennedy and his advisers were "preoccupied" with finding alternatives to nuclear weapons, but they were unwilling to give up their deterrent value or take on the foreign and domestic constituencies that depended on them.[38] Declaratory policy on the threshold was neither unambiguously offensive nor defensive.

The rapid tactical nuclear buildup during the early 1960s was, however, clearly oriented toward continuity and harder to reconcile with preferences for a high threshold. The number of TNWs in Europe increased almost threefold during the Kennedy-Johnson years, from 2,500 to 7,200.[39] The additional weapons were already in the pipeline in early 1961, but why did the new administration allow the shipments to proceed? Halperin suggests an organizational answer: TNW deployment was determined by the rate of weapons construction, and the Army, having had its forces cut during the 1950s and having invested heavily in battlefield nuclear weapons, was unwilling to give them up.[40] Like all such explanations, this one suffices only if political leaders were unwilling to impose different preferences. Even then, their reasons may better explain the policy outcome than bureaucratic momentum. McNamara had strong sentiments on this issue, which the president shared. Years later he said, "we should have stopped the increases. If I could do it differently, I would have acted to reduce the numbers of tactical nuclear weapons in Europe."[41] The question, then, is why he did not.

The administration felt that it had to reassure several constituencies that better conventional capabilities would not vitiate the nuclear guarantee. Kennedy himself saw how difficult it was to adjust the numbers "under the eyes of watchful allies always doubtful of the American will to defend them if necessary with nuclear weapons.'' There was no explicit reference to Finlandization, but the allies were seen as very dependent on the nuclear crutch. McNamara believed that efforts to raise the threshold depended on physical proof that the U.S. would honor existing commitments. Moscow was also then building up its theater arsenal. Finally, in view of McNamara's heavy agenda at the time—managing the U.S. buildup, decreasing the vulnerability of strategic forces, rationalizing the Pentagon's planning and procurement systems, and "educating" the allies about FR—he understandably wished to avoid another fight with the Joint Chiefs at home.[42]

Washington's new strategy was therefore "defensive" as well as "offensive," although the changes and controversies were naturally emphasized at the time. Because they were under little domestic pressure, policymakers were able to use sophisticated incremental strategies. The constraints they felt were external and long-term. Partly because of mounting disagreements with France over FR and other issues, Washington was unwilling to risk a major split within NATO to implement its policy. In 1967, McNamara officially revealed that the United States stored nuclear weapons in Europe, partly to rebut charges that Washington aimed to "denuclearize" NATO.[43]

Flexibility above the Threshold

The Kennedy administration also moved quickly to make the SIOP's attack options for general war more flexible. Some have seen this as incompatible with efforts to raise the threshold: if policymakers doubted that a tactical nuclear war could be limited, how could they assume a central strategic one could be?[44] The paradox disappears if their objective was capability to control conflict at *all* potential levels. Kennedy and McNamara were especially concerned about the risk of uncontrolled escalation. Since general nuclear war was possible, they sought ways to control it.

This meant the ability to limit a war to counterforce targets. Although there was nothing new about planning to strike Soviet nuclear targets, several RAND analysts became especially interested in the problem during the 1950s. Their objectives differed somewhat: Brodie was concerned mainly with damage limitation in a general war, Kaufmann with the credibility of extended deterrence. The two came together in practice. The least likely scenario for a nuclear strike on U.S. territory was a bolt out of the blue; it was *extension* of the nuclear umbrella that multiplied risks. Once the United States was vulnerable to a Soviet retaliatory strike, it appeared to many that first use would be viable only if the counterattack could be blunted.

Kaufmann began serving as a consultant to McNamara soon after the new administration assumed office. Previously he built support in the Air Force for discriminate counterforce targeting policies by playing on interservice rivalries.

In a letter to the Air Force Chief of Staff, also circulated on Capitol Hill, he argued that

A strategic force primarily or totally dependent on Polaris [the submarine-launched missile] will increase the difficulty of defending allied areas, particularly Western Europe. ... placing our bets essentially on Polaris would appear almost to invite the Soviets to engage in limited aggression. Certainly the risks would look far less against a submerged, city-busting system than against a widely dispersed, protected, land-based system which appeared capable of conducting a counterforce campaign.[45]

The "NATO Problem" that moved Kaufmann toward so-called "no cities" options would similarly affect Schlesinger a decade later as defense secretary. The Acheson task force, in arguing that such options would dispel European doubts that a U.S. president would sacrifice his cities for Europe's, made the same point.[46]

As Kaufmann realized, Air Force support for this idea, particularly within the Strategic Air Command (SAC), was valuable: SAC had seen a single massive strike as its only feasible option during the 1950s. Withholding some part of the force appeared militarily imprudent at that time, since piecemeal sorties were unlikely to penetrate Soviet air defenses, and reserve bombers on the ground would be vulnerable to a second strike. By 1962, U.S. early-warning systems had been improved, SAC's airborne alert had begun, and Soviet offensive and air defense capabilities were seen to be weaker than had been feared, which seemed to remove those obstacles.[47]

McNamara found controlled counterforce appealing. His first briefing on the original SIOP left him shaken: the minimum attack option used 1,400 weapons, and the only other choice was to launch varying levels of additional forces, all within 24 hours. None of the options distinguished between counterforce and countervalue targets, no reserve forces were designated, and there was no option for refraining from attacks on individual countries. This experience made him more receptive to the no-cities doctrine than he might otherwise have been, given his general skepticism about nuclear war fighting.[48] McGeorge Bundy, Kennedy's National Security Adviser, gave the president a similar assessment of existing war plans. McNamara later recalled that his main objective was to create smaller attack options, or "withholds." They were built into SIOP–63, which provided for completely avoiding urban-industrial targets and specific individual countries.[49]

These changes helped to resolve a key ambiguity in U.S. declaratory deterrence policy. In his first defense address to Congress, Kennedy pledged that the United States would not strike first in a war. This did not entirely rule out preemption, which remained an option in the revised SIOP. Nevertheless, the emphasis on second-strike survivability was designed to bolster stability in a crisis. The option of first use in an ongoing war was, as mentioned above, specifically reaffirmed. One motivation for controlled counterforce was the ability to respond, if necessary, to Soviet conventional attacks if they could not otherwise be contained. In a 1961 memorandum to the president, McNamara explicitly recommended against a countervalue "minimum deterrent posture" on the grounds that this would make it difficult to deter Soviet attacks on allies.[50]

Another misunderstanding developed, however. Both the Air Force and Pentagon civilians soon realized that controlled counterforce placed no logical limits on the size of strategic forces. During 1963 McNamara decided to cap procurement. As a rationale, his Systems Analysis office developed the criterion of "assured destruction" (AD). The requirements—enough warheads in a secure second-strike force to absorb a full Soviet attack and then destroy half of Soviet industrial capacity and one-fourth of the Soviet population—were calculated by determining the point of diminishing damage returns to incremental force level increases. That point would be reached, it was estimated, with no more than 400 warheads. This was criticized for ignoring what would specifically deter Moscow, but that was not its point. It was a criterion for acquisitions, not war fighting. McNamara continued to program forces separately for AD and damage limitation; the revised SIOP assigned over 80 percent of the strategic force on constant alert to Soviet military targets.[51] The misunderstanding arose because policymakers eschewed public discussion of controlled counterforce until the early 1970s.

Clear limits on strategic forces were appealing for two reasons. First, more nuclear forces meant fewer conventional forces, and McNamara was determined to raise the nuclear threshold as high as possible.[52] He was convinced by the mid–1960s that general nuclear war was a most unlikely scenario. This may explain why he did not direct the target planners to create more refined SIOP options after the mid–1960s. The counterforce options in SIOP–63 were still very large, giving little promise that a general war could be controlled, and there was still resistance within the military to a controlled response policy in general war. Although McNamara by this time was consumed by Vietnam and may not have wished to spend political capital on the issue,[53] the issue itself seems to have receded in his mind.

Second, after 1963, the Soviets markedly accelerated deployment of TNWs in Europe as well as ICBMs. They were hardening their land-based missiles and beginning research and development on a sea-based deterrent. These developments indicated that the capacity to limit damage was fading quickly. Kennedy and Johnson were thus advised,[54] and presumably concurred. That phase of American hegemonic capability was drawing to a close.

AD over the next years was roundly criticized, from both ends of the ideological spectrum, for providing no options other than counter-city incineration after a nuclear attack. That assumed that because *disarming* counterforce was now impractical, counterforce itself had been abandoned.[55] This was not true, as we have seen. McNamara was trying to communicate both the unlikelihood of nuclear war and its utter senselessness as a policy tool. In this sense, it is arguable that he was further chipping away at first use. As discussed in Chapter

6, if nuclear war is irrational, *no one* will rationally approach the brink. That outlook is difficult to reconcile with the requirements of first use.

CENTRAL COMMAND AND CONTROL: THE HEGEMON'S PREROGATIVE

A controlled strategic nuclear war was probably chimerical; Soviet doctrine apparently precluded it, at least during this period. It was, nevertheless, one logical response to the nascent Soviet intercontinental nuclear capability—a situation in which U.S. first use was potentially suicidal yet politically indispensable. After reading Barbara Tuchman's *The Guns of August*, an account of the origins of World War I, Kennedy became particularly concerned about accidental war. The fledgling French nuclear force was viewed as an obstacle to central command and control within NATO, and the administration tried to talk Paris out of it. The results bore even less fruit than Washington's missives about stronger conventional forces.

McNamara articulated the strategic objections to nuclear proliferation in the Athens and Ann Arbor presentations that made the case for FR. While European forces were "dangerous, expensive, prone to obsolescence, and lacking in credibility as a deterrent, . . . the United States [sic] nuclear contribution to the Alliance [is] neither obsolete nor dispensable." If deterrence failed, "our best hope lies in conducting a centrally controlled campaign against all of the enemy's vital nuclear capabilities, while retaining reserve forces, all centrally controlled."[56] France's *force de frappe* precluded unilateral American control of NATO military policy. Before the two speeches, Kennedy emphasized to McNamara that the allies should understand the U.S. position: if they believed they could drag America into a nuclear war by firing their weapons first, the nuclear pledge would be terminated.[57]

Proliferation was also seen as wasteful, robbing NATO of badly needed conventional forces. Acheson, in an unofficial statement of the administration's position, preferred to see "Europe . . . furnish the bulk of the conventional power and the United States the nuclear power, as well as very substantial conventional forces."[58] McNamara denies that such a division of labor was U.S. policy.[59] Officially he was correct, considering the 50 percent buildup of conventional forces over which he presided. But since the European conventional balance was closer than had been thought, Washington emphasized that French funds would be more productively spent on nonnuclear forces.

Although Britain's nuclear force was also considered anachronistic and wasteful, Washington's feelings about it were more ambivalent. Nitze's early optimism about the nuclear balance, already referred to, specifically included Britain's contribution. For various reasons, Washington had treated London differently. The British had been closely involved in the Manhattan Project that produced the first atomic bomb. Eisenhower felt that the Atomic Energy Act of 1946, which prohibited any transfer of nuclear information, was unduly restrictive, since Moscow had the technology in any case. Congress loosened it somewhat with amendments in 1954 and 1958, but intended that nuclear cooperation take place only with Britain: before a country could receive American help, it needed to have made "substantial progress" on its own. The French program was then just getting underway, while Britain had already exploded a fusion bomb.[60] This suited the British, who wanted to prolong the "special" wartime relationship with Washington. London soon began to receive U.S. nuclear information and coordinate targeting plans with the Pentagon. In return for a submarine base in Scotland, Eisenhower agreed to sell the Skybolt missile to Britain, which led eventually to deals involving Polaris and Trident submarine-launched missiles. Kennedy downplayed but did not end these relationships.[61]

De Gaulle would probably have refused such an arrangement. U.S. behavior presumed that commitments were nonsituational: how else could Washington expect France to give up its independent force? De Gaulle, on the other hand, had always viewed commitments as situational.[62] French thinking carried FR to its logical conclusion: nuclear statemate vitiated all extended nuclear deterrence pledges. Since only national nuclear forces were fully reliable, France needed to pursue its program unconstrained. De Gaulle also had a broader purpose. Nuclear weapons symbolized national assertion and were necessary to be taken seriously in a bipolar world. Washington and Paris literally talked past each other.

Johnson, like Kennedy, opposed nuclear collaboration with France. But he was less adamant and directed a "ceasefire" on the issue in 1965. U.S. behavior changed much more sharply after 1969, as shown in the next chapter. Yet the early 1960s again stands out as a time when Washington aggressively redefined intra-alliance policy, threatening NATO's cohesion. Perhaps some in the Kennedy administration took European docility for granted. Like his successors, Kennedy believed that any apparent lack of American resolve over Berlin could drive Bonn, and perhaps all Western Europe, into neutralism.[63] In any case, Washington's other nuclear initiative, the Multilateral Force (MLF), more unambiguously fits Hypothesis 5. It was purely defensive, designed to quell the desire for national nuclear forces by giving the appearance of nuclear decentralization.

The MLF grew out of suggestions by SACEUR Lauris Norstad and Christian Herter, Eisenhower's second secretary of state, that a number of Polaris submarines be assigned to NATO pending agreement on operational control and implementation of conventional force objectives. The latter, as we have seen, were not taken very seriously before 1961. Eisenhower's objectives, however, were shared by his successors; they too wished to neutralize fears about the U.S. nuclear guarantee and establish a basis for consultation on nuclear strategy.[64] Another concern, especially within the State Department, was "containing" the Federal Republic's presumed desire for its own nuclear weapons. The other allies were so skittish about Bonn that Rusk believed that too rapid an increase in German *conventional* forces would be destabilizing.[65]

The MLF was redefined to comprise surface ships when Congress refused to allow allies other than Britain access to American submarine technology. Other than this, the main obstacles to the idea were abroad. Johnson, who felt he would want an independent nuclear capability were he in Germany's position, initially allowed planning to proceed.[66] But no one except the Germans and Italians were really interested, and even Bonn recognized that sharing would be cosmetic as long as Washington retained a veto on use. Johnson dropped the idea and the next U.S. initiative, for a NATO Nuclear Planning Group, aimed to redefine the problem of allied nuclear participation from weapons access to strategic consultation. This suited McNamara, for it gave him another opportunity to "educate" the allies. He still believed that they would see the merits of a higher nuclear threshold once they were exposed to the details of targeting and warfighting. He made some progress, as discussed in the next chapter, but the learning process was very slow.

THE GROWING IMBALANCE OF PAYMENTS

As we have seen, Kennedy inherited a weakening balance-of-payments situation that became a major preoccupation. Deficits averaging $2.4 billion during 1958, 1959, and 1960 had led to more than $3 billion in losses of official gold reserves, with a third of the loss reportedly traceable to European expenditures. "[The deficit] became a symptom and a symbol of nation's fading ability to pay for all it wanted to do in the world."[67] In 1959 the Treasury Department and Budget Bureau nearly convinced Eisenhower to withdraw two divisions and seven fighter-bomber squadrons. Strong opposition from State and SACEUR killed the idea, but the option was left open.[68]

Although Eisenhower was depicted as torn by "his last and cruelest dilemma"—a choice between halting the gold outflow and maintaining the existing troop deployment—he was less troubled than some of his successors would be.[69] By his account, he had tried to trim the garrison as soon as allied economies had recovered from the war, but had been dissuaded repeatedly by diplomatic considerations. As the original SACEUR, he viewed the 1951 troop commitment as an interim measure. He was prepared for major cuts by the end of the decade: "one division in Europe," he later said, "can 'show the flag' as definitely as several."[70]

Just before leaving office, Eisenhower took three interim measures of his own. Over the opposition of the Joint Chiefs, he ordered home more than half of all overseas military dependents. The administration also planned to request that U.S. contributions to NATO's infrastructure program, a resource pool for common construction projects, be reduced from 37 percent of the total.

The third involved a trip to Bonn by Treasury Secretary Robert Anderson and Undersecretary of State Douglas Dillon. They sought help in reducing U.S. military exchange costs, and Bonn's large foreign exchange reserves were a tempting target. The Germans were reassured that no troop cuts were planned, although rumors to that effect abounded. The mission was badly coordinated and poorly prepared: Anderson had supported the troop cut that Dillon had opposed,[71] and even though the envoys recognized Bonn's extreme reluctance to provide direct reimbursement, likened to occupation costs, they came with no other option. Not surprisingly, they were turned down.

Anderson emphasized that any American administration would protect the dollar as its first priority, and that a solution to the problem would require some German compensation. In this, he reflected the president's sentiments as well as his department's charge to safeguard the currency. One indication that Bonn got the message was its subsequent counteroffers, which included increased military procurement from the United States.[72]

Stopgap Measures: Offset and "Perimeter" Defenses for the Dollar

If Bonn had been watching presidential hopeful Kennedy over the previous years, it could have expected him to press the issue firmly. Hobbled by a paper-thin popular mandate and committed both to domestic economic expansion and less external pressure on the dollar, Kennedy believed himself tightly constrained. He was determined to prove his economic orthodoxy and release U.S. strategy from the constraints of a weak dollar.

Shortly before the election, after a surge in the price of gold on the London market, Kennedy pledged categorically to defend the dollar at the official parity. His first balance-of-payments message to Congress was in the same vein, characterizing the United States as "principal banker of the free world" and asserting that external financial constraints would be a most important criterion in economic policy for the foreseeable future. Aides were ordered not to even mention a possible dollar devaluation outside his office; it would disrupt the system and, especially important to Kennedy, leave the president's economic competence in doubt. There were substantive as well as symbolic reasons for firmness. If the dollar were devalued once, foreigners would have to hedge against another devaluation, and its reserve asset value would erode. Nothing else, it was assumed, could replace it in this role. Exchange controls and reductions in development or security assistance were also ruled out.[73]

This left few exits for a rather dire situation. Kennedy had suggested one in a 1959 speech: Europe's new wealth, he believed, should be used for "common purpose[s]," including aid to underdeveloped countries and relief for the dollar.[74] This, of course, was just what Anderson and Dillon were later unable to do in Bonn. Soon after taking office, Kennedy sharpened the problem by rescinding the order on military dependents, citing military morale as a vital national interest. Each federal department was shortly thereafter required to calculate carefully and minimize the foreign exchange costs of its activities (Hypothesis 3). This became known as the "gold budget." The Pentagon came under heavy pressure to cut its gold expenses, virtually ensuring renewed pressure on the allies.

Soon a bilateral agreement was struck whereby Bonn "offset" through military procurement most incremental U.S. payments costs that arose from the troop deployment. The Germans, who had suggested military purchases when they sent Anderson and Dillon away, agreed to pay $600 million for weapons, supplies, and training. McNamara's deputy Roswell Gilpatrick, who worked the bargain out with German Defense Minister Franz-Josef Strauss, was surprised at the ease with which they reached agreement. Since Bonn planned procurement on that scale in any case, Strauss was able to bypass his finance ministry.[75] It also solved the Pentagon's problem: McNamara's "gold-budget" debits would be reduced, and the Germans, who he argued were underarmed in any case, would be contributing to the collective good both ways.[76] Both governments' short-term needs were met, and Gilpatric obtained smaller packages from Italy and France, the latter on a one-time basis.

Even though it was understood that Bonn would develop its own arms industry and that military offsets were not a long-term solution, no alternative was conceived at the time. Arguments that the payments problem should be addressed in the context of multilateral monetary reform failed to convince Kennedy, who felt that he needed a quick fix. This was preferable, he believed, to long, drawn-out discussions over principles not yet accepted abroad.[77] A new two-year agreement for $1.3 billion in military purchases was reached without trouble in August 1963, but Bonn's appetite was soon sated. In late 1965 and early 1966, the German's informed Washington that their defense buildup was nearly complete and requested some other way to offset the troop costs. This precipitated serious problems between the two governments, as discussed in Chapter 5. Just as Bonn's tolerance for military offsets was wearing thin, the "temporary expedient" became "institutionalized" in American policymakers' minds.[78]

Bundy explicitly linked German purchases and American troops in a memorandum to Johnson: the [German] "Chancellor," he said, "should be left in no doubt that [this offset] performance is indispensable for our continued six division presence."[79] If this assertion reflected presidential policy, the terms of the troop commitment had changed: there was no firm quid pro quo in 1951. But the administration was divided and it is uncertain how firm the link actually was. Johnson later reluctantly found it necessary to withdraw a fairly small number of troops with the understanding that the rest would be safe. Offset thus began as the sort of adjustment predicted by Hypothesis 2 and may for some time have defined the limits of the troop commitment itself.

The administration's other strategy even more clearly exemplified adjustment within existing commitments. Treasury Undersecretary Robert Roosa played a key role in constructing what he called "outer perimeter defenses" of the dollar. "Operation Twist" referred to market operations that eased the outward flight of short-term capital while encouraging domestic investment and housing starts. Short-term interest rates were gradually raised (and foreign dollar deposits exempted from Federal Reserve interest rate ceilings) while downward pressure was put on longer-term rates. Another, a series of "swap lines" (bilateral credit arrangements with foreign central banks), was designed to redeem foreign dollar holdings that might have been used to purchase gold, driving down the dollar's value. So-called "Roosa Bonds" at premium interest rates were issued by the Treasury. A "gold pool" was established among eight major financial centers to stabilize the London free-market price. Finally, Roosa and the Federal Reserve were instrumental in negotiating the General Agreements to Borrow, an expanded credit pool available through the International Monetary Fund.

Capital controls were gradually added to the list of ad hoc measures, breaking the spirit of Kennedy's pledge not to institute exchange controls. In July 1963, a tax was proposed on purchases of foreign securities by Americans as another way of stemming the dollar outflow. Although the Interest Equalization Tax (IET) achieved its immediate objective, a prescient prediction by Treasury Secretary Dillon also came to pass. Dillon told a house subcommittee that partial measures would fail: funds would seep out through other channels in anticipation of further barriers, eventually requiring comprehensive controls.[80] Two years later Johnson proposed that the IET, originally scheduled to terminate at the end of 1965, be extended another four years and broadened to cover both bank loans and all lending of more than a year's duration. By 1968, in the wake of the payments deficits growing out of the Vietnam War, all dollar flows to finance direct investment in continental Western Europe and other developed nations were prohibited. The Treasury and Commerce departments worked hard in the interim to get U.S. firms to curtail voluntarily their lending, investment, and deposits abroad.

Means had seemingly become ends in themselves. Richard Cooper, later a high Carter administration official, reminded Congress at the time the IET was instituted that maintaining the fixed dollar price of gold was only "an efficient means to serve our real ends"—efficient international exchange and investment.[81] Although, in Martin Mayer's words, "something had to give," it turned out to be the principle of unimpeded capital movement rather than the formal Bretton Woods commitment.[82] By the mid–1960s, adjustment within the terms of fixed exchange rates had seriously chipped away at that principle. Of course, no other country maintained capital markets as free or efficient, behavior typical of benevolent hegemony. And once even a tenuous link was made between offset and U.S. troop levels in Europe, Kennedy's pledge not to interfere with security or development assistance was lost as well.

Governments can be constrained by obligations they assume as well as by the distribution of capabilities. What Keohane and Nye call "sensitivity" interdependence often amounts to living and adjusting within existing commitments.[83] In the early 1960s, the United States was vulnerable only under the existing monetary rules. Its underlying position actually improved during the first half of the decade, when the trade and services accounts were in surplus. A 1963 Brookings report commissioned by the administration predicted that the "real" international trends were in America's favor. By 1968, it argued, repatriated profits from direct foreign investment made over the previous decade would be paying off and Europe would be losing the price competition.[84] Neither, it turned out, could neutralize the inflation created by Vietnam.

Planning for Troop Cuts

Beginning in 1962, public hints that some troops might be brought home from Europe became unmistakable. The *New York Times* reported several times that high-level Pentagon civilians and the president himself favored cuts. Kennedy publicly maintained that the United States could not sustain simultaneously its strategic forces, extensive naval deployments, a variety of ground force commitments, and "such a large presence in Western Germany."[85] "Big Lift," an exercise in which an entire armored division was airlifted to Germany in October 1963, caused even more concern in Europe. Gilpatric observed that improved force mobility was an important part of a "series of evolutionary changes in the composition and disposition of military units stationed overseas," and implied that some ground support and tactical air units might be withdrawn. Leaks attributed to the Pentagon said that cuts of up to a division were being seriously considered and that Gilpatric's speech was a trial balloon.[86]

Germany worriedly sought clarifications and was given the standard reassurances that no major changes were planned. Bonn's concerns were on Rusk's mind when he saw an advance copy of Gilpatric's speech. He was convinced that public discussion of such plans would lead irreparably to a loss of allied confidence and tried to soften the hints about troop cuts. He was turned down: Bundy had cleared the speech, which reflected White House sentiment.[87]

Kennedy proceeded cautiously in the few weeks before November 22. Just after Gilpatric's speech, he ordered a series of minor force reductions and redeployments for balance-of-payments reasons while directing Rusk to reaffirm publicly the six-division commitment. Withdrawal of fighter squadrons and B–47 bomber units from France, Britain, and Spain was approved, to take place by the end of fiscal year 1966. He further directed that "possible redeployment of U.S. forces under consideration within the government should not be discussed publicly or with the allies until a decision has been made and a politico-military plan for action approved."[88]

Whether major withdrawals had been approved at the time of his death is unclear but quite possible. Although National Security Action Memorandum 270, just quoted, stated that "the United States will maintain in Germany ground forces equivalent to six divisions as long as they are required," Kennedy requested a Pentagon plan for returning two divisions in 1964 or 1965 and did not involve State in the assigment. After his death, it was reported that the Europeans would be given eighteen months to improve their forces, after which the U.S. would review the situation. If the real motivation was the payments problem, complaints over burden sharing may have been an additional sop to Congress. In any case, Johnson apparently did not issue the ultimatum, which was leaked to lock the new president into a plan of action approved by his predecessor.[89]

Like Eisenhower's, Kennedy's preferences are inconsistent with Hypothesis 1 in this regard. More than his successors, Kennedy was willing to "pull back" selectively rather than devalue the dollar, apparently believing that the cuts could be explained to Europe. Europe was an exception; as discussed in Chapter 2, Kennedy and Johnson both preferred overcommitment to falling dominoes. Nevertheless, consistent with Hypothesis 4, Kennedy's flexibility on European troop levels stands in striking contrast to his administration's unwillingness to change publicly and fundamentally its policies on tactical nuclear deployments and the height of the nuclear threshold.

CONCLUSIONS

Alongside their public optimism and ambition, the Kennedy and Johnson administrations recognized that America's early postwar predominance was eroding. The days when dollars could be spread freely abroad or nuclear war threatened over marginal pieces of real estate had passed. Both men understood that as the productivity and competitiveness of America's major allies approached its own, U.S. leadership would become harder to sustain.[90]

Reasonably coherent strategies for dealing with these problems emerged during the early 1960s. FR was a prudent adjustment to a situation in which challenges could be expected below the nuclear threshold and controlling risks, particularly the risk of escalation, was critical. Because America would not renounce earlier pledges, the credibility of extended deterrence commitments was a powerful motivation for a new military strategy. More vigorous balance-of-payments discipline was also perceived as necessary to remain, in Dillon's words, "banker of the world." In both cases, the aim of adaptation was a more viable hegemony.

To this end, U.S. policy was more "offensive" and less incremental than would be expected from Hypothesis 5. FR asked the Europeans to change comfortable behavior they had adopted by following the American lead during the 1950s. Kennedy's attitude toward wealthy countries in balance-of-payments surplus may have been "fair," but its rationale—that creditors as well as debtors have responsibilities for payments adjustment—had been rejected by Washington at the founding of Bretton Woods. In general, there was a crusading mentality in Washington during the 1960s that often implied a made-in-America solution for every problem.

In several ways, this behavior coincides with the gradual adjustment predicted by Hypothesis 2. First, Washington's ambivalence about nuclear weapons was reflected in a preference for a higher threshold at the same time that thousands of new battlefield nuclear weapons were deployed in Europe. Whatever policymakers' private preferences, they publicly retained first use. Second, since external financial adjustment was ruled out, the main U.S. strategy for containing the payments deficit, Roosa's "perimeter" dollar defenses, was intended simply to prevent further deterioration. The same was true of offset. In both cases, myopic strategies were chosen to deal with what were then believed to be short-term, correctable stresses. The closest Washington came to changing the terms of the conventional commitment was the link between offset and troop level. Although Congress later insisted on it, there was little such pressure during the early 1960s. If this had become presidential policy, the commitment had indeed changed. Since Kennedy died before he might have acted, we cannot be certain.

Neither Kennedy nor Johnson was willing to change fundamentally the U.S. world role or the key commitments that supported it in Europe. The "Grand Design," to this end, was intended to make Western Europe a "united, faithful helpmate."[91] The allies had specific roles to play: they were to bear the brunt of the conventional buildup and help compensate America for its expenses as a hegemon. To the extent that Washington acted "offensively," policymakers were trying to redefine (or, in their minds, rationalize) the trans-Atlantic division of labor. Conventional commitments were therefore more vulnerable than nuclear ones (Hypothesis 4). Washington's tactics disrupted the status quo, but its aims were defensive.

The payments deficit was a good gauge of tolerable overextension under the existing rules, and Kennedy's vigilance is therefore somewhat inconsistent with Hypothesis 1. While his successor would be no less publicly concerned, mainly for symbolic reasons, he was also far less disciplined, with far-reaching consequences for U.S. NATO policy.

NOTES

1. Gaddis, *Strategies of Containment*, p. 218.

2. "Outline for Talk to NSC, January 18, 1962," January 17, 1962, National Security File, Box 313, John F. Kennedy Library.

3. Quoted in Walter Isaacson and Evan Thomas, *The Wise Men* (New York: Simon and Schuster, 1986), pp. 631–632.

4. William Park, *Defending the West: A History of NATO* (Boulder, Colo.: Westview, 1986), p. 28.

5. Ibid., p. 29.

6. Richard K. Betts, "A Nuclear Golden Age? The Balance Before Parity," *International Security* 11, no. 3 (Winter 1986/87), pp. 17–18.

7. David P. Calleo, "Since 1961: American Power in a New World Economy," in William H. Becker and Samuel F. Wells, Jr., *Economics and World Power: An Assessment of American Diplomacy Since 1789* (New York: Columbia University Press, 1984), pp. 407, 410.

8. Interview with Dean Rusk, September 27, 1984.

9. "Summary of the President's Remarks to the National Security Council—January 18, 1962," National Security File, Box 313, John F. Kennedy Library.

10. "Summary of the President's Remarks to the National Security Council"; Frank Costigliola, "The Failed Design: Kennedy, de Gaulle, and the Struggle for Europe," *Diplomatic History* 8, no. 3 (Summer 1984): 227–229.

11. Calleo, "American Power in a New World Economy," p. 396.

12. Ibid.

13. Gaddis, *Strategies of Containment*, pp. 205–214.

132   The Declining Hegemon

14. Interview with William Kaufmann, February 14, 1985; Fred Kaplan, *The Wizards of Armageddon* (New York: Simon and Schuster, 1983), Chap. 12.

15. John Prados, *The Soviet Estimate: U.S. Intelligence Analysis and Soviet Strategic Forces* (Princeton: Princeton University Press, 1986), pp. 183–184.

16. Robert Jervis, *The Illogic of American Nuclear Strategy* (Ithaca, New York: Cornell University Press, 1984), p. 31.

17. Smoke, *National Security and the Nuclear Dilemma*, pp. 91–92.

18. See Jervis, *The Illogic of American Nuclear Strategy*, pp. 31, 33. The term "stability-instability paradox" was developed by Glenn Snyder; see "The Balance of Power and the Balance of Terror," in Paul Seabury, ed., *The Balance of Power* (San Francisco: Chandler, 1965).

19. Prados, *The Soviet Estimate*, pp. 188, 192.

20. Brodie, "What Price Conventional Capabilities in Europe?" p. 25.

21. Interview with Harlan Cleveland, October 27, 1984.

22. Park, *Defending the West*, p. 89. One of the most candid statements came from John Kennedy before the 1960 election. Speaking about tactical nuclear war, he said, "If it is applied locally, it can't necessarily be confined locally. [The] Russians would think it a prelude to strategic bombing of their industrial centers. They would retaliate—and a local use would become a world war." Quoted in Jane E. Stromseth, *The Origins of Flexible Response: NATO's Debate Over Strategy in the 1960s* (New York: St. Martin's Press, 1988), p. 27.

23. Interviews with William Kaufmann, February 14, 1985, and Robert S. McNamara, June 19, 1982; William Kaufmann, *The McNamara Strategy* (New York: Harper and Row, 1964), pp. 120–121; Alain C. Enthoven and K. Wayne Smith, *How Much Is Enough? Shaping the Defense Program, 1961–1969* (New York: Harper and Row, 1971), pp. 132–142. See also Schwartz, *NATO's Nuclear Dilemmas*, p. 150.

24. Gaddis, *Strategies of Containment*, p. 217.

25. "A Review of North Atlantic Problems for the Future, March 1961" (Acheson Report), quoted in Stromseth, *The Origins of Flexible Response*, p. 32.

26. Schwartz, *NATO's Nuclear Dilemmas*, p. 155.

27. Stromseth, *The Origins of Flexible Response*, pp. 39–41.

28. Interview with Robert S. McNamara, June 20, 1983; Stromseth, *The Origins of Flexible Response*, p. 67.

29. Brodie, "What Price Conventional Capabilities in Europe?" p. 27.

30. Halperin, *Nuclear Fallacy*, p. 112, emphasis in original.

31. Gaddis, *Strategies of Containment*, p. 211.

32. "Draft Memorandum for the President, The Role of Tactical Nuclear Forces in NATO Strategy," January 15, 1964, p. 37. Quoted in Scott D. Sagan. *Moving Targets: Nuclear Strategy and National Security* (Princeton, N.J.: Princeton University Press, 1989), p. 39.

33. Robert S. McNamara, "The Military Role of Nuclear Weapons: Perceptions and Misperceptions," *Foreign Affairs* 62, no. 1 (Fall 1983):79.

34. Interview with Robert S. McNamara, June 19, 1982.

35. Park, *Defending the West*, p. 89.

36. See, for example, U.S. Congress, Senate, Committee on Armed Services, *Military Procurement Authorization, Fiscal Year 1964*, February 21, 1963, pp. 178–179.

37. Frank Costigliola, "The Pursuit of Atlantic Community: Nuclear Arms, Dollars,

and Berlin,'' in Thomas G. Paterson, ed., *Kennedy's Quest for Victory: American Foreign Policy, 1961–1963* (New York: Oxford University Press, 1989), p. 45.

38. Gaddis, *Strategies of Containment*, p. 220; Halperin, *Nuclear Fallacy*, p. 18.

39. Stromseth, *The Origins of Flexible Response*, p. 89.

40. Halperin, *Nuclear Fallacy*, p. 18; Park, *Defending the West*, p. 40.

41. Quoted in Stromseth, *The Origins of Flexible Response*, p. 94.

42. This paragraph draws mainly on Stromseth, *The Origins of Flexible Response*, pp. 90–93.

43. Halperin, *Nuclear Fallacy*, pp. 17–18.

44. The question is raised in Park, *Defending the West*, p. 88, and Halperin, *Nuclear Fallacy*, pp. 15–16.

45. Quoted in Kaplan, *The Wizards of Armageddon*, p. 238.

46. See Schwartz, *NATO's Nuclear Dilemmas*, p. 151.

47. David Alan Rosenberg, ''U.S. Nuclear Strategy: Theory vs. Practice,'' *Bulletin of the Atomic Scientists* (March 1987), p. 24.

48. Rosenberg, ''U.S. Nuclear Strategy,'' p. 23; Kaplan, *The Wizards of Armageddon*, p. 272; Sagan, *Moving Targets*, p. 25.

49. Rosenberg, ''U.S. Nuclear Strategy,'' p. 24; Sagan, *Moving Targets*, p. 29.

50. Halperin, *Nuclear Fallacy*, p. 20.

51. Colonel Richard G. Head, ''Technology and the Military Balance,'' Foreign Affairs 56, no. 3 (April 1978): 549; Costigliola, ''The Pursuit of Atlantic Community,'' p. 32.

52. Henry S. Rowen, ''Formulating Strategic Doctrine,'' Vol. 4, Appendix K of the *Commission on the Organization of the Government for the Conduct of Foreign Policy: Adequacy of Current Organization, Defense and Arms Control*, p. 231.

53. Sagan, *Moving Targets*, p. 36.

54. Kaplan, *The Wizards of Armageddon*, p. 316; Cordesman, ''American Strategic Forces and Extended Deterrence,'' pp. 461–463.

55. Betts, ''Elusive Equivalence,'' p. 104.

56. ''The United States and Western Europe: Concrete Problems of Maintaining a Free Community,'' Commencement Address by Robert S. McNamara, University of Michigan, June 16, 1962, reprinted in *Vital Speeches*, August 1, 1962, p. 628. The Ann Arbor address was a sanitized version of the presentation to NATO's foreign and defense ministers the previous month.

57. Kaplan, *The Wizards of Armageddon*, pp. 284–285; Edward A. Kolodziej, *French International Policy Under De Gaulle and Pompidou: The Politics of Grandeur* (Ithaca, N.Y.: Cornell University Press, 1974), p. 108.

58. Dean Acheson, ''The Politics of Partnership,'' *Foreign Affairs* 41 (January 1963): 258, cited in Kolodziej, *French International Policy*, p. 107.

59. Interview with Robert McNamara, June 19, 1982.

60. Richard H. Ullman, ''The Covert French Connection,'' *Foreign Policy* no. 75 (Summer 1989): 3–8.

61. *New York Times*, June 24, 1962. Shortly after the Ann Arbor speech, McNamara indicated that his critique of independent nuclear forces applied only to those targeted independently. See, on this point, Stromseth, *The Origins of Flexible Response*, p. 48. See also Costigliola, ''The Pursuit of Atlantic Community,'' p. 31.

62. Weinstein, ''The Concept of a Commitment in International Relations,'' pp. 48–52.

63. Costigliola, "The Pursuit of Atlantic Community," p. 26.

64. Kolodziej, *French International Policy Under DeGaulle and Pompidou*, p. 114.

65. Interview with Dean Rusk, September 27, 1984. For Walt Rostow, head of the Department of State's Policy Planning Staff before he took Bundy's job in 1966, controlling the allies, especially Germany, was "equally" important to containing the Communists. Rostow believed that the integration of allied troops on German soil was essential in keeping Bonn "on a collective course with the U.S. and the West." Rostow to Rusk, September 17, 1963, President's Office Files, John F. Kennedy Library, quoted in Costigliola, "The Pursuit of Atlantic Community," p. 28.

66. Philip Geyelin, *Lyndon B. Johnson and the World* (New York: Praeger, 1966), p. 168.

67. Costigliola, "The Pursuit of Atlantic Community," p. 26.

68. *New York Times*, January 16, 1960; October 22, 1960; October 23, 1960; November 5, 1960.

69. *New York Times*, November 5, 1960.

70. Dwight D. Eisenhower, "Let's Be Honest With Ourselves II," *The Saturday Evening Post*, October 26, 1963, p. 27; see also the *New York Times*, October 19, 1963.

71. Gregory Treverton, *The "Dollar Drain" and American Forces in Germany: Managing the Political Economics of Alliance* (Athens: Ohio University Press, 1978), p. 33; *New York Times*, October 22, 1960. Details of the division within the administration can be found in Martin Mayer, *The Fate of the Dollar* (New York: New American Library, 1981), p. 72, and in *New York Times*, November 25, 1960, p. 15.

72. *New York Times*, January 18, 1961.

73. Robert Solomon, *The International Monetary System, 1945–1981* (New York: Harper and Row, 1982), pp. 39–40, 61.

74. Costigliola, "The Pursuit of Atlantic Community," p. 27.

75. Interview with Roswell Gilpatric, November 30, 1984.

76. Confidential interview, November 9, 1984.

77. Interview with Gilpatric, February 28, 1985; confidential interview, November 9, 1984.

78. Paul M. Johnson, "Washington and Bonn: Dimensions of Change in Bilateral Relations," *International Organization* 33, no. 4 (Autumn 1979): 465, 469.

79. McGeorge Bundy to President Johnson, "Basic Talking Points for the President with Erhard," December 27, 1963, No. 1979 (471A), Declassified Documents Reference Service, Carrollton, Press,; "U.S.-German Military Cooperation: Status, Including Offset Arrangements, Sale of PERSHINGS/SERGEANTS, German MAP," June 11, 1963, President's Briefing Book, June 1963 European Trip, No. 1979 (305B), Ibid. Cited in Castigliola, "The Pursuit of Atlantic Community," pp. 35–36.

80. Dillon's testimony is cited in Mayer, *The Fate of the Dollar*, p. 109.

81. Richard Cooper, in "The United States Balance of Payments," materials submitted to the Joint Economic Committee, United States Congress, U.S. Government Printing Office, Washington, D.C., 1963, p. 111, cited in Solomon, *The International Monetary System*, p. 61.

82. Mayer, *The Fate of the Dollar*, p. 109.

83. See Keohane and Nye's distinction between sensitivity and vulnerability interdependence in *Power and Interdependence*, pp. 12–19.

84. Walter Salant et al., *The United States Balance of Payments in 1968* (Washington, D.C.: Brookings Institution, 1963).

85. *New York Times*, June 28, 1962. See also *New York Times*, May 5, 1962, and May 20, 1962.

86. *New York Times*, October 20, 1963, and October 23, 1963.

87. Christopher S. Raj, *American Military in Europe: Controversy Over NATO Burden-Sharing* (New Delhi: ABC Publishing House, 1983), p. 216; Interview with McGeorge Bundy, December 13, 1984; interview with Roswell Gilpatric, November 30, 1984.

88. National Security Action Memorandum No. 270, October 29, 1963, National Security File, declassified and sanitized NSAMs, Lyndon B. Johnson Library.

89. Interviews with McGeorge Bundy, December 13, 1984, and Roswell Gilpatric, November 30, 1984. See also *New York Times*, December 18, 1963.

90. Calleo, "Since 1961," p. 397.

91. Costigliola, "The Pursuit of Atlantic Community," p. 27.

5 The United States and European Defense, 1966–1973

OVERVIEW

The seven years after 1965 were unusually stressful for American foreign policymakers. Many of the problems derived in some fashion from Vietnam; the war cost much more than the lives and other resources directly consumed there. Vietnam was a "test case" for nonnuclear FR.[1] It failed dramatically, setting in motion or speeding up many other changes in the U.S. world position, all of which affected the major NATO commitments to some degree.

After 1965, it was clear that U.S.–Soviet nuclear parity was only a matter of time, with uncertain but undoubtedly difficult consequences for extended deterrence. While Moscow would almost certainly have caught up in any case, Vietnam meant that Washington was unable to slow down the erosion in its relative position. It also led to a hemorrhage in the balance of payments that "perimeter defenses" were unable to contain. Along with a growing general feeling in Congress that the country was seriously overextended, this led to the most serious challenge to the NATO troop commitment since the early 1950s. Senior policymakers devoted considerable attention and energy during the late 1960s and early 1970s trying to prevent major withdrawals. But this was only part of a larger contest between the branches over the substance and control of foreign involvement—one that has occasionally gone into remission, but never really ended.

In each major area that affected Europe—nuclear deterrence, the balance of payments, and domestic pressures on military involvement—direct or indirect effects of eroding hegemony meant that Johnson and Nixon had fewer viable exits than Eisenhower and Kennedy. After 1964, for example, the Soviets began the rapid ballistic missile buildup that many had expected several years earlier.

As we saw in Chapter 4, U.S. declaratory policy increasingly emphasized AD rather than the damage-limiting mission for strategic forces after mid-decade. This meant that civilian policymakers gradually understood that "meaningful and lasting" nuclear superiority was beyond their reach. It was better, they believed, to stabilize the arms race and prevent any important *inferiority* from developing.[2] This has remained the consensus view among strategists and, except for a brief period during the Reagan administration, government policy.

The implications for extended deterrence commitments were less clear. The significant damage-limiting capability that existed in the early 1960s was gone by mid-decade. McNamara's emphasis on a high nuclear threshold and his public AD rhetoric moved first-use threats further and further into the background, as intended. An important school of thought, consistent with the stability-instability paradox, developed: nuclear stalemate (assured second-strike forces) necessarily dissuades the major challenges that would prompt first use. On the other hand, if this was true, a disarming first strike in support of NATO was out of the question. While stalemate would thus augment crisis stability, Nixon, Kissinger, and Schlesinger found the growing disjunction between weapons and strategy disturbing. NATO had traditionally relied on the nuclear shield to compensate for Soviet geographic and manpower advantages.

Official enthusiasm for controlled nuclear warfighting plans changed significantly, waning during the late 1960s and then waxing under Nixon and Kissinger's tutelage. "Usable nuclear options," then, was the other response to the decline of nuclear hegemony. Whereas McNamara emphasized a high threshold and the growing irrelevance of nuclear threats, his successors were preoccupied with finding ways to buttress first use.

If Vietnam and de Gaulle's withdrawal from NATO in 1966 dramatically indicated America's decreasing ability to get its way in the world, the weakening dollar was another signal.[3] Kennedy's payments deficits were small enough to be managed by financial manipulations and offset. The story of Johnson's insistence on his war in Vietnam and expensive social programs, both without higher taxes, has been told before and need not be repeated here; once he decided to have his cake and eat it too, the deficit swelled and ad hoc exits for dealing with it were closed. When diplomatic pressure on U.S. creditors to continue holding dollars met increasing resistance, capital controls tightened and the administration sought a new international reserve asset that would, it was hoped, take pressure off the dollar. But Special Drawing Rights did not appear until 1970, and the gold-dollar link finally snapped the next year. This would ultimately take most of the pressure off the conventional troop deployment.

Congress vigorously pursued the burden-sharing theme during these years, putting both administrations on the defensive. While hardly of a single mind on these issues, many legislators saw the deficits as indicators of allied free riding and American overextension. Johnson, Nixon, and their close associates in turn saw this weariness as neo-isolationism, which may have been true of Senator Mansfield, leader of the movement. They feared European Finlandization and a snowballing process of retrenchment. These factors, more than the specifics of European defense, explain their resistance to troop cuts. The uncertain status of America's own troops also left them in a weak position to press Europeans for a higher nuclear threshold. In sum, U.S. policy toward Europe was increasingly constrained in every relevant way.

As before, the superpower nuclear balance and balance of international payments were the critical variables. This time, since both the nuclear and conventional commitments were under more severe strain, Hypothesis 2 would predict attempts to change the terms of commitments. We might thus expect allies to be more aggressively pushed to share hegemonic responsibilities, evidence of which would support Hypothesis 5.

NUCLEAR STRATEGY AND EXTENDED DETERRENCE, 1966–1973

The long-expected surge in Soviet ballistic missile deployment began in 1965 and 1966. Intelligence reports indicated that Moscow was working on enhanced early-warning radars, was preparing to deploy ICBMs for the first time in dispersed underground silos, and was preparing to deploy at least three new land-based missiles. Personnel in the Strategic Rocket Forces increased by over 180,000 between 1964 and 1965. Each year after mid-decade, the intelligence projection of future Soviet ICBM forces was revised upwards, and intense debate emerged within the intelligence community over the meaning of this mass of technical evidence (Hypothesis 3).[4]

By about 1966, well before Moscow achieved what came to be called loosely nuclear "parity," it had attained a significant AD capability against the United States and an even more pronounced one vis-à-vis Europe. The buildup of medium and intermediate-range missiles made NATO's nuclear forces particularly vulnerable. After 1963 American Thor and Jupiter missiles and older B–47 bombers were withdrawn, leaving only a limited number of British bombers, some inaccurate and unreliable cruise missiles, and a fairly large number of U.S. attack fighters equipped solely for a nuclear role. McNamara had no use for a replacement land-based nuclear system. The growth in Soviet theater forces was especially destabilizing, since NATO had to assume that planes not on Quick Reaction Alert would be lost. SACEUR thus planned to preempt on warning of attack.[5]

This obviously put pressure on the link between theater and central-strategic nuclear forces. If SACEUR preempted, all SIOP forces not in the AD reserve would have to be launched as well—exactly what FR had been designed to prevent. This led NATO military planners to worry about undue delay in authorizing nuclear use, but it had, at least temporarily, just the opposite effect in Washington.[6]

Reintegrating Nuclear Weapons into Strategy

The Johnson administration drew significant and broad political conclusions from these changes in the nuclear balance, mainly because it was becoming too expensive and technically difficult to maintain nuclear warfighting superiority. While American advantages in numbers and quality of strategic weapons were expected to last for a time, maintaining pre–1964 damage-limiting capabilities soon became impossible. Furthermore, command, control, and intelligence capabilities (C^3I) were simply too primitive: every aspect, such as damage assessment and retargeting, took too long to fight a truly controlled nuclear war.[7] Similar technical problems constrained the flexible use of such theater forces as the Pershing I. During this period, high accuracies required a fixed silo-based configuration, which would raise the cost to ICBM levels and do nothing to solve the vulnerability problem.[8]

The administration preferred to cap strategic forces at the number of launch vehicles programmed in the early 1960s and control the arms race through agreements with Moscow. (The Multiple Independent Reentry Vehicles— MIRVs—deployed on ballistic missiles after 1970 did not further this goal. They were especially destabilizing, since they increased the vulnerability of fixed-based missiles and thus incentives to preempt in a crisis.) This should be possible, it was reasoned, if each understood that the other had a secure second-strike capability.

It was now argued that AD also buttressed extended deterrence: any nuclear conflict in Europe would involve the United States and invite destruction of the USSR. We saw in chapter 4 how this reasoning helped dissuade McNamara from trying to reduce further the minimum size of attack options in the SIOP. It signaled unmistakably that Washington now regarded nuclear war as virtually unthinkable and that more refined FR options above the threshold had a low priority. As Anthony Cordesman put it,

the U.S. ended its era of superiority in assured destruction capability without any clear plan for executing strategic strikes in support of extended deterrence. If anything, she regarded the improvement of NATO conventional forces as a much higher priority for ensuring the overall deterrence of Warsaw Pact aggression than any possible action she could take to improve the capability of either her own nuclear forces or NATO's. The U.S. also continued to rely on the risk of strategic nuclear war to deter the Soviet Union without having any limited options in the SIOP beyond demonstrative use. . . . The United States did stress counterforce in the sense of striking more and more Soviet military targets; what it did not stress was flexibility and restraint.[9]

In one sense, this was a shrewd attempt to turn declining hegemony to advantage. Both sides' fear of Armageddon would cover a multitude of contingencies, as U.S. threats had in the days of American dominance. But it left few plausible choices if deterrence failed and assumed that conflict at lower levels could be "hermetically sealed" from the nuclear threshold.[10] In openly embracing NFU, McNamara has since renounced even these risks.

His desire to push nuclear threats into the background turned out to be the exception rather than the rule. The next administration tried to restore extended deterrence by very carefully lowering the threshold at which *some* nuclear weapons *might* be used. Kissinger wanted to change what he later called "the McNamara attitudes," meaning a sharp, even impenetrable threshold between the use of conventional and tactical nuclear weapons. This suggested, as he put it, that the United States had "in effect abdicated from the serious defense of Europe. How could [it] hold its allies together as the credibility of its strategy eroded?"[11] (Hypothesis 2). After 1969, priority was given to reconnecting weapons to strategy; as discussed below, this ruled out a "serious" nonnuclear defense of Europe. Kissinger was upset that there were over 7,000 tactical nuclear weapons in Europe and "no coherent" plans for their use. According to one official, he "wore out" the Joint Staff with demands for usable warfighting plans.[12]

Despite these concerns, senior policymakers paid only intermittent attention to nuclear strategy during this period. Vietnam, the overall Soviet military buildup, changing political relationships with the USSR and China, and congressional attacks on defense programs were the major preoccupations. But Nixon and Kissinger were interested in grand strategy, and nuclear weapons played a key role. At a National Security Council (NSC) meeting in August 1970, Kissinger compared the prevailing strategic balance unfavorably with that existing during the 1962 Cuban Missile Crisis (Hypothesis 3). There were also specific concerns about emerging ICBM vulnerability as well as a general sense that AD undercut domestic support for nuclear modernization programs.[13] Under orders from the White House, the bureaucracy began studying ways to bolster extended deterrence, although the results were not announced until 1974.[14]

U.S. Nuclear Policy in NATO

Washington spent six difficult years convincing the rest of NATO to accept FR. MC 14/3, adopted in May 1967, provided at least on paper for symmetric responses to deterrence failure. NATO would meet hostilities at the level initiated by the Warsaw Pact and escalate deliberately if necessary. A general nuclear response was promised explicitly if the Pact used strategic weapons and implicitly if battlefield defenses failed.[15]

In some respects, it was a Pyrrhic victory. MC 14/3 was an ambiguous compromise between Europeans' preferences for quick escalation and U.S. insistence on a lengthy conventional pause. NATO's version of FR did provide for an initial nonnuclear response, but both its length and the precise role of tactical nuclear use if it failed were left glaringly unclear. Washington, as we saw, wanted NATO to have conventional forces capable of blunting even a major attack without crossing the threshold; the allies, especially Germany, wanted a promise of early use of strategic weapons.[16] Although both sides got half a loaf, Americans began with higher hopes. The U.S. had interpreted FR to mean the capacity for 90 days of conventional combat; Europe, as a House subcommittee critically noted, had stockpiled barely a week's worth of ammunition and spare parts.[17]

In other respects, the alliance as a whole and the United States in particular were better off with MC 14/3. It was at least some compensation for six years of trans-Atlantic argument and French withdrawal from NATO's integrated command. Washington had also come to understand the allies better. McNamara recognized by the mid–1960s that the Europeans would not make the conventional improvements he had hoped for, and the United States could not do so alone. Washington thus backed off from its earlier insistence on a military posture that could hold off almost any conventional attack, and admitted that under some "highly unlikely" conditions it might cross the threshold.[18] This signified that a hegemon could qualify the terms of a commitment for which it was effectively the monopoly supplier, but it could not force others to compensate by supplying more troops.

NATO's Nuclear Planning Group (NPG) dealt successfully with these issues at the diplomatic level. It has been comprised of defense ministers representing the United States, Britain, West Germany, Italy, and three other members rotated at eighteen-month intervals. Washington sponsored it so that the allies could participate in nuclear planning without necessarily acquiring the weapons themselves. It "ended talk of the Multilateral Force" once Johnson abandoned that idea and made it politically possible for Bonn to sign the nuclear nonproliferation treaty, a key U.S. objective.[19] It also gave the allies, especially Germany, more information about nuclear matters and a clearer understanding of the constraints under which tactical nuclear weapons might be used (Hypothesis 2). The Germans, for example, had regarded FR as a step toward the denuclearization of Europe. After participating in the NPG, Bonn agreed that 7,000 battlefield weapons were enough.[20] Kissinger for similar reasons found the NPG useful, although it could not resolve deep differences in outlook between the United States and the continental Europeans.[21]

Nixon and Kissinger went off in an entirely different direction by *helping* France develop nuclear weapons. Since they would exist in any case, the Kennedy-Johnson policy seemed counterproductive: it was in NATO's interest that the French force be as survivable and efficient as possible. Washington had also come to believe that multiple centers of nuclear decision making increased Soviet strategic and targeting uncertainties and bolstered deterrence. This led to a close program of nuclear assistance, limited in Washington only by the strict letter of the Atomic Energy Act and bureaucratic resistance that determined senior officials finally overcame.[22]

This turning point partly compensated for a smaller American role. Fifteen years later, France and Britain were publicly urged to continue their nuclear programs, of particular value in light of a shrinking U.S. nuclear presence.[23]

THE CONVENTIONAL COMMITMENT, 1966–1973

Vietnam took its toll first on the troops stationed in Europe and then on virtually the entire defense budget. For domestic political reasons, Johnson tried but failed to conceal its costs. Although he believed that NATO commitments were fragile and could easily unravel if America or Britain reduced its contribution, he felt pressure, some from Pentagon civilians, to bring home some of the troops. His strategy was to signal the allies that he was resisting internal pressures while making the smallest possible reduction.[24]

Congressional pressures reached their zenith during the Nixon administration, which was even more determined to resist them. This was accomplished through some Byzantine tactics that made U.S. policy seem incoherent: Europe was reaffirmed as the hub of U.S. global strategy and the principal military theater at the same time that the administration's burden-sharing rhetoric escalated and hints of cuts circulated in Washington. But Nixon and Kissinger had clear priorities. They appeased domestic pressures just enough, in their judgment, to contain them.

Vietnam, the Mansfield Challenge, and Problems with Offset

Vietnam directly affected troop levels and readiness in Europe, although the Johnson administration insisted the opposite. Nearly identical statements— McNamara to the North Atlantic Council in December 1965 and Undersecretary of State Ball to the Senate Foreign Relations Committee in June 1966—promised that no "major units" would be transferred from NATO-committed forces. Officials were at first evasive and defensive about the scale and effect of the transfers. Press reports that the Seventh Army in West Germany was being stripped of occupational specialists were first denied, then confirmed a few weeks later. Thirty thousand trained personnel removed during the first half of 1966 were replaced by half as many untrained forces; the former, McNamara explained, were support troops in excess of the ordinary U.S. commitment.[25]

This was consistent with other steps taken to defuse opposition to the war by minimizing its visible costs. Johnson refused to mobilize the reserves, raise taxes to stem inflation until 1966, or request an income tax surcharge to pay for the war until 1967. It was pointed out that most of the personnel squeeze could be attributed to the reserves decision: the regular Army usually depended on them for combat support and training, so that failure to mobilize meant that the services had to create and train new support forces—ordnance and engineering units, for instance—from within regular units.[26] Skeptics wondered whether European or Asian requirements could be satisfied simultaneously (Hypothesis 1).

They could not, and the erosion of conventional readiness in Europe seriously undercut Washington's message about FR. By 1966, U.S. forces in Europe were smaller and weaker than at any time since the last Berlin Crisis; it was reported a year later that one of the five divisions pledged for reinforcement would be sent to Asia. An unnamed official claimed that "since none of our allies believes a war would last anything like sixty days, we don't think word of our temporary shortage of troops will cause any trauma over there."[27] Between 1962 and 1970, U.S. personnel in Europe dropped from 416,000 to 291,000 and over $10 billion worth of equipment was removed.

Mike Mansfield, the Senate majority leader, still believed that there were too many troops in Europe. Beginning in 1966, he and other burden-weary legislators put the Johnson and Nixon administrations on the defensive with efforts to bring some of them home. Offset ceased to be an ad hoc expedient useful to both sides and became a highly politicized symbol of relative burdens. Mansfield underscored his point by attaching his resolution calling for a "substantial reduction" of U.S. forces permanently stationed in Europe to Senate Resolution 99, which had authorized the additional divisions sent in 1951. He repeatedly argued over the next eight years that Europe had recovered and could do more for itself.

The administration rejected these arguments. Dean Rusk's view, shared by Johnson, was that a victory for Mansfield would vindicate de Gaulle's claim that Europe could not depend on the United States. France was just then leaving NATO's integrated command and further erosion was feared.[28] Walt Rostow, Bundy's successor, later recalled that

At about this time I attended a meeting at the State Department of Democratic Senate Leaders, chaired by Dean Rusk . . . one could see the makings of a powerful isolationist coalition: those, like Senator Russell, who felt that more than twenty years after the war Europe should be able to defend itself; isolationists or neo-isolationists like Frank Church and Mike Mansfield; those obsessed with the balance-of-payments problem, like Stuart Symington; those, like John Pastore, furious with the European allies for their failure to support the United States in Southeast Asia.[29]

The administration pointed to advantageous offset agreements, suggested the possibility of negotiated East-West troop withdrawals, argued that NATO was too fragile to withstand the cuts, and pleaded for patience. Neither Mansfield nor the others were persuaded. Although his resolution was not put to a vote until 1971, Johnson felt pressed by the sentiments it tapped.

One reason was strong pressure from the Pentagon and Treasury to cut exchange costs in Europe. McNamara believed that the payments problem would hobble the entire U.S. defense role if it was not brought under control. The 1967 deficit was $3.5 billion, the largest since 1960. The administration responded by cutting embassy staffs abroad, a step that was later judged to have impeded intelligence collection.[30] Symington's riposte was a measure that would have prohibited funding for more than 50,000 troops in Europe after 1968. Johnson countered by imposing the first mandatory controls on foreign investment in American history.

As with the ad hoc dollar defenses, policymakers preferred the security of quick fixes. McNamara refused to sign off on a proposed NATO Military Payments Union under which surplus countries would issue IOUs to those in deficit; the obligations could then be satisfied in ways other than military purchases. The latter, which drove down U.S. unit costs and helped amortize research and development, were strongly preferred in the Pentagon. More effective outside the Pentagon was McNamara's argument that broadening the issue-area would dilute leverage the U.S. derived from tying troop level to offset. For these reasons, the proposal was never considered at the presidential level.[31] Bonn might not have accepted the idea in any case, as this would have increased its total liability, but Washington's insistence on continuing the original offset formula helped precipitate a serious problem in NATO and U.S.-German relations.

McNamara was also impatient with allied defense efforts and believed the U.S. was too tied down in Europe. His tough stance with Bonn might therefore also have been intended as a pretext for cuts. He told a Senate subcommittee that by "any measure, whether it be men or money or military effectiveness, the contributions of our allies are not sufficient and do not represent an equitable distribution of the burden." He knew this would "provide ammunition to those of us who wish to reduce our support of the common defense."[32] He believed that tough bargaining would induce the allies to do more and favored a two-division withdrawal. This was a minority view: others feared that if the U.S. cut too deeply, the allies would become demoralized and move toward neutralism.[33] State's position was that offset and troop level should be kept separate.

By 1966 Bonn's military buildup was about completed, and the Ludwig Erhard government wanted to shift some of its committed but unspent offset funds to civilian goods. This occurred around the same time that London decided, also for balance-of-payments reasons, to withdraw any portion of *its* 51,000 troops in Germany (called British Army on the Rhine, or BAOR) not fully covered by offsets. The administration feared that Congress would cut the U.S. garrison out of pique if the British went ahead. German Chancellor Erhard gambled on a personal appeal to Johnson, but the president, beset by intragovernmental and congressional pressures, insisted that only *future* agreements were open for discussion. Erhard's coalition fell at year's end without a resolution of the problem.

Johnson wanted the record to show that he had kept major NATO commitments intact.[34] The White House proposed a "trilateral" framework to negotiate interconnected offset and troop deployment agreements with the other two governments. Britain reluctantly agreed to the format under U.S. pressure.[35] Johnson chose John McCloy as his personal representative to these difficult talks, which began in October 1966.

McCloy, enormously popular in Germany, was thought to have the stature and flexibiliby in both countries to drive a bargain that would pass congressional muster. To ensure that he understood the White House's pressures, Johnson arranged for him to hear Mansfield's view at a meeting of the congressional leadership. The president by this time was inclined toward a one-division cut as a way to preserve the rest.[36] It was a delicate balancing act; since McCloy had been chosen to soothe Bonn, and some feared he would be *too* sympathetic, his negotiating instructions were fairly tough. In a letter dated March 1, 1967, Johnson told his envoy, "In the absence of a financial solution, and especially in light of the large German payments surplus, Congressional and public opinion would be intense, and the Germans should recognize that the situation might get out of hand."[37]

The ploy worked. The Trilateral Negotiations began in October of the previous year, recessed while the new cabinet in Bonn was organized, and resumed in March. Three issues were resolved: troop cuts were kept fairly small, Washington and Bonn agreed on a broader definition of acceptable balance-of-payments compensation, and the executive branch reaffirmed an *implicit* link between such payments and troop level.

A force "rotation" plan had been developed in the Pentagon's bureau of International Security Affairs (ISA) and was promoted by a member of McCloy's staff on loan from ISA who wanted to minimize the military impact of any cuts.[38] Rusk had favored a one-division, three air-wing cut as the least unpalatable alternative that could be sold to Congress; McNamara wished to double that. McCloy favored the rotation plan because it camouflaged the withdrawal: ground forces and supporting air units would be brought back to the U.S. to save foreign exchange, but would leave equipment behind and return annually for exercises. The number of troops actually removed from Europe under this bargain was only two-thirds of a division, 35,000 men (although the total number withdrawn after 1965, including those sent to Vietnam, was almost 60,000).[39]

Johnson found this acceptable. He could then tell critics that he had received a detailed report, considered the issue carefully, and concluded that larger cuts would imperil NATO.[40] Rusk reassured skeptical senators that the forces were still committed to Europe and would not be sent to Vietnam.[41] Once Bonn understood how British decisions impinged on U.S. opinion, it made a better offset offer to London and a bargain was struck between those two, filled out with a modest amount ($19 million) of U.S. military procurement in Britain.[42]

Considering his constraints, the compromises reflected Johnson's objective. McCloy and Rusk wanted to promise the allies no further cuts without allied agreement and Soviet concessions; McNamara wanted that option left open. The assurance was made, facilitated by the no gold-conversion pledge noted later.[43] On the other hand, offset was by now linked to the number of troops Washington would commit to keeping in Europe. While "hard-liners" believed this was the only way to get attractive payments compensation, everyone involved believed that Congress demanded it. Separating the two was never considered.[44] When it was recognized that a full military offset was out of the question, purchases of U.S. government securities were accepted as an alternative, despite congressional complaints that the U.S. was borrowing to support its own troops. Rusk could not refute this, claiming that since the forces were vital to U.S. security, the costs should be shared.[45]

Another compromise was Bonn's promise not to purchase gold from the U.S.

Treasury. This simply codified what Washington had already agreed upon informally with several developed countries, and the Germans had not in fact been making sizable purchases.[46] A threat to withdraw troops absent an agreement seems to have been made, although one participant believes a face-saving compromise would have been reached even without it.[47] In any case, the public promise was valuable to the administration. It made provocative or panic-driven behavior that could have closed the gold window less likely, sent a signal to international financial managers, and was an example to the French.[48] By 1967 continued confidence in the dollar was critical: the prospect of large claims on the gold stock would have closed the window within twenty-four hours.[49]

In its last months, the Johnson administration tried unsuccessfully to get direct support from Bonn for the troops. It was calculated that the United States would save over $400 million a year in marks if Bonn would pay the salaries of German workers at U.S. bases and $30 million if it operated some minor facilities such as anti-aircraft stations. Washington's special negotiator got the same negative answer as Anderson and Dillon a decade earlier.[50] Bonn argued that direct support implied that only Germany benefited from American troops; the issue, it claimed, was one for the entire alliance.

These adjustments support the major arguments of this book. Johnson's support for the rotation plan, broadened offset, and a formal no-gold-conversion pledge reflected serious consideration of the strategic stakes, not just a compromise between the McCloy and McNamara positions.[51] The bargaining link between German offset and U.S. troop levels reflected congressional pressure and thus supports Hypothesis 5. Rusk's concern about the diplomatic consequences of a successful troop-cut resolution, especially in light of French behavior, supports Hypothesis 3.

The broader pattern of American behavior during the late 1960s also supports Hypotheses 1 and 2. Policymakers deliberately overextended themselves in Vietnam and tried to hide that from NATO allies and the American people. Rather than rethink basic priorities, they adjusted the terms of the gold-dollar and troop commitments. Under siege, the United States ceased to behave as a benevolent hegemon.

Nixon's Answer: Europe First and the End of Bretton Woods

Richard Nixon's election as president was largely due to public weariness with Vietnam, but he soon realized that more than that was under assault. After thirty years of executive dominance, portions of the disengagement faction in Congress wanted to reclaim a larger foreign-policy role as well as redefine its substance. They confronted an administration determined to limit and control the retrenchment.

Executive-branch priorities were challenged mainly through the defense budget. Between fiscal years 1970 and 1975, Congress cut defense requests an average of 6 percent while adding an average of nearly 5 percent to nondefense obligational authority. Pentagon requests were cut by 22 percent in constant dollars between 1968 and 1975. In contrast, between fiscal 1950 and 1969, defense reductions averaged 1.7 percent and nondefense reductions averaged 9.2 percent.[52] Congress also reduced the Pentagon's budgetary autonomy in three ways: additional lines in the budget across which the executive branch had little authority to reprogram funds; "special interest items," for which no reprogramming was allowed; and "action items," specific directives that might not relate to the budget. During the first half of the 1970s, line items increased from 155 to 720, special interest items from none to 436, and action items from 107 to 350.

The administration adjusted in two ways. First, it gave up plans to fight "two and a half wars" simultaneously—major wars against Russia in Europe and China in Asia, and a smaller one elsewhere. This both recognized and was intended to exploit the Sino-Soviet split and signaled the administration's evolving approach to Mainland China. It was also in part an attempt to rationalize strategy: there were never enough forces to fight three wars, even before Vietnam, and pretending otherwise seemed pointless when Congress was cutting the defense budget.[53] But its main purpose was to appease congressional critics, which it did not.

Another change, more widely discussed at the time, was the Nixon (Guam) Doctrine. In declaring that America would no longer provide land forces for Asian wars, Nixon drew a narrow "lesson" from Vietnam. He insisted that existing treaty commitments would be kept, and intentionally left vague how that would be done in gray areas between conventional and irregular warfare. The purpose, as suggested in Chapter 2, was to change the terms of continuing commitments as little as possible and concede some ground to domestic critics while reassuring front-line states that their interests were not being sacrificed (Hypothesis 2).[54]

Decision makers assumed nonnegligible policy risks to achieve this. How else could commitments be maintained as capabilities shrank and the public insisted on no more Vietnams? In effect, the administration gambled that détente would stabilize the Third World enough to obviate U.S. intervention (Hypothesis 1).[55]

Senior officials during these years saw themselves as constantly on the defensive. Nixon's first annual foreign-policy report to Congress emphasized the distinction between interests and commitments, indicating a somewhat more situational view than Kennedy's or Johnson's. It also stressed the importance of a sustainable posture; as the president explained to two British correspondents, the administration had to "withstand the present wave of new isolationism."[56] But this applied mainly to *new* commitments; since existing ones would be kept, capabilities had to be stretched. Defense Secretary Melvin Laird, who faced smaller budgets while Soviet forces were growing rapidly, laid responsibility for the consequences at Congress's door.[57]

Although Mansfield and his supporters might have wanted the Nixon Doctrine to apply to Europe, this was not its intent. Yet domestic pressures for cuts peaked during Nixon's presidency, and his first foreign policy report promised only to maintain existing troop levels for eighteen months. The precise meaning of this signal is unclear from the public record. It might have been an honest warning, but could also have been intended to scare other NATO members into taking their troop commitments more seriously or doing enough to appease Congress. In either case, it illustrates myopic incrementalism.

A Europe-first policy was explicitly articulated and, to the extent possible, implemented. Balance-of-power considerations were paramount. Moscow achieved nuclear parity at the same time that NATO's posture was weakening: inflation-adjusted U.S. spending for NATO had declined steadily between 1964 and 1969, just as five more Soviet divisions were deployed in the aftermath of the Czech invasion. Over the next decade, at least 6,000 additional Soviet tanks were stationed in Eastern Europe.[58]

The new priority was underscored in two ways. Nixon unambiguously reaffirmed the nuclear guarantee as "unique" and "irreplaceable" for reasons discussed earlier.[59] Conventional procurement was also emphasized for Europe. For example, by fiscal 1972 ground forces had shrunk to levels maintained in the late 1950s without reductions in those pledged to Europe beyond the earlier Vietnam-induced attrition. Planners de-emphasized Army helicopters, which were better suited for Asia.[60] Rebuilding weapons stockpiles (over $10 billion worth of equipment had been transfered to Asia) was less visible and hence less politically vulnerable than other major programs; Laird did so and called on the allies for comparable efforts. Improved conventional air ordnance, anti-armor capabilities, and conventional artillery were also procured for Europe. As Laird put it, it was decided early in Nixon's term to save U.S. forces, especially ground troops, for "special priority commitments such as NATO or for cases of dire emergency."[61]

The administration also reversed course by separating German offsets from U.S. troop levels. This is perhaps clearer in hindsight than it was at the time, when Congress pressed the issue and the administration was obliged to give evidence of hard bargaining. In light of the piecemeal reductions, a policy review on military posture recommended against troop cuts in Europe. Also in 1969 the administration decided to go "easy" on the allies to avoid the public bickering of the Johnson years. A compromise offset agreement was reached that year reflecting those priorities.[62]

Mansfield made this difficult. His advisory resolution attracted 51 co-sponsors in 1970, perhaps because there would be no vote. The executive branch was worried enough to request several more National Security Study Memorandums (NSSMs) examining possible combinations of reductions and force postures. Nixon's decision late that year to stand firm against cuts moved the majority leader to change tactics, and in May 1971 Mansfield introduced an amendment requiring half the forces in Europe to be cut by the end of the year.[63] The administration was concerned enough to employ many of the "big guns" of postwar policy to lobby against it, including Acheson, McCloy, Rusk, and Johnson.

On May 14, five days before the vote, Soviet leader Leonid Brezhnev invited NATO and the Warsaw Pact to negotiate mutual force reductions, calling attention to a hint dropped in March at the Twenty-fourth Communist Party Congress. NATO had been urging talks since 1968 as a logical continuation of the Harmel Report's emphasis on the "twin pillars" of defense and détente. Moscow had meanwhile been urging an all-European security conference to legitimize the postwar boundaries and regimes. Each had approached the other's proposal cautiously; now, however, the Kremlin was worried about destabilization in Europe if U.S. troops were withdrawn.[64] Washington responded with alacrity, although only to defeat Mansfield, who lost by a vote of 36 to 61.[65]

Two years later, Mansfield's amendment for a 40 percent cut in all foreign-based land forces (483,000) was barely defeated, as was a cut of 110,000 sponsored by Senators Humphrey and Cranston. But a House-Senate conference committee on the defense bill retained the Jackson-Nunn Amendment, which would have forced the withdrawal of any U.S. forces committed to NATO whose exchange costs were not offset by the allies. This became moot the next year, as discussed in chapter 6.

These pressures were also reflected in offset bargaining after 1969 and the administration's ambiguous signals about troop levels. In September 1970, Nixon told NATO Secretary-General Manlio Brosio that the U.S. preferred European defense improvements to compensation for itself. This made strategic sense and might have mollified congressional troop cutters. But Washington had no lever on internal European expenditures as the previous decade had made clear. The administration thus took a "tougher" position on direct support the next year, and the 1971 offset agreement provided for German renovation of U.S. barracks. This was popular with service personnel and countered congressional complaints that in buying U.S. securities, Bonn was making profitable investments rather than sharing costs.[66] Washington's inconsistencies on the type of compensation it desired reflected fear of how Congress might react, not a lack of strategic priorities. At one point officials refused to offer a dollar figure for direct support, fearing further pressures for cuts if the allies failed to meet it (Hypothesis 4).[67]

Nixon decided to press direct support again two years later for the same reason.[68] As discussed in chapter 6, offset's days were numbered, although no one suspected that at the time. There would be only one final agreement after 1973.

No one save Treasury in the Nixon administration *wanted* to press the allies or withdraw troops; containing the reputational damage from Vietnam required the opposite. Moreover, no figure comparable to McNamara wanted to redistribute the conventional burden fundamentally. Since the administration was trying to negotiate with Moscow from a position of declining hegemony, the appearance of strong alliance ties and domestic support for the president were deemed to be critical.[69] In this light, some of its tactics, which were interpreted in just the sense it wished to avoid, demonstrated the vulnerability of conventional troop commitments (Hypothesis 4).

Laird, for example, proposed trimming NATO-committed forces in September 1969. He suggested a larger list of cancellations and cuts the following year; this culminated in an NSC meeting in November 1970 at which he proposed withdrawing from 20,000 to 40,000 troops. According to Kissinger, Laird wanted the cuts to affect NATO immediately: the Atlantic constituency would protest, Laird reasoned, and the cuts would be restored. Kissinger suggests that these tactics, while effective, were unsettling at a time when foreigners believed that the United States was abandoning wholesale its postwar world role. Others claim that Kissinger supported the ploy, despite his disavowals. This maneuvering was intended to buy time, defuse congressional pressures, and induce greater European efforts (Hypothesis 4).[70]

Nixon had a hand in this, although the details are murky. There had been rumors abroad about cuts from the beginning of his term, and by the end of the next year many Europeans believed them to be imminent.[71] Careful yet explicit signals to that effect emanated from the White House.[72] Although German Chancellor Willy Brandt claimed in a 1969 interview that Washington had promised no substantive changes in deployments during the current offset agreement, Nixon allowed speculation about them to continue and avoided publicly reaffirming the existing force level until well into 1970.[73] Even after that, leaks of planned cuts continued without an authoritative response.

Nixon had other pressing concerns, and since Mansfield's resolutions had until then been nonbinding, he might have wished to avoid another public brawl with Congress. Given his habit of thinking in terms of bargaining chips, he seems to have used the uncertainty he could not control to scare the Europeans into making concessions.[74]

The Demise of Bretton Woods. Nixon, who was as bored by economics as he was fascinated by grand strategy, avoided a dollar crisis for two years. But the political and economic costs of defending the dollar had mounted since the mid–1960s, and when it weakened once more in 1971, the gold-dollar link was discarded. As Kissinger explained, "the United States abandoned gold convertibility in order to secure a more realistic and defensible set of exchange-rate relationships."[75] It was indeed striking, given the government's earlier acrobatics, how easily a different mentality developed: that the Bretton Woods obligations unfairly handicapped the United States and had to be replaced.

The economic causes were inflation and the American political business cycle. The Federal Reserve followed a tight money policy during 1969 and 1970 but abandoned it when recession threatened. Nixon was happy for political reasons, especially when Republicans did relatively poorly in the off-year elections. Inflation crept up and the trade balance in spring 1971 went into deficit for the first time since the nineteenth century. Speculators attacked the dollar, the mark was floating by May, and a major dollar devaluation appeared necessary.

It seemed so on political grounds as well. A reserve-currency country had no control of its exchange rate, since if it devalued, others could simply follow suit and erase the advantage. The dollar had originally been overvalued deliberately to aid European and Japanese recovery, but there had been no basic adjustment among the dollar, mark, and yen since the 1950s. As the dollar grew more overvalued, its defense had cost the domestic economy dearly. Analogies were drawn to Britain, another country whose systemic monetary responsibilities had impeded domestic growth.[76] It was increasingly argued that benevolent monetary hegemony had become too expensive.

These considerations loomed larger as economic power diffused among the industrial democracies. Japan and Germany had become economic powerhouses during the 1960s, penetrating the American market and competing effectively elsewhere. Britain's imminent entry into the Common Market would enlarge what looked more and more like a protectionist club. Increasing evidence that U.S. preeminence was waning was linked to long-standing arguments for a major overhaul of Bretton Woods. By early August 1971, protectionist pressures were increasing and the administration, facing reelection in just over a year, was paying attention.[77] Economic nationalism, long officially dormant in the United States, rather suddenly became respectable.

Nixon and John Connally, his Treasury Secretary, thus agreed with the administration's economic experts that exchange rates had to be realigned. On August 15, Nixon announced a 10 percent import surcharge, temporary wage-and-price controls, and an end to gold convertibility. There was somewhat less here than met the eye: the dollar had for several years been inconvertible de facto, and the administration was using the crisis to force the issue.

By this time the administration preferred a system of floating rates, that is, a renunciation of Bretton Woods. It was temporarily in a strong bargaining position, since the dollar would float until there was agreement on new parities.[78] But Kissinger worried that monetary disarray would spill over into geopolitics and convinced Nixon to resolve the issue. For diplomatic reasons, Paris was chosen as the bridge to the other industrialized countries. President Georges Pompidou was willing to settle, but in return for accepting a substantial dollar devaluation and the end of the gold link he demanded fixed parties and U.S. defense of the new rate. This fell short of a completely new regime, although that was not the way it was interpreted.[79] The Smithsonian Agreement reached by the Group of 10 finance ministers in December 1971 was based on this pledge.

This agreement too would not last; by 1973 U.S. officials were seeking their second devaluation. Although it was not immediately recognized, they had committed themselves to floating rates, since intervention currencies were not being accumulated to support the dollar at any particular level. This angered former policymakers who believed that America was obligated to seek a solution that would protect large holders of dollars.[80] Two years later, floating rates were legitimized and the dollar effectively "crowned" as the major international reserve asset. This took pressure off the troop deployment in Europe, as discussed in the next chapter.

Beliefs and Fears about Europe

Congressionally imposed troop cuts were nevertheless quite possible in the early 1970s, and the administration worried about the consequences. It feared Finlandization or, even worse, bandwagoning toward Moscow. Europeans *were* evidently satisfied with existing NATO arrangements and concerned about U.S. staying power. This was to be expected in view of the overall stability in Europe since late 1940s, the congressional and public support NATO had enjoyed, and the weariness Mansfield seemed to be tapping. But the leap to Finlandization scenarios went beyond this evidence and arguably indicated U.S. inclinations toward such beliefs.

That Europe was accustomed to the status quo had long been apparent. George Kennan, an early advocate of containment who disavowed its later militarization, believed that allied leaders rejected his 1957 proposal for mutual Soviet-American troop reductions because keeping U.S. forces was more important to them than Soviet withdrawals.[81] In late 1971 the *New York Times's* Max Frankel dispatched this from London:

Reliance upon credible American protection has made for a "nice and comfortable" balance on the Continent and stability in Western Europe, as they put it at the British Foreign Office. The alternative, as it is imagined in London, Paris, and Bonn is "Balkanization"—meaning fragmentation—and eventually "Finlandization," meaning an uncomfortable susceptibility to Soviet influence . . . as several influential officials and observers here remark, the desire to keep the United States militarily engaged in Europe is so great that the allies will take—and give—a good deal for it. . . . It is commonly felt that if the United States reduces its forces in Europe, even in exchange for Soviet withdrawals, then West Germany will feel compelled to demobilize some of its forces while the smaller countries in the Alliance relax their modest efforts even further.[82]

In this context the administration was initially concerned about Brandt's *Ostpolitik*, the policy of rapprochement with the East bloc. The White House at first viewed it as incipient Finlandization, a fear born of the fact that Moscow held the key to German reunification. Bonn might, after all, believe that its future lay not with the West but with what Germans call "Mitteleuropa." Italian, British, and French leaders gave Kissinger a similar message: Germany's overtures to the East resulted at least partly from diminished U.S. credibility; if America did not deal with Moscow from strength, all Europe might follow.[83]

Worries on both counts were overdrawn. Germany did not relax its defense efforts between 1966 and 1973, years of uncertainty about America's future intentions and capabilities in Europe. Between fiscal 1967, when forces were transferred to Vietnam, and fiscal 1969, when the rotation plan was implemented, German expenditures dropped but quickly rebounded. Between 1971 and 1978, while U.S. military spending dropped 2.7 percent in constant prices, the average non-American NATO member's expenditures grew 3.14 percent.[84]

These data do not unambiguously show that the allies *balanced* U.S. retrenchment. America's shrinking share of NATO expenditures during the 1970s reflected a smaller overall defense establishment and withdrawal from Vietnam,
not Europe. True balancing would be indicated by the latter and, simultaneously,
larger allied efforts. Europe nevertheless hedged its bets during these years, a
time when America retreated part way from global containment and accepted
nuclear parity with Moscow.

The administration eventually realized that Bonn was not pursuing *Ostpolitik*
as a supplicant, although officials were initially predisposed to see flexibility as
open-ended accommodation.[85] The Social Democrats, those most in favor of
rapprochement, believed that strong defenses provided bargaining leverage and
would not accept neutralization as a price for better relations with the East. In
a 1972 *Foreign Affairs* article Brandt said that a major reduction of U.S. forces
in Europe "must be part as well as a result of decreasing tension between East
and West." Bonn also refused to ratify the Soviet–West German normalization
treaty until an acceptable agreement on Berlin was reached.[86]

The analytically important issue is how much American behavior can be
explained by Finlandization beliefs. To what extent have they made policymakers
especially concerned about reassurances and resistant to troop cuts imposed by
Congress? As discussed in Chapter 3, it is easy to claim that beliefs are autonomous and causally powerful. Showing either is difficult. Since we cannot know
what decision makers really thought, what follows is an indirect argument.

Autonomous beliefs have an independent cognitive or affective basis and do
not simply rationalize preferences. One indication is willingness to pay for more
security than would follow from a "balancing" model; Finlandization beliefs
are demanding in this regard. The executive branch, to illustrate, had a range
of choices in responding to Mansfield. Nixon might have been able to compromise
on a smaller reduction (as Johnson did) that would have gained him political
capital and perhaps left the remaining troops untouchable.[87] For example, two
of McNamara's former staffers suggested cuts of about a third, as compared
with Symington's proposed 80 percent cut. They contended that a successful
withdrawal would depend on convincing the allies of two things: that the remaining forces could be sustained, and deterrence could be preserved by adjusting
relative contributions. Washington, they said, would have to listen carefully to
allied reactions rather than make a priori assumptions about them. After all,
most American officials ignored allied appeals that U.S. credibility was not, as
far as they were concerned, at stake in Vietnam.[88]

Beliefs causually affect behavior if they diverge significantly from reality or
(a corollary) if actors behave differently on the basis of different beliefs.[89] Chapter
2 showed that a hegemon's inclinations about commitments will be risk-averse.
Although Finlandization is improbable, it seems not to have appeared so in
Washington during the early 1970s. In fact, what has most distinguished Finland's benign neutrality toward Moscow is its uniqueness. Finland is small,
borders on the USSR, was once connected to the Czarist empire, and fought

three wars with the Bolshevik regime. Aside from West Germany, European NATO shares none of these features (save British and French participation in the Soviet civil war). Germany has fought Russia, but its size and distance from the heart of Russian power make direct coercion problematic. It would thus be implausible for Moscow to claim or enforce an analogous relationship with Bonn. This applies a fortiori to the rest of NATO Europe; dominating it would require many highly improbable conditions.[90]

Finlandization scenarios were apparently misapplied to Western Europe. Those who took them seriously failed to reexamine old images and thus recognized only half of the "alliance security dilemma": allies' twin fears of being abandoned in a crisis and trapped involuntarily in a conflict initiated by their protector. Europeans have oscillated between fear that the United States will not risk destruction for them and fear that it will act belligerently. Correspondingly, America is often seen, sequentially, as too conciliatory *and* too tough on arms reductions. This leads to cycles of anxiety: allied fears of abandonment lead first to American reassurances, then typically to a reaffirmation of the nuclear link, then to fears of entrapment, and finally to renewed American efforts to compensate for that. The cycle may then start over.[91]

Americans have been far quicker to recognize fears of abandonment and have treated them much more seriously, not usually recognizing that this is only one side of a dependency syndrome. Some confirmatory evidence, to be sure, was available during the early 1970s. There were fears in Europe that the Nixon Doctrine signified neo-isolationism, despite the administration's signals to the contrary.[92] This might have seemed to be the result of America's past inability to define a selective, sustainable role in world politics—exactly what Nixon was trying to do. In any case, even if allies' perception of abandonment is more damaging to the United States than a feeling of entrapment, it hardly follows that abandonment will produce Finlandization. In a balance-of-power model— the one U.S. officials use to interpret the behavior of Moscow, Beijing, and Tel Aviv, among most others—just the opposite should occur.

Specific cognitive errors have contributed to this. In an uncertain environment, risk-averse decision makers have applied an "availability" heuristic (decision rule) that predicts outcomes by extrapolating from the most easily remembered example. Finland has garnered much Western sympathy and its fate has been readily recalled. Invoking it in dissimilar situations ignores such key statistical decision criteria as prior baseline probabilities associated with the relevant outcomes (e.g., Finlandization or successful maintenance of autonomy) as well as the validity of the salient example itself. Predictions that Europe would respond to declining U.S. hegemony by reducing its own arms assumed that the outcome would resemble the catalyst, despite the logic of balance-of-power theory. This exemplified the "representativeness" heuristic, another predictive bias.[93]

This special sensitivity to bad outcomes, however, did not affect everyone. People can avoid confronting value trade-offs by believing that their preferences are supported by various logically independent considerations. This occurs frequently in political decision making when important values clash; Americans seem unusually prone to it.[94] Both the executive branch and its critics showed evidence of it. Symington, for example, found the costs of U.S. troops in Europe unbearable; an administration witness professed them cost-effective. A Senate subcommittee counsel differed strongly with an administration witness as to whether a 50 percent cut in the U.S. Seventh Army would have a major military effect.[95]

Probability estimates seem to be linked to these preferences by the same cognitive consistency mechanism. This too applied equally to the administration and its critics. Martin Hillenbrand, an assistant secretary of state, predicted that major U.S. troop withdrawals would lead to Soviet domination. Kennan, who had long opposed the militarization of the NAT, thought this unlikely. Even if the Soviets attempted it, they would back down "against a firm European resistance."[96]

CONCLUSIONS

Many of the problems faced by American foreign policymakers during the late 1960s and early 1970s were of their own making. It proved impossible simultaneously to fight a major war in Vietnam, maintain the original troop garrison committed to NATO, preserve the gold-dollar link, and pay for fairly ambitious (at least by American standards) social programs. Although America's enormous initial postwar advantages were bound to erode, overextension significantly accelerated the process.

Some of the consequences are easily interpreted through a systemic model of declining hegemony. As Keohane and Nye put it more generally, an "atmosphere of crisis and a proliferation of ad hoc policy measures" were evident in Washington during the late 1960s and early 1970s, and dissenters wondered a great deal about the costs (and benefits) of hegemonic leadership. The other NATO countries, especially France, no longer accepted a one-sided dependence or the American lead on most issues.[97] They were not very understanding about the payments deficit, accepted FR only grudgingly and incompletely, and were indifferent or worse to America's cause in Vietnam.

These contraints did not affect the nuclear employment planning that bore on extended deterrence. The bureaucracy was able to work away, largely unhampered by Congress or the allies. The fruits of these labors are discussed extensively in the next chapter.

Up to a point, the policy response to these problems fits the general model of chapters 2 and 3. In accepting the rotation plan, demanding a link between offset and troop level, and insisting on a formal no-gold-conversion pledge from Germany, the Johnson administration was able to continue deliberately overextending itself by changing the terms of these commitments (Hypotheses 1 and 2). Pushed by Congress, the administration could no longer afford the "benevolence" of offsets that met the needs of *both* Washington and Bonn (Hypotheses

4 and 5). While no one was fooled, it camouflaged a fairly small troop cut as a "rotation" and resisted calls for larger, explicit cuts in order to retain America's dominant roles in NATO agenda formation, mobilization, decisionmaking, and administration.

The next administration followed essentially similar policies. It pushed hard on offset when that was necessary for internal reasons, allowed the allies to wonder about troop cuts for most of a year (Hypotheses 4 and 5), and broke the gold-dollar link. Under the circumstances the Nixon Doctrine was a conservative adjustment, thereby increasing the risks of overextension as forces shrunk (Hypotheses 1 and 2). This illustrated Washington's ambivalence about overcommitment—preferring it as a matter of course, but worrying lest it erode key commitments (Hypotheses 1 and 3). The administration's economic tone was openly nationalistic, for both internal and external reasons.

Nixon did, however, restore Europe's place in U.S. strategy for self-proclaimed balance-of-power reasons. Whereas Johnson and McNamara accommodated nuclear parity by essentially *refusing* to adjust within the terms of first use, Nixon and Kissinger emphasized the fundamentally political role of extended deterrence in a hegemonic security system. While Johnson fought in Vietnam at the expense of Europe, Nixon gave up a military role on the Asian mainland to restore the military presence on the European continent.

Systemic models are not much help in explaining such choices. Incipient nuclear parity and FR implied a standoff in Europe, freeing a global hegemon to operate elsewhere. On the other hand, as the main theater of the U.S.–Soviet cold war, Europe could be interpreted as the major, continuing test of American resolve, especially given the country's historic isolationism and the unmistakable challenge from contemporary neo-isolationists. Intuitively, we can see that policymakers cut their losses in Asia after 1969 and concentrated on refurbishing the U.S. position where there was an established structure and strong public support. But theoretically, this is an ad hoc explanation.

This returns us to the inherent limits of single-exit models. In the absence of a burning building, there is always more than one option. Between 1966 and 1973 the superpower rivalry appeared to have stabilized, especially if one imputed those purposes to Moscow's major nuclear buildup. In this context Washington first found a remote threat, could not tame it, and then found its geopolitical bearings in Europe again. Nixon and Kissinger preferred, when pressed, to risk falling dominoes in Asia rather than Europe. Beginning in the early 1970s, Moscow's expansionist notion of détente made the main adversary look more ominous, and NATO commitments took on even more meaning as tests of resolve.

NOTES

1. See Gaddis, *Strategies of Containment* (New York: Oxford University Press, 1982), Chap. 8.

2. Smoke, *National Security and the Nuclear Dilemma* (New York: Random House, 1987), pp. 126–127.

3. Calleo, "Since 1961," p. 409.

4. Prados, *The Soviet Estimate* (Princeton: Princeton University Press, 1986), pp. 189–191.

5. Cordesman, "American Strategic Forces and Extended Deterrence," p. 462.

6. Ibid., p. 463.

7. Ibid., p. 463; Rosenberg, "U.S. Nuclear Strategy," p. 24.

8. Cordesman, "American Strategic Forces and Extended Deterrence," p. 464.

9. Ibid., p. 466.

10. Robert Jervis, "Strategic Theory: What's New and What's True," in Roman Kolkowicz, ed., *The Logic of Nuclear Terror* (Boston: Allen and Unwin, 1987), p. 55.

11. Henry Kissinger, *White House Years* (Boston: Little, Brown, 1979), pp. 391, 216. Nevertheless, for obvious reasons, there was no wholesale attempt to return to massive retaliation.

12. Interview with Martin Hillenbrand, Assistant Secretary of State for European Affairs, 1969–1972, November 20, 1984.

13. Laird, "A Strong Start in a Difficult Decade: Defense Policy in the Nixon-Ford Years," *International Security* 10, no. 2 (Fall 1985): 11.

14. Prados, *The Soviet Estimate*, p. 194; Anthony Cordesman, "American Strategic Forces and Extended Deterrence," in David Kaufman et al., eds., *U.S. National Security: A Framework for Analysis* (Lexington, Mass.: D.C. Heath and Co., 1985), p. 467; Henry Kissinger, *White House Years* (Boston: Little Brown, 1979), p. 217.

15. J. Michael Legge, *Theater Nuclear Weapons and the NATO Strategy of Flexible Response*, Report R–2964-FF (Santa Monica, Calif.: RAND Corporation, 1983), p. 9, cited in Jane Stromseth, *The Origins of Flexible Response* (New York: St. Martins, 1988) p. 175.

16. Kissinger, *White House Years*, p. 219.

17. U.S. Congress, House of Representatives, Committee on Armed Services, Special Subcommittee on North Atlantic Treaty Organization Commitments, *Report: The American Commitment to NATO*, 92nd Cong., 2nd sess., August 17, 1972, p. 14972; Stromseth, *The Origins of Flexible Response*, p. 177.

18. Robert S. McNamara, Draft Memorandum for the President, 16 January 1968, Subject: NATO Strategy and Force Structure, p. 4, Department of Defense, Freedom of Information Act, cited in Stromseth, *The Origins of Flexible Response*, p. 178.

19. The words in quotes are McNamara's; see "Summary Notes of 566th NSC Meeting," December 13, 1966, Lyndon B. Johnson Library. See also Roger Morgan, *The United States and West Germany, 1945–1973: A Study in Alliance Politics* (London: Oxford University Press, 1974), p. 182.

20. Stromseth, *The Origins of Flexible Response*, p. 144.

21. Kissinger, *White House Years*, pp. 219–220.

22. Richard Ullman, "The Covert French Connection," *Foreign Policy* no. 75 (Summer 1989), pp. 8–13.

23. *New York Times*, July 20, 1989, p. 4.

24. Lyndon B. Johnson, *The Vantage Point: Perspectives of the Presidency, 1963–1969* (New York: Holt, Rinehart and Winston, 1971), p. 309.

25. U.S. Congress, Senate, Committee on Foreign Relations, *Hearings: United States*

Policy Toward Europe (and Related Matters), 89th Cong., 2nd sess., 1966, p. 110; Raj, *American Military in Europe*, p. 106; *New York Times*, April 8, 1966.

26. *New York Times*, April 8, 1966, p. 4.

27. *New York Times*, October 11, 1967, p. 2.

28. Interview with Dean Rusk, October 27, 1984.

29. W. W. Rostow, *The Diffusion of Power: An Essay in Receent History* (New York: Macmillan, 1972), p. 396.

30. *New York Times*, November 28, 1989.

31. On the proposed NATO Military Payments Union, see Gregory Treverton, *The "Dollar Drain" and American Forces in Germany* (Athens: Ohio University Press, 1978), p. 116.

32. Testimony of Robert S. McNamara, U.S. Congress, Senate, Combined Subcommittee of the Foreign Relations and Armed Services Committees, *Hearings, United States Troops in Europe*, 90th Cong., 1st sess., April 26, 1967, p. 19.

33. Confidential interview.

34. Confidential interview.

35. *New York Times*, November 10, 1966, and December 13, 1966; confidential interview.

36. Morgan, *The United States and West Germany*, p. 179; confidential interview.

37. Letter from Johnson to McCloy, Collection IT34, Box 6, Lyndon B. Johnson Library. Not only did Johnson want to push McCloy somewhat toward "toughness," but Johnson was also concerned that the record show *him* to be "tough" (confidential interview).

38. Treverton, *The "Dollar Drain,"* pp. 124–125; *New York Times*, April 13, 1969, p. 3.

39. Kissinger, *White House Years*, p. 394.

40. Confidential interview.

41. See testimony by Rusk in *United States Troops in Europe*, pp. 67–75.

42. Treverton, *The "Dollar Drain,"* p. 152.

43. John W. Finney, "Compromise on Troops," *New York Times*, May 7, 1967.

44. Treverton, *The "Dollar Drain,"* pp. 143, 145, 149, 156.

45. See testimony by Rusk, *United States Troops in Europe*, p. 80.

46. Treverton, *The "Dollar Drain,"* p. 131. By 1967 and 1968, heavy diplomatic pressure was put on the central banks of America's major creditors to go on accumulating dollars even though it had become *de facto* unconvertible. See Calleo, "Since 1961," p. 411. Nixon's rupture of the gold-dollar link was consequently later seen as a break of faith by some in the preceding administration.

47. Confidential interview.

48. Treverton, *The "Dollar Drain,"* p. 131.

49. Confidential interview.

50. Treverton, *The "Dollar Drain,"* pp. 40–41.

51. Ibid., p. 150.

52. Lawrence J. Korb, *The Fall and Rise of the Pentagon: American Defense Policies in the 1970s* (Westport, Conn.: Greenwood Press, 1979), p. 34; *New York Times*, November 22, 1989, p. 12.

53. See Kissinger, *White House Years*, pp. 220-222; see also *New York Times*, January 26, 1973, p. 12.

54. Henry Brandon, *The Retreat of American Power* (New York: Doubleday, 1973), pp. 80–81; Kissinger, *White House Years*, p. 225.

55. Robert S. Litwak, *Detente and the Nixon Doctrine: American Foreign Policy and the Pursuit of Stability, 1969–1976* (Cambridge: Cambridge University Press, 1984), pp. 126, 136.

56. Richard Nixon, "First Annual Report to the Congress on United States Foreign Policy for the 1970s," February 18, 1970, in *Public Papers of the Presidents of the United States: Richard Nixon* (Washington, D.C.: U.S. Government Printing Office, 1971), pp. 118, 119; Brandon, *The Retreat of American Power*, p. 81.

57. See *New York Times*, August 22, 1969, and December 27, 1969. The Nixon Doctrine moved Asian allies in the direction of providing for their immediate territorial defense. This gave Laird—who was looking for ways to reduce overseas deployments enough to contain pressures for even larger cuts—an opportunity to withdraw one of the two U.S. divisions in Korea. But as long as the commitments themselves were retained, especially to countries that faced some real threat of attack, the price was a lower nuclear threshold. See Earl C. Ravenal, "The Nixon Doctrine and Our Asian Commitments," *Foreign Affairs* 49, no. 2 (January 1971): 202, 216.

58. Laird, "A Strong Start in a Difficult Decade," pp. 18–19.

59. Nixon, "First Annual Report to Congress on Foreign Policy for the 1970s," p. 129.

60. Edward Fried, "The Financial Cost of Alliance," in John Newhouse et al., eds., *U.S. Troops in Europe: Issues, Costs, and Choices* (Washington, D.C.: Brookings Institution, 1971), p. 121; *New York Times*, December 27, 1969.

61. Interviews with Melvin Laird, July 15, 1982, and September 18, 1984; Laird, "A Strong Start in a Difficult Decade," pp. 19, 23.

62. Treverton, *The "Dollar Drain*," pp. 42–43.

63. See John Yochelson, "The American Military Presence in Europe: Current Debate in the United States," *Orbis* 15, no. 3 (Fall 1971): 785, and Phil Williams, *The Senate and U.S. Troops in Europe* (New York: St. Martin's Press, 1985), p. 184.

64. Raymond L. Garthoff, *Detente and Confrontation: American-Soviet Relations from Nixon to Reagan* (Washington, D.C.: Brookings Institution, 1985), pp. 114–116.

65. Kissinger, *White House Years*, pp. 399–402, 947–948.

66. Interview with Martin Hillenbrand, November 20, 1984.

67. *Washington Post*, October 9, 1970; *New York Times*, October 9, 1970.

68. Treverton, *The "Dollar Drain*," pp. 46–47.

69. For an account of the administration's rationale, see Kissinger, *White House Years*, pp. 939–949. For Nixon's statement of the geopolitical consequences of withdrawals, see "Fourth Annual Report to the Congress on United States Foreign Policy," May 3, 1973, *Public Papers of the Presidents of the United States: Richard Nixon* (Washington, D.C.: U.S. Government Printing Office, 1975), p. 409.

70. See Kissinger, *White House Years*, pp. 395–397; *New York Times*, December 1, 1970, and December 25, 1970; John Yochelson, "The American Military Presence in Europe," *Orbis* Vol. 15, no. 3 (Fall 1971), p. 795; Treverton, *The "Dollar Drain*," p. 44. A former defense official disagrees, claiming Laird's intentions were not benign and that Laird was "playing games" with U.S. NATO deployments (confidential interview, June 5, 1984). Circumstantial evidence supports Kissinger's interpretation. Laird's proposed cuts, like the additional 30,000 planned late in the Johnson administration and cancelled by Nixon, would have affected support and logistics rather than combat units. This emphasized political rather than military considerations, since European morale

depended most on visible evidence of combat strength. In contrast, if cuts were unavoidable, military men favored pulling out combat troops and leaving intact the infrastructure that could equip and maintain combat reinforcements flown in from the U.S. On these points, see *New York Times*, August 20, 1970.

71. Treverton, *The "Dollar Drain,"* p. 44.

72. Kissinger, for example, cautioned some European visitors against attributing undue significance to the current numerical strength of the U.S. garrison. See *New York Times*, February 4, 1970.

73. Phil Williams, *The Senate and U.S. Troops in Europe* (New York: St. Martin's, 1985), p. 162.

74. Interviews with Martin Hillenbrand, November 20, 1984, and Elliott Richardson, former Undersecretary of State, July 3, 1985.

75. Kissinger, *White House Years*, p. 962.

76. Calleo, "Since 1961," p. 419.

77. Kissinger, *White House Years*, pp. 952, 953.

78. Mayer, *The Fate of the Dollar*, p. 171.

79. Kissinger, *White House Years*, p. 961. Whether the Smithsonian Agreement restored or disposed of Bretton Woods depends on whether the regime's key rule was simply fixed rates or gold convertibility as well. David Calleo seems confused on this point: see "Since 1961," pp. 420–421.

80. Martin Mayer, *The Fate of the Dollar* (New York: New American Library, 1981), pp. 185, 209, 212. Johnson's Treasury Secretary Henry Fowler was particularly vocal on this point.

81. George F. Kennan, "Europe's Problems, Europe's Choices," *Foreign Policy* no. 14 (Spring 1974): 12.

82. *New York Times*, December 21, 1971, p. 11.

83. See Richard Barnet, *The Alliance: America, Europe, Japan—Makers of the Postwar World* (New York: Simon and Schuster, 1983), p. 318; *New York Times*, December 21, 1971, and November 10, 1989; Kissinger, *White House Years*, p. 922.

84. Two qualifications should be noted in interpreting the overall NATO figures. The aggregate figure for non-U.S. NATO is an average that does not weight for a country's size or military importance in the alliance. Second, the average includes large increases for two countries, Greece and Turkey, which during this period were engaged in conflicts outside NATO's area of responsibility. If they are removed from the group, the overall growth in spending is 2.15. If Luxembourg, a tiny member whose expenditures grew 6.3 is also removed, the non-U.S. NATO members' spending increased by just 2.3 percent. This at least throws Finlandization arguments into question. The German figures are from a Department of Defense, May 16, 1984, mimeo; the other data are from U.S. House of Representatives by the Congressional Research Service, *NATO After Afghanistan, Report Prepared for the Subcommittee on Europe and the Middle East of the Committee on Foreign Affairs*, October 27, 1980, p. 46, Table VIII.

85. Brandon, *The Retreat of American Power*, pp. 76–77.

86. The Brandt quote is from "Germany's Westpolitik," *Foreign Affairs* 50, no. 3 (April 1972): 420; see also Seyom Brown, *New Forces, Old Forces, and the Future of World Politics* (Glenview, Ill.: Scott, Foresman, 1988), pp. 110, 122.

87. Denis Healy, then a Labor cabinet minister in Britain, thought a 20 percent reduction, approximately one division, would have accomplished this. See *New York Times*, December 21, 1971. See also Brandon, *The Retreat of American Power*, p. 214.

88. Alain C. Enthoven and K. Wayne Smith, "What Forces for NATO? And from Whom?" *Foreign Affairs* 48, no. 1 (October 1969): 95, 96. See also Litwak, *Detente and the Nixon Doctrine*, p. 118.

89. Jervis, *Perception and Misperception in International Politics*, pp. 14–15.

90. Kennan, "Europe's Problems," pp. 9, 15.

91. Jane M. O. Sharp, "Arms Control and Alliance Commitments," *Political Science Quarterly* 100, no. 4 (Winter 1985–1986): 648–652.

92. Litwak, *Detente and the Nixon Doctrine*, p. 137.

93. Amos Tversky and Daniel Kahneman, "Judgement Under Uncertainty: Heuristics and Biases," *Science* vol. 185 (September 27, 1984).

94. Robert Jervis, *Perception and Misperception in International Politics* (Princeton: Princeton University Press, 1976), pp. 136–137. A general discussion of this topic is found on pp. 128–142.

95. U.S. Congress, Senate, Committee on Foreign Relations, *United States Security Agreements and Commitments Abroad: United States Forces in Europe*, 91st Cong., 2nd sess., 1970, pp. 2203–2206, 2212.

96. Ibid., p. 2213; Kennan, "Europe's Problems," p. 16.

97. Robert Keohane and Joseph Nye, *Power and Interdependence* (Boston: Little, Brown, 1977), p. 45.

6 The United States and European Defense, 1974–1980

OVERVIEW

As Henry Kissinger predicted, managing the consequences of Moscow's emergence as a military superpower was the major American challenge of the 1970s. In certain respects, U.S. officials faced fewer constraints after mid-decade than before. As a result, NATO benefited from substantial and dependable U.S. support. But America's relative weight in the world clearly shrank during these years, making it difficult to fulfill some commitments and prompting an extending academic and political discussion of hegemonic decline.

Conventional forces in Europe were less politically vulnerable than a few years earlier, for two reasons. The loose monetary regime that followed Bretton Woods released the United States from an obligation to defend the dollar at any particular level and largely removed balance-of-payments considerations from security policy. Congressional pressures against the American presence in Europe and defense spending in general also eased considerably due to disillusionment with détente and a substantial Soviet military buildup.

Washington had "accepted" nuclear parity during the late 1960s by sidestepping arms races both in defensive damage-limiting systems such as antiballistic missiles (ABMs) and in nuclear delivery vehicles. By the early 1970s, the Soviets had a secure AD capacity and were on their way to surpassing the United States in delivery vehicles. These results, codified in the 1972 ABM Treaty, meant that the United States would not try to limit the death and destruction that Moscow could cause it in a central strategic war. This left open how Washington would adjust, if at all, the major purposes for which it deployed nuclear weapons: basic deterrence, extended deterrence of nuclear attack, and extended deterrence of conventional attack.[1] Because the implications of future

nuclear parity were not recognized when these objectives were formulated, nuclear strategy was most clearly the area in which the United States, as a declining
hegemon in the late 1970s, had a choice among "exits."

Washington, however, saw a massive Soviet buildup that seemed to rule out
a relaxed view of U.S. security requirements. While the U.S. total of ICBMs,
SLBMs, and long-range bombers dropped slightly between 1970 and 1975 (from
2,260 to 2,142, or 5 percent), the Soviet total increased dramatically (from 1,730
to 2,537, or 47 percent). Moscow surpassed the United States in the number of
ICBMs by 1970, the number of SLBMs by 1974, and the total number of strategic
nuclear launchers by 1973.[2] Although these numbers and the size of Soviet
missiles mainly indicated Russia's technological weakness, the buildup appeared
sinister, and when Moscow deployed MIRVs sooner than expected, fears of an
effective Soviet counterforce capability gained currency.

The Soviet conventional buildup, especially its naval deployments, appeared
even more ominous. During the 1970s, the USSR produced about five times as
many tanks, three times as many armored personnel carriers, eight times as many
artillery pieces, and twice as many aircraft of all types as the United States. A
major shipbuilding program, begun in the late 1960s, meant that by 1973 the
Soviet Union exceeded the United States in total number of warships and was
soon able to maintain a sizable presence in the Indian Ocean and carry on
exercises as far away as the Gulf of Mexico. Since the USSR requires neither
open sea lanes for much of its trade nor as extensive a fleet as the United States
for lift or reinforcement, this raised serious questions about its long-term
intentions.[3]

To the extent that Moscow achieved overall military parity—and that judgment
has been controversial, given the quality of Soviet weapons—it represented a
dramatic erosion of America's relative hegemonic capability. U.S. policymakers
during the 1970s were acutely conscious of how that decline was accelerated by
Vietnam. Robert Komer, Undersecretary of Defense for Policy during the Carter
administration, calculated that Vietnam cost almost half a trillion 1985 dollars,
equivalent to at least seven years' worth of defense investment. This, he claims,
was "why the military balance shifted against us to the extent it did."[4] Since
Soviet leaders seem to have decided after Khrushchev's ouster to catch up
whatever the costs, the outcome was probably inevitable. The steady, unrelenting
character of the buildup made it all the more notable.[5] U.S. leaders were concerned during the late 1970s not to concede unilaterally any more ground, especially since they needed to sell a new strategic arms treaty to a skeptical
Senate.

Not surprisingly, then, NATO was strongly emphasized after the mid–1970s
and less demanding security alternatives were political nonstarters. The United
States changed none of its major nuclear objectives despite the adverse changes
in its nuclear position.[6] Instead, credible first-use nuclear options became a major
emphasis, as did improved rapid reinforcement capabilities. When some of the
allies reneged on their commitments to a common rearmament program agreed
to in 1978, Washington effectively continued to cooperate unconditionally.

As before, the superpower nuclear balance was a critical variable, as were Soviet conventional capabilities: Americans were troubled by Soviet "meddling" in the Third World at a time when Congress sharply constrained U.S. involvement. Although the balance of payments ceased to matter much after 1975, even this was not an unmixed blessing, as it removed a source of discipline on fiscal, monetary, and security policies. Under such circumstances—salient external threats and lessened constraints at home—Hypothesis 2 implies that a hegemon should adjust within the terms of existing commitments.

NUCLEAR STRATEGY AND EXTENDED DETERRENCE, 1974–1980

Nuclear parity affected some of the means rather than the ends of American policy. As just noted, the three major purposes of U.S. strategic forces—basic deterrence, extended deterrence of nuclear attacks, and extended deterrence of conventional attacks—were left unchanged. In particular, the Soviet nuclear buildup did not cause policymakers to back away from plans for first use in defense of Western Europe.[7] They decided, unlike McNamara, to adjust explicitly within the terms of existing commitments (Hypothesis 2).

They pursued this through more, and more varied, preplanned SIOP options employing less than the entire strategic arsenal. Although McNamara had introduced options for withholding attacks from certain countries and target categories, he abandoned the pursuit of additional flexibility above the nuclear threshold for reasons discussed earlier. The SIOP was still limited to attacks involving thousands of warheads when he left office.[8] In subsequent years, the growth of Soviet power led U.S. planners to look for ways short of all-out nuclear war to respond to limited nuclear attacks on the United States or an attack on Western Europe. Unlike McNamara and his associates, they feared that mutual AD ("MAD") would not restrain Soviet expansionism and that the perception of shifting power would lead to allied Finlandization. Parity sharpened but did not create these concerns and incentives, since an all-out nuclear war would have been extremely destructive even in the early 1960s.[9]

Nuclear planning was largely unconstrained by Congress, despite its stakes and controversies. It turned out that modernization programs already underway provided most of what was necessary to add more flexibility to the war plans. Despite the extent of America's relative military decline during the 1970s, there was little change in the intellectual underpinning or political purposes of American nuclear deterrence policy (Hypotheses 4 and 5).[10]

Renewed Emphasis on Credible Options

In mid–1972 Nixon commissioned National Security Study Memorandum 169 to review additional nuclear weapons options. That led to National Security Decision Memorandum (NSDM) 242, which authorized Defense Secretary Schlesinger's policy guidance to the target planners. By this time, U.S.–Soviet arms control negotiations had pushed nuclear acquisition and employment policy to the center of official attention, and the future of U.S. strategy was then being closely examined. The Soviet buildup, especially the unexpectedly rapid progress in MIRV technology, kept this review going at an intensive level (Hypothesis 3).[11] NSDM 242 emphasized the need for escalation control—that is, the possibility of limited nuclear use—as well as the targeting of Soviet "recovery resources" rather than urban or industrial targets per se. The changes were reflected in the new SIOP that took effect at the beginning of January 1976.

NSDM 242 and the associated Nuclear Weapons Employment Policy (NUWEP) reemphasized flexibility *above* the nuclear threshold. Under MAD conditions this required, Schlesinger argued, that deterrence be reinforced "across the *entire* spectrum of risk."[12] Deterrence was not seen suddenly as unstable. But as the Defense Secretary explained the rationale for limited nuclear options (LNOs), or what became known as the "Schlesinger Doctrine,"

It is our judgement that this change in targeting doctrine shores up deterrence. A targeting doctrine which stresses going only against cities is not an adequate deterrent for most purposes when the Soviet Union, as is the case today, has a counter-deterrent which is beyond the capability and, I believe the desire of the United States to take away. . . . So what the change in targeting doctrine does is give the President . . . the option of limiting strikes to a few weapons. It is to be understood that if the United States were to strike the Soviet Union in response to some hypothetical act on their part, this would not have to be a massive response. . . . I think this will shore up deterrence in those few areas in which there is weakness.[13]

This was partly a straw man, since the president was hardly limited to counter-city retaliation. Decision makers wanted selective signals that Moscow would understand as something other than an all-out attack. Convincing the Soviet Union that the United States would not be "self-deterred" in situations of limited but serious aggression—for example, limited nuclear attacks or nuclear blackmail of allies—was an explicit motivation for the changes and their public presentation.[14]

Another major purpose was to reaffirm the possibility of first use against conventional aggression. As Schlesinger told a BBC interviewer, U.S. strategic forces remained coupled to Western Europe, and "that is a major reason behind the change in our targeting doctrine last year."[15] LNOs, for instance, were used to support forces in Europe. Whereas escalation from the immediate battlefield to deep attacks within Pact territory had previously been emphasized, additional Poseidon SLBMs were now assigned to selective, intermediate, tactical missions near the front lines (Hypothesis 2).[16]

Such statements and publicly emphasized deployments served at least as much a psychological as a military function. Policymakers understandably worried about self-deterrence and sought options that *they* believed they might implement in a crisis.[17] They might also have projected those fears onto allies. Washington worried less that Moscow would use its new power than that allies might accommodate it for fear that the United States would no longer protect them. If so, it is evident why U.S. officials did not, as was suggested, explain matter-of-factly that they had built forces capable of denying the Soviets any meaningful advantage from nuclear threats or use.[18] If they really feared allied Finlandization or bandwagoning, technical presentations of war outcomes would have been beside the point at a time when Soviet power was growing more visibly than American power.

There was also a coercive bargaining rationale for LNOs. Such strikes are not very militarily useful as such but might, it was thought, credibly demonstrate resolve. By brandishing the threat of uncontrolled escalation, they warn an adversary unmistakably. Schlesinger knew that a war-winning capability was beyond America's reach, given the Soviet buildup. Instead, by calling Moscow's explicit attention to the possibility of further escalation, LNOs could signal that the U.S. was determined not to "lose" in a serious crisis.[19]

This return to a flexible strategy reflected the growth of Soviet power. As long as a state or bloc is significantly stronger than another, it can simply invoke that superiority to make its threats credible, as the United States did before the early 1960s. Parity shifts deterrence strategies toward emphasis on the defender's resolve and the possibility of escalation if the other does not back down. The prospect of uncontrolled escalation underlying LNOs, then, has been one of Washington's principal methods of reaffirming first use in an age of nuclear parity (Hypothesis 2).[20]

For several reasons, NSDM 242 and the NUWEP did not assign a major role to theater nuclear forces in the new targeting options. The executive branch at this point still faced congressional pressures for troop cuts, and Schlesinger found it expedient to offer *reductions* in U.S. theater weapons in return for cuts in Soviet conventional forces. He tried to show Congress that the administration was serious about conventional options and that one was within reach for NATO (Hypothesis 4). (Considering the buildup of theater forces during the early 1960s, some reductions might have been militarily justifiable in any case.) He also found it easier to program LNOs through the strategic systems which Washington controlled unilaterally than to subject theater planning to the lengthy and complex process of inter-allied agreement in the NPG (Hypothesis 5).[21]

The more pronounced coercive tone evident in Schlesinger's explanations of NSDM 242 also characterized the so-called "counter-recovery strategy." Under the guidance associated with this concept, 70 percent of the industrial resources that the Soviets would need to recover after a nuclear war were targeted. This became the highest single priority in the SIOP after 1974.[22]

Neither Jimmy Carter nor most of his advisers entered office in 1977 with these preoccupations. They tended to be skeptical of nuclear FR assumptions and close to the AD position. But by this time, the growth in Soviet forces and a nascent consensus among specialists in favor of flexible nuclear-war-fighting options made it difficult to return to the "McNamara attitudes." For one thing, continuous improvements in Soviet ICBM missile accuracies, reliabilities, and fractionation capabilities were found during this period. In 1977, Moscow tested a significantly improved reentry vehicle for the SS-19 missile. This apparently furnished a rationale for further revision of nuclear doctrine. During Carter's nuclear planning review, evidence of an extensive Soviet program for protecting the leadership during a nuclear war was interpreted as an important indication of the regime's war aims (Hypothesis 3).[22] Carter also felt pressure from hardliners to take the Soviet military threat seriously.

Official thinking thus came to parallel that of the early 1970s to a greater degree than might have been expected. In August 1977, the administration ordered a major policy study, the Nuclear Targeting Policy Review (NTPR). It found that little had been done to translate NSDM 242 into specific war plans.[24] In June 1980 the review resulted in new guidance in the form of Presidential Directive (PD) 59. When presented by Secretary of Defense Harold Brown, it was called the "countervailing strategy."

As the administration saw it, however, the problem was not primarily a military one. No one thought a limited Soviet counterforce attack was likely, certainly not out of the blue. Instead, the countervailing strategy stems from "a combination of conventionalization and fear that the stability-instability paradox could enable the Soviets to expand, especially if they are willng to run significant risks."[25] "Conventionalization," a term coined by Hans Morgenthau, refers to beliefs that nuclear weapons can be treated essentially like conventional ones. Conventionalization is one necessary condition for strategies such as "countervailing" which envisage the possibility of a protracted nuclear war. Another is the belief, shared by Carter's National Security Adviser Zbigniew Brzezinski and Brown as well as Schlesinger and Kissinger, that NATO could be coerced in a crisis if it lacked a wide range of "usable" military options. Some officials held this view earlier than others, or took it further, but all held it to some extent. Even the appearance of weakness could be dangerous, whatever the military situation.[26]

While Brown publicly defended PD 59 as a refinement of the Schlesinger Doctrine, and it did not make major changes in the structure of the SIOP, strategy is more than an enumeration of targets. PD 59, in setting new priorities, went beyond NSDM 242. There was more public emphasis on preparing to fight a prolonged nuclear war if necessary, and on denying the Soviets "victory" at any intermediate rung of the escalation ladder envisaged under FR. Correspondingly less emphasis was placed on the bargaining and signaling aspects of escalation control. Brown thus admitted that PD 59 furnished no clear way to end a nuclear war.[27] New options were prepared for defending Europe, some in heretofore conventional contingencies. FR above the nuclear threshold seems to lower that "firebreak," contradicting other aspects of the general strategy.[28]

The SIOP was changed in three ways as a result of PD 59. One increased the emphasis on "counterleadership targeting" by singling out what Soviet leaders presumably valued most: the Communist and Great Russian instruments of control. Protected civilian and military shelters were emphasized.[29]

Another reemphasized what was now called "countermilitary targeting." The problem was that the rapid growth in Soviet strategic forces and the increased hardness of its ICBMs had eroded relative U.S. counterforce capabilities (the ratio of U.S. warheads to Soviet launchers) significantly during the 1970s, despite the addition of MIRVs to most of the U.S. missile arsenal. Countermilitary targeting thus implied some new "hard target kill" capabilities and better command and control systems. It was intended not for offensive damage limitation, which was seen as impossible, but to enhance deterrence by impeding Soviet war aims (Hypothesis 2).[30]

The third change further refined criteria for identifying valued Soviet assets other than military or leadership targets. An alternative strategy relying more on AD was rejected on the grounds that this might not be a sufficient deterrent. The Carter and Reagan administrations chose instead to concentrate on those resources necessary to sustain war. This obviously strengthened the linkage between U.S. strategic forces and the contingencies under which NATO would fight, and was one of its purposes (Hypothesis 2). It was also more easily done, it turned out, than trying to impede recovery.[31]

Congressional Impact. Since external constraints and perceptions of risk or opportunity indicate only the executive's preferences, its ability to implement them depends on whether it controls the necessary policy instruments. As discussed in Chapter 3, this in turn varies with the issues involved as well as the central state's general institutional capacity vis-à-vis other domestic actors. Extended deterrence is effectively nonrival within NATO; conventional protection is not. This means that conventional strategies are more constrained by force size than nuclear strategies. Congress should thus be able to affect the former more than the latter. Was this true during the 1970s? Did the executive have a fairly free hand in adjusting nuclear employment policies?

Aside from the Senate's participation in approving SALT I and II, Congress twice threatened to complicate the overall nuclear planning process. In neither instance, however, was the impact more than marginal. FR was in both cases flexible enough to accommodate itself to these disruptions.

One initiative sought to rationalize theater nuclear weapons in Europe and the associated doctrine. We saw in earlier chapters that the weapons were deployed largely for purposes of political reassurance and that NATO's "doctrine" for their use was an uneasy compromise between U.S. and continental European perspectives. One of the three NATO-related amendments offered by Senator Sam Nunn in 1974 addressed this problem. It froze the size of the theater stockpile pending Pentagon review of its role in NATO strategy and its relationship to conventional preparedness. As Nunn explained,

The point is that nobody is certain about what would happen [in a nuclear war]. Some reduction of the size and alert status of the tactical nuclear weapons force in Europe, if done very selectively, could still produce an effective deterrent and enhance the conventional capability by providing troops for conversion to [conventional] combat forces . . .

nuclear deterrence of major conventional attacks has been weakened by overall nuclear parity. This places more reliance on effective conventional forces to stop and contain a conventional attack, or to require that the conventional attack be so large and overwhelming as to demand the use of nuclear weapons.[32]

This conformed closely to official FR thinking; Nunn was working with the administration to rationalize the theater nuclear and conventional postures.[33] A year later he successfully opposed Senator Gravel's amendment to reduce the tactical stockpile and impose a no-first-use constraint on it.[34]

Gravel's NFU amendment lacked wide support and, as an infringement of the president's power as commander-in-chief, was probably unconstitutional. Whether reductions in the theater stockpile would have raised the nuclear threshold depended, as always, on which weapons were removed and whether NATO commanders felt they could afford to wait longer before firing them. In short, Gravel's legislative instrument was blunt and rather ineffective (Hypothesis 4).

Another legislative effort reflected fears that a commitment to nuclear FR would justify destabilizing weapons systems. Preferences for "hard target kill" capability had shifted several times between the branches; under McNamara, the Pentagon canceled a warhead specifically designed for that purpose. Then, in the early 1970s, when launchers rather than warheads were limited by SALT I, the Senate refused to authorize funds for a counter-silo-capable MIRV. Work nevertheless continued under another program.[35] A few years later Senator Thomas McIntyre, who particularly objected to counterforce capability for the submarine-based leg of the strategic triad, introduced amendments to cancel research and development funds. He succeeded in committee but lost on the Senate floor.[36] Although the SIOP changes authorized by NSDM 242 did not require silo-busting warheads, the Mark 12A, which had such capability, was funded. By 1974, U.S. strategic forces could hit many of the hardest targets, even if all of the most protected ones could not be struck at an "efficient" ratio.[37]

Schlesinger repeatedly distinguished between different employment policies and specific hardware improvements. Although new systems were requested (e.g., a refined guidance system for the Minuteman III, cleaner warheads to reduce collateral damage, the MX ICBM, and the Trident I and II SLBMs), he knew that even if Congress refused to fund them, ongoing tests and scheduled research and development would improve missile accuracies somewhat.[38] NSDM 242 did not prescribe a strategy that would threaten most of the hardest Soviet targets; it instead sought options for demonstrating resolve and restraint. These less demanding criteria explain why the SIOP could be modified using the nuclear arsenal as it stood during the early 1970s. Schlesinger was unsure what Congress would approve, but proceeded as far as possible within existing capabilities and foreseeable improvements.[39]

Technological momentum was indeed on his side. The American military services have essentially become procurement organizations that buy as much state-of-the art technology as budget ceilings allow. This is especially true of the Navy and Air Force, which "own" virtually all U.S. strategic weapons. Systems are deployed only after lengthy gestation periods.[40] Meanwhile, Congress has usually economized by stretching out production schedules, not by canceling programs. The nuclear arsenal became so diversified in the 1960s and plentiful in the 1970s that it was difficult for Congress to affect strategy through the budget except at the margins. Strategic warheads, for instance, doubled between 1970 and 1976, enhancing the flexibility with which the entire Soviet target base, especially conventional military targets, could be attacked.[41] In contrast, the Army's uncertainty during the early 1970s about how many divisions Congress would leave in Europe made fashioning a strategy suitable for nuclear parity difficult (Hypothesis 5).[42]

Under conditions of nuclear plenty and rapid technological change, then, targeting priorities and escalatory guidelines are only loosely tied to specific hardware characteristics. Surprisingly, this has been true of command, control, communications and intelligence capabilities (C^3I), which might instead be assumed to drive those plans. In March 1974, Schlesinger told Congress that the $33 million requested for the Command Data Buffer System, designed to retarget Minuteman III missiles in under an hour, was the *largest* single expenditure related to NSDM 242. The system was proposed simply as a technical aid; only later was its strategic utility recognized. Desmond Ball contends that it is difficult to identify any C^3 project that "derived from or was affected in any specific way by the policy revisions of the mid- and late–1970s."[43] Correspondingly, because no one expected a nuclear war, strategy was allowed to outrun existing monitoring capabilities. NATO might even rationally *de-emphasize* the C^3 improvements conducive to fighting a limited nuclear war, since they might weaken deterrence by making uncontrolled escalation less likely.[44]

FR is an especially supple doctrine. Various versions emphasize different escalation paths and, as we have seen, somewhat different targeting priorities. A variant can be found for almost any contemporary force configuration. For example, Carter's NTPR revealed that how one would impede Soviet recovery from a nuclear war was not well understood. It did, however, indicate that a major emphasis on counter-recovery targeting would require far more warheads that were in or programmed for the U.S. arsenal. The analyst who directed the review argued that in contrast to *recovery* from a war, SIOP planners "better understood" which industries and logistics provided immediate *support* for a Soviet war effort, and that those ought to be emphasized. Not coincidentally, emphasizing war industries allowed thousands of industrial targets to be dropped from the SIOP.[45] FR assumptions would seem to support either emphasis.

In sum, Congress affected the shift to flexible nuclear war-fighting strategies very little during the 1970s. Congress can of course prevent a major emphasis on countermilitary targeting by refusing to fund the requisite weapons. But it can hardly refuse to approve expenditures for C^3 improvements, however the

Pentagon plans to use them. The executive branch during the 1970s tried to bolster extended deterrence in the face of a significant, adverse power shift, and did so in a stable, long-term planning context (Hypotheses 2 and 5).

The Debate Over Nuclear Strategy During the 1970s

The national dialogue on nuclear strategy Schlesinger called for in announcing the new targeting priorities was already underway, spurred by Senate consideration of the SALT I agreements and the Soviet buildup.[46] Its focus was the requirements for credible extended deterrence. In part, as would be expected in a declining hegemon, "dissenters" questioned the risks of system leadership. But in this case, unlike that of the dollar or troops in Europe, there was major disagreement over the nature of the requirements themselves.

One wing of the nuclear-war-fighting school, exemplified by Colin Gray, embraces what others consider "conventionalization" and has seen Moscow as relentlessly expansionistic. Accordingly, strategic superiority defined as escalation dominance is required for credible extended deterrence: Moscow must believe that the United States would up the ante on behalf of its allies rather than see them overrun. Since MAD raises the prospect that the U.S. would be self-deterred in a crisis, it is incompatible with foreign defense commitments. To maintain them, extensive counter-silo targeting is required, as well as active and passive nuclear defenses. The latter might hold U.S. casualties to 20 million in an all-out war which, according to Gray, "should render U.S. strategic threats more credible."[47]

U.S. policy was less demanding and more realistic. Ballistic missile defense was jettisoned during the 1970s, making American leaders far less willing to contemplate all-out nuclear war than Gray. American leaders repeatedly disavowed interest in a first-strike capability and declared it beyond reach in any case; for all practical purposes, nuclear superiority as Gray defined it could not be regained either. Yet they acknowledged that U.S. commitments *did* require that Moscow be *denied* a capacity for escalation dominance. As one Carter administration official put it,

it would be critical that the Soviet Union continue to believe that there is no intermediate level of escalation at which [tactical nuclear] use could be successful. This is especially important in an Alliance context, where the United States needs a doctrine for its nuclear forces that is consistent with and supportive of proclaimed U.S. willingness to resort to nuclear escalation if conventional defense fails.[48]

This provided the impetus for PD 59.

For McNamara, MAD or parity came to imply the obsolescence of traditional military doctrines above the nuclear threshold. First, he assumed that while weapons could be partially protected, this might neither work nor be cost-effective. People, in any case, could not be protected. Second, even the most limited use of nuclear weapons could lead to all-out war. Third, for these reasons, the nuclear threshold must be fairly high and reinforced in every way possible. Fourth, following from this, nuclear-war-fighting options lower the threshold by treading on the conventionalization fallacy. Deterrence is most stable if policymakers harbor no illusions about surviving *any* nuclear war. Fifth, nuclear force improvements beyond a secure second-strike capability have little value. This has also been called the "stable balancer position"; it is one general response to the loss of nuclear hegemony.[49]

One group of stable balancers has seen extended deterrence as essentially unaffected by hegemonic decline because the *mutuality* of MAD means that any major challenge to the status quo could lead to total war. Whereas full-blown war fighters of Gray's school as well as less extreme advocates of nuclear FR have often been bemused by fears that the Soviets could launch a major non-nuclear challenge and expect the U.S. to be self-deterred from major retaliation, what McGeorge Bundy calls "existential deterrence" and Robert Jervis simply calls AD dismisses this. According to Bundy, "existential" deterrence should be distinguished "from anything based on strategic theories or declared policies or even *international commitments*":

What keeps the peace in Europe, then, is the whole range of consequences that aggression would entail, even if in some initial stage it might "succeed." As long as the Americans cannot be defeated—as long as the deterrence of their survivable forces is strong—there is no attraction in the choice of war.[50]

But he does not believe that the risk of escalation can be entirely ruled out and thus favors NFU. Jervis takes Bundy's argument to its more straightforward conclusion: "the resulting deterrence covers a lot more than attacks on one's homeland."[51]

In Jervis's version, this view implies that adaptation within the terms of existing deterrence commitments is not problematic. Societal vulnerability is the key and immutable characteristic of the nuclear age; American resolve cannot be bolstered by more flexible options or better weapons, since the chief inhibiting factor cannot be removed.[52] But since these constraints induce tremendous caution on both sides, major challenges are fairly easily deterred in a MAD world. Aside from the arguments that a controlled nuclear war cannot be fought and that preparing to do so is destabilizing, stable balancers find the elaborate strategies discussed in this chapter essentially unnecessary.

Another group of stable balancers concludes that extended deterrence is not viable over the long run. It agrees with Gray that MAD is incompatible with extended deterrence, but sees the former as immutable. Self-deterrence is the most rational option in a crisis and the likeliest possibility. George Ball thus calls extended deterrence commitments a "cosmic bluff" because "whether we like it or not, the deterrent value of our weapons will steadily diminish as mounting public concern decreases the likelihood that any president would ever use them unless the Russians used them first.''[53] David Garnham finds flaws in each of the other positions: the invulnerability required for escalation dominance is gone forever; controlled nuclear wars are chimerical; existential deterrence neither precludes total war nor furnishes an acceptable way to deal with it. America must "decouple" from Europe, he argues, for "even a miniscule probability of an infinitely tragic outcome is too large.''[54]

By 1980 the controlled-war fighters had "won" the debate. Only they seemed to have practical answers to Kissinger's earlier question: what would hold NATO together if U.S. strategy lacked credibility? Their approach suffered a glaring ambiguity: the "shot across the bow," or nuclear warning, could lead to a limited nuclear war, which Brown admitted might spin out of control. Yet only the war fighters seemed ready to *do* something about the Soviet buildup, the critical issue during the 1970s.

The stable balancers appeared too relaxed about a Soviet threat that looked very real to Washington at this time, and they too were divided by key assumptions about nuclear weapons. Some, such as Jervis, favored the deterrent value of an ambiguous nuclear threshold. Others, such as Bundy, Ball, and Garnham preferred an unambiguous threshold that would minimize risks of escalation and rationalize a strategy that to them lacked credibility. Since these groups had different ends, the split between them was more profound than differences among the warfighters. But it mattered less, since policy had swung in the other direction.

The Long Range Theater Nuclear Forces Decision

The SALT process had a disquieting effect on some Europeans. Its major import, superpower strategic parity, had to be considered alongside Moscow's buildup in virtually every other military category. From 1971 to 1976, years in which real U.S. military spending fell, Soviet spending increased 4 percent to 5 percent annually.[55] Europeans liked the more relaxed atmosphere and commercial advantages of detente, but some, at least, feared abandonment through a superpower deal. In a highly publicized 1977 speech, German Chancellor Helmut Schmidt said, "strategic arms limitations confined to the United States and the Soviet Union will inevitably impair the security of Western European members of the alliance vis-à-vis Soviet military superiority in Europe parallel to the SALT negotiations.''[56] In effect, Schmidt challenged the Carter administration to revitalize the nuclear guarantee.

A specific concern was the triple-warhead missile code named SS–20 by NATO. It was mobile, had a range of 1,500 miles, and was clearly intended to intimidate Western Europe. By the end of Carter's term one was being deployed each week and all but 23 of the 180 were targeted at Western Europe (Hypothesis 3).[57] Schmidt worried that NATO had no comparable weapon and that the "Eurostrategic balance" was shifting to the Soviets.

The administration initially took the position that a military response was unnecessary. National Security Adviser Zbigniew Brzezinski observed that there never had been a Eurostrategic nuclear balance.[58] He might also have noted that such a notion was hardly in Europe's interest, since it implied the possibility of a prolonged theater war; why else would the local nuclear matchup matter? Secretary of State Cyrus Vance assured the allies that existing plans to modernize NATO's theater arsenal would continue. Although, at Moscow's insistence, a protocol to the SALT II Treaty constrained cruise missile deployments through 1981, Vance promised that the U.S. would reject any so-called "nontransfer" provision that would impede NATO's future plans.[59]

But this did not suffice after the neutron bomb episode. The enhanced radiation weapon, as it was technically designated, was designed to minimize blast effect and long-term radiation, instead releasing neutrons at ground zero with relatively little collateral damage. Unlike "dirty" tactical nuclear weapons, using this one against massed Warsaw Pact armored formations appeared eminently credible (Hypothesis 2). Carter's advisers expected him to approve deployment. He refused, although not because the neutron bomb could have eroded the nuclear threshold.[60] Perhaps he half believed the Soviet propaganda characterizing it as a "capitalist weapon" designed to destroy lives rather than property. Bonn was angered at the seeming policy reversal.

The Long Range Theater Nuclear Forces (LRTNF) Decision, taken by NATO in December 1979, was in part a response to this diplomatic fiasco. A special unit working under the auspices of the NPG, the High Level Group, had been formed two years earlier to formulate a response to the Soviet nuclear buildup. The solution was to replace 108 U.S. Pershing 1-A missiles in Germany with Pershing IIs and to deploy 464 ground-launched cruise missiles in Britain, Germany, Italy, the Netherlands, and Belgium. NATO would try to negotiate the SS–20s away, obviating the deployment, but few were optimistic that this could be done.

With good reason, few took seriously the military rationale for the so-called "dual-track decision." The administration had not suddenly decided that Europe needed new land-based nuclear systems. Instead, it was felt that after the imbroglio about the neutron bomb, Washington needed to demonstrate its competence to manage nuclear affairs and lead the alliance. The dual-track solution seemed a decisive yet prudent response. Some officials feared a gradual process of Finlandization if the Soviet deployment went unanswered; as one put it, "we could not let the Europeans depend on Moscow for their security." New theater-based systems would also end talk about SALT constraints in areas of interest to NATO, removing one argument against the Treaty.[61]

These reassurances, however, had a military price. Politically effective nuclear "coupling," the object of the deployment, required missiles based on European territory, since this would involve them in any attack. Because they could hit Soviet territory, the Pershings might either be attacked early or fired preemptively in a crisis; either way, the threshold to a major nuclear war would be lowered and U.S. control reduced. This was acknowledged, even though it contradicted the logic of FR.[62]

Ironically, the military rationale for the LRTNF was closer to AD, which "stresses the importance of commitment, relies on irrationality, and denies the need to match a wide variety of Soviet provocations with an equal range of Western options." It almost *had* to be incoherent, since the missiles were provided only to soothe allied insecurities.[63] The U.S. nuclear commitment has played several potentially incompatible roles in NATO: deterrence, defense, and political reassurance. Solutions to one problem can thus exacerbate others: greater risks if deterrence failed were accepted to avoid political risks.

THE CONVENTIONAL COMMITMENT, 1974–1980

All else equal, hegemonic decline should narrow the options available to the foreign policy executive. This was only partly true with respect to the conventional commitment between 1974 and 1980, reminding us that specific situational constraints and opportunities can create conditions differing significantly from the baseline prediction.

First, as we saw in Chapter 5, Nixon's decisions of August 1971, together with the oil embargo and price increases, set in motion events that led to general exchange rate floating among the currencies of the major reserve centers. Although American policymakers had actively resisted this development, its benefits became obvious. Along with greater general policy flexibility, the government no longer had to concern itself with an official settlements balance, and the rationale for European payments offsets disappeared. At least temporarily, the costs of U.S. forces in Europe ceased to be a domestic political issue, and an irritant in U.S.-German relations was removed.

A second constraint, congressional pressures for troop cuts, also eased after 1974. Legislative concerns about burden-sharing became manifested in initiatives for more effective, streamlined forces. But the executive shared these priorities: Senator Nunn's attempts to rationalize NATO's conventional and nuclear postures were seen as constructive. Schlesinger vigorously emphasized stronger conventional forces in view of the Soviet nuclear buildup, and the Carter administration was later characterized (by a participant) as the most coalition-minded since Truman's.[64] The new congressional mood even allowed the Carter Pentagon to implement much of the most comprehensive program to strengthen NATO since the 1950s.

On the other hand, growing Soviet power narrowed the politically acceptable choices. Moscow, it was thought, could not be allowed geopolitical advantages from its improved position. For example, despite plans to reorient defense strategy toward Europe, attention shifted at the end of the decade to Soviet intentions in the Persian Gulf. This was Europe's oil lifeline; the problem of growing Soviet interest and presence in the region became NATO's, although it was an out-of-area issue under the NAT. A new U.S. commitment to protect the Gulf exacerbated the rivalness of conventional forces and raised congressional ire about burden sharing.

According to hegemonic stability theory, declining hegemons will try to redistribute burdens under these conditions.[65] This, however, did not occur. The Carter administration cooperated unconditionally with the allies, again highlighting the importance of beliefs about fragile European resolve.

The End of Offset

There was significant uncertainty about the future shape of the international monetary system between 1971 and 1974. During 1972, the Treasury Department regarded the Smithsonian exchange-rate realignments (an average dollar depreciation of about 8 percent against all OECD countries) as inadequate; Secretary George Shultz believed that at least another depreciation was necessary to accommodate long-term structural changes in the world economy.[66] As explained in chapter 5, the administration by now favored a system of floating exchange rates. It was this change that removed the financial constraint on foreign troop levels.

The proximate cause of the floating-rate regime was a set of European decisions in March 1973 to float currencies against the dollar. To be sure, it was the overvalued dollar rather than fixed rates as such that really hurt the United States.[67] But it was the difficulty in adjusting obsolescent parities that finally made the previous system intolerable. One official described the implications of this new-found autonomy:

Pursue fiscal and monetary policies which will lead to sustainable economic expansion with reasonable stability of prices, and accept the balance-of-payments results . . . under this policy, we will not attempt to keep the exchange rate at any particular figure or within any particular zone or range.[68]

He might have added that almost any fiscally acceptable level of overseas military spending could also now be accommodated.

Offset thereby died an abrupt death in mid-decade. This development, like the payments problem more generally, was only somewhat a product of the U.S. world position. Instead, "the deficit was the result of large official transfers that could not be offset by private commercial or capital flows given the exchange rates that had been encouraged by the United States [in the late 1940s]."[69] More precisely, balance-of-payments offset was an indirect effect of hegemonic decline. Domestic actors *did* increasingly question the asymmetric costs of coalition leadership after the mid–1960s; foreign-exchange costs incurred through policies that benefited others were seen this way, even though they benefited the hegemon as well. Offset thereby became thoroughly politicized, hardly what Gilpatric expected in 1961.

These problems dissipated with the monetary changes of 1971 through 1973. Most obviously, growing dollar balances abroad were no longer destabilizing. The combined effects of devaluation and petrodollar capital flows into the United States put the balance of payments in the black; the balance on current account showed marked improvement from 1973 to 1976 as compared with 1971 and 1972.[70] This gave Bonn its most politically persuasive argument for ending the process.[71] The military payments problem also lost overall economic salience: by the mid–1970s, the $1 billion in foreign-exchange costs attributable to troops stationed in Europe seemed small compared to hugh inflows of oil money. Most important, under flexible exchange rates the government needed to defend the dollar only under circumstances that threatened normal market transactions. This made an official reserve assets or settlement balance much less meaningful, politically as well as economically.[72]

These implications were not immediately evident. The Jackson-Nunn Amendment, requiring the withdrawal of troops whose exchange costs were not compensated, was passed in the fall of 1973. Edward Fried, who had worked on the problem while an NSC staffer, said several months earlier,

To the extent that military foreign exchange outlays are not offset by cost-sharing and military procurement, the international adjustment mechanism will have to do the work. This, too, is not a question of burden-sharing, but of improving the degree to which the monetary system facilitates international activities that nations wish to carry on.[73]

These conditions were just then taking hold. Fried told the Pentagon Comptroller's office that payments adjustment would now take care of itself. Preoccupation with it had become so ingrained in official Washington that the problem virtually disappeared without most Americans realizing it.[74]

Bonn also became more assertive about the issue. The Germans, especially Helmut Schmidt, had long resented offset; Schmidt's background as Finance Minister and Defense Minister made his arguments especially credible. Not only did he now have the economic logic on his side, but the reduced domestic pressure for U.S. troop cuts, discussed later, made further U.S. demands untenable. In mid–1975, he refused to make another offset agreement, offering instead to pay most of the costs to move a U.S. combat brigade to the northern part of the country. Washington accepted this as the best it could do under the circumstances.[75]

Ironically, the demise of Bretton Woods indirectly accelerated the decline of American resources and global influence. The high dollar that allowed Washington to finance huge budget deficits during the 1980s put added strain on U.S. exports, especially those from older industrial sectors. "Deindustrialization" proceeded faster than it might have otherwise. And the new floating rate system worried Europeans, who feared the effects of fluctuating parities on their trade. Their response, the European Monetary System (EMS), has in practice been a Deutschmark zone, in which Bonn's customary monetary stability has become the continental norm.[76] Under the impetus of the Single European Act, the EMS promises to be the nucleus of a financially cohesive Europe and a pillar of a more pluralistic world economy.

Rebuilding Conventional Forces in Europe

Although each administration during the 1970s emphasized the rebuilding of NATO's conventional capabilities, a supportive congressional consensus developed only slowly. Mike Mansfield nearly passed his amendment in 1973. Even a few years later, when troop cuts were no longer debated, Congress remained skeptical about resource allocation. When Schlesinger tried to convert thirteen support-heavy Army divisions into sixteen leaner ones that would be better equipped for the likeliest conflicts, he was accused on Capitol Hill of "backing into" the change to avoid detailed legislative oversight. The charge was probably correct.

The domestic politics of defense thus were more complex than during the Kennedy buildup. Congress was more hawkish than in the early 1970s, but also more attentive to the way defense dollars were spent. After Vietnam and Watergate, legislators and their staffs were more inclined to trust their own judgment rather than uncritically accept the executive's. Their increased institutional capacity to play this role was a significant development during this period. A Congressional Budget Office was established; the resources and responsibilities of the Congressional Research Service, Office of Technology Assessment, and General Accounting Office were increased. By the late 1970s, members of the House and Senate had, respectively, 750 and 350 policy-oriented assistants; this amounted to a seven- and four-fold increase over a decade earlier.[77] Congress thus could be a more effective partner or a more troublesome adversary for the executive. These opportunities and constraints helped shape the conventional commitment for the balance of the decade.

The New Congressional Mood. Several factors coalesced between late 1973 and mid-decade to end legislative pressure for troop cuts in Europe. The improved U.S. financial position, growing disenchantment with détente and worries about Soviet behavior, a belief that intra-alliance conflict had gone far enough, and the fall of South Vietnam all contributed. The last was pivotal; even Mansfield's strongest supporters hesitated to signal further retreat after the dénouement in Vietnam.[78]

More effective opposition to cuts in the Senate also played a role. Nunn became a recognized specialist on defense issues; he was hawkish, yet skeptical enough of the Pentagon's institutional priorities to be respected by virtually all his colleagues. He gradually (albeit temporarily) changed the terms of the debate from comparative burden sharing to efficiencies in the use of available resources. He offered a cogent rationale for adequate conventional forces in Europe: the importance of a reasonably high nuclear threshold in an era of nuclear parity.

Nunn shepherded three NATO-related measures to passage. One, an amendment to a FY 1976 Pentagon appropriations bill, required U.S. equipment to be "interoperable" with that of other NATO members. It had been estimated that the alliance wasted billions of dollars annually on disparate fuel, ammunition, and spare parts components. A second, discussed earlier in this chapter, tried to rationalize U.S. tactical nuclear doctrine. The third, an amendment to a procurement authorization bill, required a cut of 18,000 support personnel in Europe, although these could be replaced by an equivalent number of combat troops. It was worked out indirectly with the Pentagon or, at least, had Schlesinger's full support.[79]

These efforts bore significant fruit. Two years later, a Senate report issued after one of Nunn's trips to Europe helped build a consensus for the Carter administration's comprehensive force improvement initiatives (Hypothesis 5).[80]

The Changing Military Balance and Force Improvements. Had the congressional mood remained unchanged, Washington could not have responded coherently to the growth of Soviet military power during the 1970s. In addition to dramatic gains in the nuclear balance, Moscow challenged long-established U.S. advantages in force-projection capabilities and sea power. Brown warned that this "[has] created a substantial shift in military strength that has already had profound political consequences." Schlesinger worried about "the cohesion of our alliances should we allow the Soviets to substantially exceed us."[81]

The Soviet buildup posed two military problems. One was familiar: Soviet military doctrine stressed surprise and a short, intense war, for which NATO was judged ill equipped. The imbalance in conventional combat power at the root of this problem simply got worse during Vietnam. While the two alliances spent comparably on conventional forces, the Warsaw Pact devoted less to personnel and was able to insist on highly standardized forces. NATO, in short, might fight only as reliably as its weakest or least integrated link. Nunn "insisted that the Europeans be told that improvements in U.S. forces 'are of little value without significant improvement in allied forces,' " and this became the basis for Carter's Long Term Defense Program.[82]

The growth in Soviet naval power presented the second problem. Aside from its main purpose—deterring attack—NATO has had two major military requirements: retaining usable military options in Europe even during a large-scale war, and guaranteeing the lines of communication between Europe and North America. After the invasion of Czechoslovakia, the Soviet buildup in Europe far outstripped NATO's efforts, making Europe even more reliant on the United States for rapid reinforcement early in a war. But just as this became evident, Moscow's naval buildup meant that NATO had lost the "undisputed naval mastery essential to reliable communication between America and Europe."[83] A security hegemon, as discussed in Chapter 2, needs global reach to perform its commitments. The Europeans drew the obvious conclusions, even if they were not Finlandized. Germany linked Soviet exercises off the Scottish coast to NATO's reduced capability to control the North Atlantic; others found NATO's strength in the eastern Mediterranean noticeably weak.[84]

Several improvements in ground forces were made after 1973 and were justified in the Pentagon's 1977 report: "The added weight in men, armor, and guns that the Soviets have been providing to a potential assault force in Central Europe is a fundamental reason why the active Army is being expanded from 13 to 16 divisions (within a constant level of manpower). We are adding two combat brigades to the European deployments (also within the manpower constraints established by Congress)."[85] This passage also indicates how European requirements drive the size of conventional forces, particularly land forces, and how Congress continued to constrain, albeit much less so than before, adjustments the executive considered necessary (Hypotheses 4 and 5).

Schlesinger's policies were underpinned by a strong programmatic coherence that continued through the decade. A central assumption was that conventional readiness was paramount in a situation of nuclear stalemate. He wished to streamline the force structure so that a short, intense war could be fought in Europe without necessarily crossing the nuclear threshold. This complemented the emphasis on LNOs above the threshold: if one's initial nuclear salvo was essentially a warning, it made sense not to be driven to it unnecessarily early. Schlesinger redirected the Pentagon toward leaner forces and regarded these programs as his major achievement (Hypothesis 2).[86]

He also realized that a renewed emphasis on conventional deterrence in Europe required corresponding changes in presentation. He had learned from McNamara's experience that nonnuclear options could be sold to the allies, if at all, only as a supplement to nuclear deterrence, not as a substitute.[87]

Carter deepened the NATO conventional initiatives taken by his two immediate predecessors; as in other areas, there were greater differences of style than substance.[88] The Pentagon announced that NATO programs would have first claim on resources; Brown told a Senate subcommittee that he aimed to "increase our defense budget in real terms, particularly that part devoted to conventional capability in Europe."[89] He also sent a strong bureaucratic signal that NATO requirements were to be given priority at every stage in the force-planning process. He named Robert Komer, a highly visible personality and RAND NATO specialist, to oversee alliance affairs, and gave him direct access to the Secretary's office.[90]

Longstanding problems were addressed. Nunn's report, essentially accepted by the administration, laid the basis for consensus on priorities. Three areas were stressed. One was "interoperability," which implied a "two-way street" in defense procurement; the days when Washington could simply sell arms to Europe without reciprocation were over. The Army decided in 1978 to use a German 120 mm gun on its new KM–1 tank, and 348 F–16 fighters were produced in Europe, drawing on 4,000 European and American suppliers and contractors.[91]

The other concerns were readiness, on the one hand, and reinforcement and sustainability, on the other. They were addressed, along with interoperability, as part of the Long Term Defense Program. Ten inter-alliance groups of specialists worked on the problems that Komer and Nunn identified. In this regard the United States was again acting as a benevolent hegemon, setting NATO's agenda, mobilizing its members and, importantly, willingly making the same sacrifices.[92] Komer suggested some redistribution of burdens but emphasized using resources already committed to the alliance most efficiently.[93]

During 1977, for example, the Carter administration sent 8,000 additional men and more equipment to Europe, continuing the proceess of replacing the specialists withdrawn for Vietnam. But since funds for conventional forces remained limited, this decreased the readiness of units based in the United States (Hypotheses 1 and 4).[94] Policymakers also saw anti-tank missiles as an equalizer against numerically superior Warsaw Pact tank forces (Hypothesis 2). As the Betts quotation in chapter 3 suggests, this was a reasonable response to constraints on force size. But it failed to account for Soviet countermeasures, and the Pact's offensive capabilities continued to concern many observers.[95]

In May of that year, Washington also secured allied agreement to 3 percent real annual increases in military spending. While not legally binding, it was the most specific pledge of its kind ever made within NATO. In light of the domestic and international politics of defense burden sharing, it served several American purposes. Since the administration was committed to NATO improvements in any case, a multilateral pledge got more for the money. Also, since Carter was at most ambivalent about overall defense increases (as opposed to those for NATO programs), a NATO-wide pledge was an effective lever for the administration within the military planning and procurement bureaucracies. A broader rationale was a recognition that meaningful improvements would have to be made collectively. Congress, if not the executive, would demand reciprocal efforts (Hypothesis 4).[96]

This prediction was correct: NATO's rearmament process was soon colored by congressional concerns about relative effort. In discussing further possible American reinforcement of NATO's central front, Nunn said, "without having our allies do their part, and unless we are sure they are, I think we would be creating disincentives."[97] Brown agreed in principle, but tried to finesse the issue by talking about common alliance objectives.[98] Such remarks were not mere window dressing to placate Congress. The administration *did* want more from the allies, precisely because it could not do what it wanted alone. But, as discussed later, it was willing if necessary to carry out its promises unconditionally.[99] This created rancor between the two branches during 1979 and 1980.

The Implications of Conventional Rivalness

By 1978 the Carter administration's determination to strengthen NATO's military posture was clear, although the rivalness and collective provision of the alliance's conventional forces caused problems. Preparing forces for Europe— for example, by "heavying up" divisions for tank and artillery warfare—made them less suited for other uses. Moreover, new commitments in the Persian Gulf stretched capabilities to the bone. In short, the marginal cost of extending conventional protection was considerable.

Other constraints were also evident. Funds to protect Europe and the Gulf were hostage to congressional perceptions that the allies were free riders; what the executive could do in either region might be limited by European efforts. At the same time, the growth in Soviet power had given Moscow what it heretofore lacked, truly global reach. Europe and the Gulf looked more vulnerable than several years earlier. Consequently, by 1980, a considerable gap separated U.S. commitments from usable capabilities.

Implications of the Southwest Asian Crisis. Even after the United States left Vietnam and adopted a one-and-one-half war criterion, it remained overstretched. In 1975 it was authoritatively claimed that the United States could not guarantee both the Gulf and the Mediterranean. NATO's Atlantic Commander (SACLANT) maintained repeatedly that he lacked the forces to meet his commitments.[100] These observations preceded the Carter Doctrine; in fact, by 1978, analysts within and outside the government debated whether the concentration on Europe would come at the expense of responses to other threats (Hypothesis 1).[101]

Southwest Asia emerged as a principal concern less than two years later. The Soviet invasion of Afghanistan was one factor; whatever it indicated about long-term Soviet expansionist intentions, it put the USSR closer to a position from which it could threaten the West's major oil supplies. The other, Iran's capture of American diplomats, was more important symbolically. But the two together exemplified American decline to friends, foes, and the U.S. public.

Under these circumstances, the Carter Doctrine severely strained U.S. capabilities: "Circumstances could arise in which U.S. resources, both men and transport, that would have gone to Europe would now go to south-west Asia. Simultaneous crises in Europe and south-west Asia would produce a shortfall in American capabilities."[102] Force size increased only slightly between 1977 and 1981; most additional defense outlays were consumed by inflation and qualitative improvements.[103] The Gulf commitment thus had to be met temporarily with existing forces. The rapid deployment strategy on which it was based, which Komer called a "one and two-half war force sizing scenario," would eventually require at least five new land and amphibious divisions and seven new air wings.[104] In the meantime, the new responsibilities were accommodated in two ways.

First, longstanding plans to shift forces from Asia and the Pacific to Europe during wartime were changed. This "swing strategy" originated during the Korean War when a Soviet attack on Europe was feared while Washington was distracted. It was reaffirmed in the late 1960s when the allies expressed concern that Vietnam might distract the United States from NATO. The issue had to be publicly addressed when the strategy, which had been known within NATO but not to Asian allies, was leaked to the press. Washington changed plans in early 1980 because the U.S. would rely, at least temporarily, on forces in the Pacific to respond in the Gulf; plans to spread these forces even further looked increasingly imprudent. Abandoning the swing strategy meant that some forces committed to SACEUR in wartime were shifted to a lower level of availability, to be used in Southwest Asia. This removed some pressure from the services, especially the Navy, although planners contended that in the long run, U.S. commitments could only be met by significantly expanding forces or getting the allies to do more.[105] Cutting commitments was not mentioned (Hypothesis 1).

The second adjustment was one of degree rather than kind: Washington pressed publicly for better burden sharing and complained loudly about the results. To be sure, the allies could do little directly in Southwest Asia. Only the British and French could provide continuing naval assistance; London had given help at the height of the Afghanistan crisis, but France was unwilling to do so. Vance talked about "free riding," and the atmosphere became rancorous.[106]

The rest of NATO could, however, have done more in Europe to compensate for a greater U.S. role in the Gulf. Among the possibilities mentioned were programs for calling up reserves to replace U.S. forces sent to the Middle East, weapons stocks sufficient for a thirty-day conventional war in Europe, and air and naval transport to replace what the United States might need elsewhere. The response was disappointing, prompting one U.S. official to complain that "if the Europeans can't strengthen themselves in Europe while we carry the can for them in the Persian Gulf, then I'm really worried about the future of the alliance."[107]

Despite this, Washington never indicated that it would stop cooperating as a result, either in Europe or elsewhere. Allied performance on the 3 percent pledge also fell short; of the fifteen NATO members, five met the target in fiscal 1979, six in 1980, and nine in 1981.[108] There were, as always, plausible explanations. Because it was superimposed on the normal force-planning cycles, governments were often unwilling or unable to meet the commitment unless they could do so within those plans. Additional efforts led to cuts in other areas, which was disappointing when the objective was to do better across the board. France, for instance, reduced its presence in Germany as the costs of nuclear and conventional modernization programs increased. And virtually everywhere except in the United States, the guns-butter trade-off favored butter.[109] This was hardly the response the administration wanted.

A Game Theoretic Interpretation. It was, nonetheless, predictable. Some simple game theoretic models indicate why. Providing NATO's conventional deterrent presents a collective action problem, since alliance members vary widely in "size" and capability. Unlike nuclear deterrence, there is no dominant provider and thus no "privileged group." Free riding is a rational strategy for most members.[110]

This situation can be modeled by a Prisoners' Dilemma game. In its single-play version, each player's dominant strategy—the one yielding the best payoff regardless of the other's—is defection. Yet this is true only if it is played once or a few times, an assumption inapplicable to many situations in international relations. In the international economy, for instance, negotiations on international monetary arrangements, trade, and energy take place continuously and are expected to continue indefinitely into the future . . . bargaining among the advanced industrial countries involves a small number of governments intensely interacting with one another and carefully monitoring each other's behavior.[111]

This description also fits NATO. Its members meet semi-annually (and in smaller groups more frequently), discuss numerous interrelated topics, and coordinate force contributions, exercises, and objectives. They might thereby surmount the collective action problem through continuous, close surveillance.

Under conditions prevailing during the period of this case study, however, this was unlikely, since Europe and the United States seem to have had fundamentally different burden-sharing preferences. For the United States, "cooperation" during this period entailed significant new Persian Gulf responsibilities without significant reductions in theater European forces or commitments; "defection" would be cutbacks in either. For the Europeans, as they pledged, "cooperation" implied consistent increases in military spending of about 3 percent; "defection" was noticeably less. The preference ordering of central decisionmakers, although not the Congress, seemed to be CC, CD, DC, DD (U.S. values first)—a strategy of unconditional cooperation.

In short, America and Europe were pursuing very different strategies: Europeans were acting as if burden sharing was a mixed-motive game, America as if it were one of pure coordination. Europe's preferences (aggregating all non-U.S. members to simplify) was either (a) DC, DD, CC, CD, or (b) DC, CC, DD, CD (Europe's values first). The ordinal matrices, with 4 being a player's highest payoff and 1 its lowest, are

		(a) Europe		(b) Europe	
		C	D	C	D
United States	C	4,2	3,4	4,3	3,4
	D	2,1	1,3	2,1	1,2

Since both players have dominant strategies in both games, the Nash equilibrium outcome is CD in either matrix (U.S. values first). But from America's perspective, the two are potentially quite different. In matrix (a) Europe's second choice, after playing the United States for a "sucker," is mutual defection; in (b) it is mutual cooperation. In (a) Europe is playing an asymmetric version of the game Snyder and Diesing call "Deadlock," although, since America continues to cooperate, this is not the outcome.[112] Since Europe here prefers defection unconditionally, the United States will not do better until it evaluates outcomes differently. For example, it could have done so by directly linking NATO outcomes to those of another game, such as international monetary coordination, in which Europe had more incentive to cooperate.

Alternatively, since Europe's second choice in (b) is mutual cooperation, the United States might have moved it to the upper left cell by cooperating initially in burden sharing talks and threatening immediate D if Europe defected. America's prior behavior would have made the threat hard to believe. But, as Schelling observes, a player can increase its bargaining leverage by visibly and credibly limiting its options.[113] In this case, the president could name an influential senator, such as Mansfield, Symington, or Nunn, as his "Special Representative for Alliance Burden Sharing." The individual would retain his or her seat in Congress, but could attend, as a member of the U.S. delegation, any meeting of the North Atlantic Council or the NATO foreign or defense ministers. More important, he or she would chair the U.S. delegation at the annual force-planning sessions, be entitled to participate in the associated interagency planning, and be given suitable staff. This would signal that an outsider had been brought into the central policymaking circle to move preferences unmistakably away from unconditional cooperation. If this were accomplished, a revised payoff matrix would be:

		Europe	
		C	D
United States	C	4,3	2,4
	D	1,1	3,2

If communicated effectively, this could shift the allies' payoffs as well, by reducing their gains from defection.[114] DC would no longer be a viable first choice, since it would immediately be followed by DD or even CD (allied values first).

Renewed Congressional Sensitivities and Constraints. By 1980, unconditional cooperation was again threatened by Congress. Half a decade earlier Williams predicted that Mansfieldesque sentiment in Congress could return.[115] It was stimulated partly by Europe's desire to maintain the bridges to Moscow built earlier in the decade. Many congressional representatives were angered when, in 1980, Europe refused to join in anti-Soviet sanctions. Statements by French and German leaders that détente was divisible did not help. Resentment was not confined to Capitol Hill: one executive branch official remarked that Bonn's preferred division of labor was "we do the fighting and they do the trading."[116] But Congress, unlike the White House or Pentagon, took action. In 1982 a move to withdraw 19,000 troops was defeated, but resentment and the desire to impose conditions on continued support were growing.

More lasting effect came from an amendment to the FY 1981 Defense Authorization Act that directed the executive branch to compare "the fair and equitable shares of the mutual defense burden(s) that should be borne by . . . member nations of [NATO] and . . . Japan," and to enumerate "efforts by the United States . . . to eliminate existing disparities." The 3 percent pledge had backfired; many of the allies were at best performing inconsistently. The administration claimed that defense budgets were higher than they would have been without it, even if some countries were falling short. This missed the point and looked like an excuse for free riding. Congress's basic ambivalence about the alliance—valuing it as an instrument of containment, yet resenting allies who defined priorities differently—was evermore evident, and the troop commitment was now a target of the hard-line right as well as the (diminished) dovish left. In part, the Carter administration's pressures on Europe were a response to these ominous rumblings from the Hill (Hypothesis 4).[117]

CONCLUSIONS

Managing hegemonic decline was the major preoccupation of the Nixon, Ford, and Carter administrations. As would be expected in a situation of salient external threats and loosened domestic constraints, each adjusted overwhelmingly within the terms of existing commitments, especially on the nuclear side. If this case is at all representative, declining hegemons have a great deal of adaptive slack. It illustrates clearly that systemic theories account much better for constraints than responses, especially for great powers.

The probabilistic adaptive framework used in this book, however, explains some policy patterns during the late 1970s. After the payments problem dissipated, the military balance of power was the major international constraint. Hypothesis 3, for instance, puts Washington's preoccupation with Soviet MIRV development, long-range theater missiles, and nuclear warfighting plans in context. These phenomena, in essence, signified critical variables because they seemed to indicate Moscow's long-term intentions. Virtually no responsible official thought it would use its growing military power physically. But it might be more resolute in a crisis, and the buildup at the very least suggested a willingness to exploit military power peacefully.

This produced a major effort to revive first use through credible nuclear-warfighting options. The prospect of uncontrolled escalation that makes LNOs a meaningful adaptive response was the principal method of reaffirming extended deterrence in a situation of nuclear statemate. "Shots across the bow" evermore refined countermilitary targeting, and the neutron bomb were the specific solutions. These targeting changes were specifically intended to reaffirm the possibility of first use against conventional aggression, a course of action from which the McNamara Pentagon had progressively backed away. Unfortunately, a high likelihood of uncontrolled escalation meant disaster if the other side *failed* to back down. Ultimately, in an effort to save first use, policymakers embraced weapons and targeting policies that contradicted FR. They willingly accepted significant policy risks of escalation to avoid what were seen as more dangerous political risks.

The executive branch was relatively unconstrained in making these changes. While the countervailing strategy called for some "silo-busting" weapons, most of the requisites involved better command and control capabilities—areas Congress could hardly refuse to fund. Moreover, LNOs could be programmed through the strategic systems Washington controlled, obviating Washington's need to work through the collegial but cumbersome NATO machinery.

Unlike the nuclear umbrella, the conventional commitment was affected by the vicissitudes of congressional opinion. The waning of "Mansfieldism" allowed Schlesinger to begin rebuilding forces in Europe, and Nunn's leadership in the Senate was used to help shape and build a consensus for Carter's Long Term Defense Program. Once again, European requirements drove the size of conventional forces, particularly land units. But despite continued force improvements and reduced responsibilities in Southeast Asia, Washington remained overcommitted. The minimum-risk force posture Kaufmann may indeed have been unrealistic, but the United States was arguably stretched thin *after* Vietnam and *before* the Carter Doctrine. Under these conditions, which may be part and parcel of the role U.S. leaders were determined to preserve, Congress took a harder line on burden sharing than the executive branch and tried to limit the latter's ability to cooperate unconditionally with the allies.

That incentive, as much of the last three chapters show, is readily explained within this book's analytic framework. As suggested by systemic and cognitive theories, U.S. officials were notably risk-averse during these years. Kissinger, Schlesinger, and Brown all worried publicly and repeatedly about "allied cohesion" in the face of Moscow's military buildup. These fears were major reasons for NSDM 242, PD 59, and the LRTNF deployment. They contradict standard balance-of-power theory in the most obvious way. Why should NATO have been anything but resolute when the adversary was getting stronger? To be sure, the allies, especially Bonn, had a vested interest in détente and made comments indicating a different view of the threat than Washington. But they also sounded the alarm about Soviet theater nuclear weapons and ultimately agreed to deploy American ones in response. It is hard to avoid the conclusion that Finlandization fears and, by extension, preference for the familiar, sharply defined bipolar world account for much of the continuity in U.S. policy.

NOTES

1. Warner R. Schilling, "U.S. Strategic Nuclear Concepts in the 1970s: The Search for Sufficiently Equivalent Countervailing Parity," *International Security* 6, no. 2 (Fall 1981): 48–58.

2. International Institute for Strategic Studies, *The Military Balance 1975–1976* (Boulder, Colo.: Westview, 1975), p. 73; Schilling, "U.S. Strategic Nuclear Concepts in the 1970s," p. 49.

3. Smoke, *National Security and the Nuclear Dilemma*, pp. 186–189.

4. Robert W. Komer, "What 'Decade of Neglect'?" *International Security* 10, no. 2 (Fall 1985): 71–72.

5. In Ibid., p. 72, note 4, Komer concedes that the loss of U.S. strategic nuclear superiority was only partly due to the military demands of Vietnam. See also Smoke, *National Security and the Nuclear Dilemma*, p. 188.

6. Schilling, "U.S. Strategic Nuclear Concepts in the 1970s," p. 58.

7. Schilling, "U.S. Strategic Nuclear Concepts in the 1970s," p. 62.

8. David Alan Rosenberg, "Reality and Responsibility: Power and Process in the Making of United States Nuclear Strategy, 1945–1968," *Journal of Strategic Studies* 9 (March 1986): p. 48.

9. Schilling, "U.S. Strategic Nuclear Concepts in the 1970s," p. 62.

10. As Schilling put it, "one could have gone to sleep during the strategic nuclear debate in 1970, awakened in 1980, and rejoined that debate with remarkably little sense of intellectual loss or confusion." See "U.S. Strategic Nuclear Concepts in the 1970s," p. 59.

11. Cordesman, "American Strategic Forces and Extended Deterrence," p. 472.

12. U.S. Department of Defense, *Report of Secretary of Defense James R. Schlesinger to the Congress on the FY 1975 Budget and the Fiscal Year 1975–1979 Defense Program* (Washington, D.C.: U.S. Government Printing Office, 1974) p. 5 (emphasis added).

13. U.S. Congress, Senate, Committee on Foreign Relations, Subcommittee on Arms Control, International Law, and Organization, *U.S.-U.S.S.R. Strategic Policies*, 93rd Cong., 2nd sess., March 4, 1974, p. 9.

14. *New York Times*, January 22, 1974; personal correspondence with a former Defense Department official.

15. Cited in Lynn Etheridge Davis, *Limited Nuclear Options: Deterrence and the New American Doctrine* (London: International Institute for Strategic Studies, 1976), p. 6, note 18; for another Schlesinger statement, see *New York Times*, July 2, 1975.

16. Davis, *Limited Nuclear Options*, p. 7; *New York Times*, June 18, 1975.

17. Thomas Powers, "Choosing a Strategy for World War III," *The Atlantic*, November 1982, p. 106. Some officials apparently saw the tactical nuclear stockpile in Europe as so large, and the possible destruction from its use so great, that NATO might be self-deterred at this level as well. See "U.S. Considers Reduction of Atom Arms in Europe," *New York Times*, September 23, 1974.

18. Schilling, "U.S. Strategic Nuclear Concepts in the 1970s," pp. 66–68.

19. Cordesman, "American Strategic Forces and Extended Deterrence," pp. 474–475.

20. Smoke, "Extended Deterrence: Some Observations," pp. 40–44.

21. Cordesman, "American Strategic Forces and Extended Deterrence," pp. 478–479.

22. Sagan, *Moving Targets*, p. 45.

23. Cordesman, "American Strategic Forces and Extended Deterrence," p. 479; Sagan, *Moving Targets*, p. 51; Powers, "Choosing a Strategy for World War III," p. 103; interview with a Carter administration defense official.

24. Cordesman, "American Strategic Forces and Extended Deterrence," p. 482.

25. Robert Jervis, *The Illogic of American Nuclear Strategy* (Ithaca, N.Y.: Cornell University Press, 1984), p. 66.

26. Ibid., p. 68.

27. Interview with a Carter Administration Pentagon official; *New York Times*, August 6, 1980; Jervis, *The Illogic of American Nuclear Strategy*, pp. 74, 79–84; U.S. Department of Defense, *Report of Secretary of Defense Harold Brown to the Congress on the FY 1981 Budget, FY 1982 Authorization Request, and FY 1981–1985 Defense Programs* (Washington, D.C.: U.S. Government Printing Office), January 29, 1980, p. 66.

28. Desmond Ball, "Counterforce Targeting: How New? How Viable?" *Arms Control Today* 11, no. 2 (February 1981): 7.

29. *New York Times*, August 6, 1980. Brown told Congress that the biggest difference between PD 59 and previous policy directives was "a specific recognition that our strategy has to be aimed at what the Soviets think is important to them, not just what we might think would be important to us in their view." See *Nuclear War Strategy*, Hearings before the Committee on Foreign Relations, U.S. Senate, 96th Cong., 2nd Sess., September 16, 1980, p. 10. Quoted in Sagan, *Moving Targets*, p. 49.

30. Sagan, *Moving Targets*, pp. 52–53.

31. Sagan, *Moving Targets*, pp. 52–53; Cordesman, "American Strategic Forces and Extended Deterrence," p. 483.

32. Sam Nunn, *Policy, Troops and the NATO Alliance*, report to the Committee on Armed Services, U.S. Senate, April 2, 1974 (Washington, D.C.: U.S. Government Printing Office, 1974), p. 4.

33. See *New York Times*, September 23, 1974.

34. *Congressional Record*, daily edition, Senate, June 6, 1975, pp. 17603–17607.

35. See Ted Greenwood, *Making the MIRV* (Cambridge, Mass.: Ballinger, 1975), pp. 70–71; Herbert Scoville, "Flexible Madness?" *Foreign Policy* no. 14 (Spring 1974): 165–166.

36. See *New York Times*, February 7, 1975, and October 19, 1975.

37. See Powers, "Choosing a Strategy for World War III," pp. 104, 106; Barry Carter, "Nuclear Strategy and Nuclear Weapons," *Scientific American* 230, no. 5 (May 1974): 25.

38. Carter, "Nuclear Strategy and Nuclear Weapons," p. 31.

39. Interview with Seymour Weiss, former director, Bureau of Political and Military Affairs, Department of State, April 3, 1986. See also Colin Gray, *Strategic Forces and Public Policy: The American Experience* (Lexington: The University Press of Kentucky, 1982), p. 100; Cordesman, "American Strategic Forces and Extended Deterrence," pp. 474–475. Davis also distinguishes between the ability to win and the ability to stop a nuclear war in *Limited Nuclear Options*, p. 21.

40. This is the argument of Graham T. Allison and Frederic A. Morris, "Armaments and Arms Control: Exploring the Determinants of Military Weapons," in Franklin A. Long and George W. Rathjens, eds., *Arms, Defense Policy, and Arms Control* (New York: W. W. Norton, 1976) and of Powers, "Choosing a Strategy for World War III."

41. Desmond Ball, "The Role of Strategic Concepts and Doctrine in U.S. Strategic Force Development," in Bernard Brodie, Michael D. Intriligator, and Roman Kolkowicz, eds., *National Security and International Stability* (Cambridge, Mass.: Oelgeschlager, Gunn, Hain, Inc., 1983), p. 55.

42. Brandon, *The Retreat of American Power*, p. 215.

43. Ball, "The Role of Strategic Concepts and Doctrine," pp. 56, 57.

44. See Jervis's discussion of this point in *The Illogic of American Nuclear Strategy*, p. 75; see also David N. Schwartz, "The Role of Deterrence in NATO Defense Strategy: Implications for Doctrine and Posture," *World Politics* 28, no. 1 (October 1975): 126.

45. Sagan, *Moving Targets*, p. 53.

46. See "Debate over Change in Nuclear Strategy," *New York Times*, January 22, 1974.

47. Colin S. Gray, "The Strategic Forces Triad: End of the Road," *Foreign Affairs*

56, no. 4 (July 1978): pp. 774, 788; Colin S. Gray and Keith Payne, "Victory Is Possible," *Foreign Policy* no. 39 (Summer 1980), especially pp. 16, 25.

48. Walter Slocombe, "The Countervailing Strategy," *International Security* 5, no. 4 (Spring 1981): 22.

49. These five points are my summary. A large literature has been produced by those who take this position. See, for example, Wolfgang Panofsky, "The Mutual Hostage Relationship Between America and Russia," *Foreign Affairs* 52, no. 1 (October 1973); Scoville, "Flexible Madness"; Spurgeon M. Keeny, Jr., and Wolfgang Panofsky, "MAD Versus Nuts," *Foreign Affairs* 60, no. 2 (Winter 1981/1982); Leon V. Sigal, "Rethinking the Unthinkable," *Foreign Policy* no. 34 (Spring 1974). The most comprehensive statement of the position is Jervis, *The Illogic of American Nuclear Strategy*.

50. McGeorge Bundy, "The Bishops and the Bomb," *New York Review of Books* 30, no. 10 (June 16, 1983): 4, 6. The emphasis is mine.

51. Jervis, "Why Nuclear Superiority Doesn't Matter," p. 619; Jervis, *The Illogic of American Nuclear Strategy*, pp. 45–46, 156.

52. Jervis, *The Illogic of American Nuclear Strategy*, p. 146.

53. George W. Ball, "The Cosmic Bluff," *New York Review of Books* 30, no. 12 (July 21, 1983): 41.

54. David Garnham, "U.S. Nuclear Policy and Extended Deterrence," in Carol Edler Baumann, ed., *Europe in NATO: Deterrence, Defense, and Arms Control* (New York: Praeger, 1986), p. 24.

55. Lawrence S. Kaplan, *NATO and the United States: The Enduring Alliance* (Boston: Twayne, 1988), p. 148.

56. Quoted in Kaplan, *NATO and the United States*, p. 153.

57. Ibid., pp. 155–156.

58. Ibid., p. 153.

59. Ibid.

60. Ibid., p. 154.

61. See especially James Thomson, "The LRTNF Decision: Evolution of U.S. Theater Nuclear Policy," *International Affairs* 60, no. 4 (Augumn 1984): 605–607. See also Richard Barnet, *The Alliance: America, Europe, Japan—Makers of the Postwar World* (New York: Simon and Schuster, 1983), pp. 371–377; Zbigniew Brzezinski, *Power and Principle: Memoirs of the National Security Adviser, 1977–1981* (New York: Farrar, Strauss, and Giroux, 1983), pp. 307–309; Kaplan, *NATO and the United States*, p. 156.

62. See comments of Assistant Secretary of State Richard Burt quoted in Jervis, *The Illogic of American Nuclear Strategy*, pp. 90–91.

63. See Ibid., p. 94, and Jervis, *The Meaning of the Nuclear Revolution* (Ithaca, N.Y.: Cornell University Press, 1989), Chap. 6.

64. See Leslie H. Gelb, "Schlesinger," *New York Times*, August 14, 1976, p. 36; Komer, "What 'Decade of Neglect'?" p. 79.

65. Keohane, "The Theory of Hegemonic Stability and Changes in International Economic Regimes," pp. 136–137.

66. See John S. Odell, *U.S. International Monetary Policy: Markets, Power and Ideas as Sources of Change* (Princeton, N.J.: Princeton University Press, 1982), p. 312. F. Lisle Widman, Deputy Assistant Secretary of the Treasury for International Monetary and Investment Affairs, outlined in 1976 the rationale for the new exchange-rate policies. He put it partly in system-structure terms:

The economies of Europe and Japan rose up from the ashes of war while we ourselves were drawn into. . . . The goals of preserving official par values for currencies were overshadowed by more powerful political forces, by governmental mismanagement, or by sheer political weakness. The par value system was not flexible enough to adapt to these pressures . . . and the United States could no longer afford to maintain an over-valued currency at the expense of its own economic welfare.

Remarks made on May 24, 1976, at the World Trade Institute, World Trade Center, New York, N.Y., reprinted in *Annual Report of the Secretary of the Treasury for the Fiscal Year Ended June 30, 1976 and Transition Quarter* (Washington, D.C.: U.S. Government Printing Office, 1977), p. 548.

67. Krasner, "American Policy and Global Economic Stability," p. 36.

68. Widman, "Remarks," pp. 549, 550.

69. Krasner, "American Policy and Global Economic Stability," p. 37.

70. *Economic Report of the President, 1980* (Washington, D.C.: U.S. Government Printing Office, 1980), p. 316, Table B–98.

71. *New York Times*, June 14, 1975, p. 14.

72. Widman, "Remarks," p. 549; interview with Clyde Crosswhite, National Security Adviser, Office of Trade Finance of the Assistant Secretary of the Treasury for International Affairs, February 24, 1986.

73. Edward R. Fried, "The Military and the Balance of Payments," *The Annals of the American Academy of Political and Social Science* 406 (March 1973): 85.

74. Interview with Edward Fried; "Off the Offset Era," *New York Times*, July 24, 1976.

75. Paul M. Johnson, "Washington and Bonn: Dimensions of Change in Bilateral Relations," *International Organization* Vol. 33, No. 4 (Autumn 1979), p. 469; *New York Times*, June 14, 1975; interviews with State and Defense Department officials.

76. Stanley Hoffmann, "The European Community and 1992," *Foreign Affairs* 68, no. 4 (Fall 1989): 30.

77. James A. Nathan and James K. Oliver, *Foreign Policy Making and the American Political System*, 2d ed., (Boston: Little, Brown, 1987), pp. 120–121.

78. Williams, *The Senate and U.S. Troops in Europe*, pp. 243–246.

79. Ibid., p. 245; *New York Times*, July 31, 1974.

80. Joshua Muravchik, *The Senate and National Security: A New Mood* (Beverly Hills, Calif.: Sage, 1980), p. 50.

81. *New York Times*, October 25, 1975; *New York Times*, February 28, 1980.

82. *New York Times*, November 4, 1979.

83. Thomas H. Etzold, "The Military Role of NATO," in Lawrence S. Kaplan and Robert W. Clausen, eds., *NATO After Thirty Years* (Wilmington, Del.: Scholarly Resources, 1981), p. 239.

84. *New York Times*, April 26, 1968; *New York Times*, January 30, 1975.

85. *Report of Secretary of Defense Donald H. Rumsfeld to the Congress on the FY 1977 Budget and Its Implications for the FY 1978 Authorization Request and the FY 1977–1981 Defense Programs* (Washington, D.C.: U.S. Government Printing Office, 1976), p. vii.

86. *New York Times*, August 20, 1975, and November 5, 1975.

87. James Schlesinger, "The Eagle and the Bear," *Foreign Affairs* 63, no. 5 (Summer 1985): 951.

88. Gaddis, *Strategies of Containment*, pp. 346–347.

89. See U.S. Congress, Senate, Committee on Armed Services, *Hearings: NATO*

Posture and Initiatives, 95th Cong., 1st sess., August 3, 1977, p. 14; U.S. Department of Defense, *Annual Report, FY 1979, February 21, 1978* (Washington, D.C.: U.S. Government Printing Office, 1978), p. 38. Such comments were heard so often that Brown felt obliged to balance them with a speech devoted entirely to Asian security issues. See "Brown Says U.S. Will Strengthen Its Forces in Asia," *New York Times*, February 21, 1978.

90. *NATO Posture and Initiatives*, pp. 8, 67; *New York Times*, March 14, 1978.

91. Kaplan, *NATO and the United States*, p. 150.

92. According to one closely involved official, Congress offered no resistance to the force additions, but did, for predictable reasons, resist the implications of a genuine "two-way street" for defense procurement. (Confidential interview, February 18, 1986)

93. Robert W. Komer, "Treating NATO's Self-Inflicted Wound," *Foreign Policy* no. 13 (Winter 1973–74): 36–37. Cited in Kaplan, *NATO and the United States*, p. 150.

94. See *New York Times*, October 19, 1977. By the end of Carter's term, there were four full U.S. divisions, three full brigades, and two armored cavalry regiments in Europe, the most since the 1960s. (Confidential interview, February 18, 1986)

95. Kaplan, *NATO and the United States*, p. 151.

96. Interview with Robert Komer, November 1, 1984; interview with a member of the Carter NSC staff, October 23, 1984; interview with James Siena, former Deputy Assistant Secretary of Defense for European and NATO affairs, May 20, 1982; Robert Komer, "Looking Ahead," *International Security* 4, no. 1 (Summer 1979): 110; *New York Times*, December 6, 1977, and December 10, 1978.

97. U.S. Congress, Senate, Committee on Armed Services, *Department of Defense Authorization for Appropriations for FY 1979*, 95th Cong., 2nd sess., March 3, 1978, p. 1905.

98. *NATO Posture and Initiatives*, pp. 17, 26.

99. Interview with Robert Komer, November 1, 1984.

100. *New York Times*, July 6, 1975; Simon Lunn, *Burden-Sharing in NATO* (London: Routledge and Kegan Paul, 1983), p. 26.

101. *New York Times*, March 24, 1978.

102. Lunn, *Burden-Sharing in NATO*, p. 25.

103. James E. Dougherty and Robert L. Pfaltzgraff, Jr., supply the figures in *American Foreign Policy: FDR to Reagan* (New York: Harper and Row, 1986), pp. 331–332.

104. Robert W. Komer, *Maritime Strategy or Coalition Defense?* (Lanham, Md.: University Press of America, 1984), p. 17.

105. *New York Times*, October 9, 1979 and May 25, 1980; confidential interview.

106. *New York Times*, February 17, 1980; Lunn, *Burden-Sharing in NATO*, pp. 26–28; interview with Cyrus Vance, June 10, 1982.

107. *New York Times*, April 14, 1980.

108. Department of Defense, *Report on Allied Commitments to Defense Spending: A Report to the United States Congress by the Secretary of Defense* (Washington, D.C.: U.S. Government Printing Office, 1981), p. 66.

109. See Lunn, *Burden-Sharing in NATO*, pp. 29–31.

110. Olson defines a privileged group as "a group such that each of its members, or at least some of them, has an incentive to see that the collective goal is provided, even if he has to bear the full burden of providing it himself." See Mancur Olson, *The Logic of Collective Action: Public Goods and the Theory of Groups* (Cambridge, Mass.: Harvard University Press, 1965), pp. 49–50. On free riding within NATO, see Gregory Treverton,

Making the Alliance Work: The United States and Western Europe (Ithaca, N.Y.: Cornell University Press, 1985), pp. 99–100.

111. Keohane, *After Hegemony*, pp. 76–77. I thank Robert Keohane for suggesting this application.

112. Snyder and Diesing, *Conflict Among Nations*, pp. 45–46.

113. These general ideas are developed in Thomas C. Schelling, *The Strategy of Conflict* (Cambridge, Mass.: Harvard University Press, 1960), pp. 22–35.

114. Unilateral strategies to reduce the costs of being exploited and the gains from exploitation are discussed in Kenneth Oye, "Explaining Cooperation Under Anarchy: Hypotheses and Strategies," *World Politics* 38, no. 1 (October 1985): 10. While the United States cannot change the game from Prisoners' Dilemma by itself, it can increase the likelihood of mutual cooperation by influencing others' payoffs. Robert Jervis applies this argument to great-power systems in "From Balance to Concert: A Study of International Cooperation," *World Politics* 38, no. 1 (October 1985): 64.

115. Phil Williams, "Whatever Happened to the Mansfield Amendment?" *Survival* 18, no. 4 (July/August 1976): 152.

116. James O. Goldsborough, "Europe Cashes in on Carter's Cold War," *New York Times Magazine*, April 27, 1980, p. 42.

117. Williams, *The Senate and U.S. Troops in Europe*, p. 271; Lunn, *Burden-Sharing in NATO*, p. 32; interview with James Siena.

7 Conclusions and Implications

We all want a relationship with the United States. But I imagine we would all prefer that it not be so hierarchical as it has been.

Sergio Romano, former Italian Ambassador to Moscow[1]

I don't know what will become of this land. . . . There will be bound to be a cooling off vis-à-vis America as the prospect of united Germany comes into view.

Klaus Bolling, former head of Bonn's mission to East Berlin[2]

[I]n a new Europe, the American role may change in form but not in fundamentals.

President Bush, November 1989[3]

CONCLUSIONS: ASSESSING THE ARGUMENT

Considering America's deep isolationist roots, the story of the last three chapters is one of dramatic departure from the past and striking policy continuity. It is no coincidence that many books about NATO or the American role in it carry subtitles such as "The Enduring Alliance" or "The Entangling Alliance." NATO was the first integrated military coalition of its kind, may well be the last, and indeed endured longer than its founders had any right to expect. Much of this continuity can be attributed to the durability of the two U.S. commitments discussed in this book.

The book presents a general argument about adaptation to hegemonic decline as well as an interpretation of the NATO case. One's confidence in the latter increases if the former is sound. Harry Eckstein argues that a good theory of political behavior should be assessed according to criteria of (1) regularity, (2) reliability, (3) foreknowledge, and (4) parsimony in addition to (5) validity.[4] By these standards, how good is the argument?

"Regularity," according to Eckstein, means identification of "rules that phenomena observe in the concrete world, as players do in games or logicians in logic." Nomothetic rather than idiographic propositions are required. The five hypotheses derived in chapters 2 and 3 meet this criterion, albeit as "probability statements" rather than "laws."[5] I have tried to show that they should be generally true of great powers that assume substantial system-wide commitments, however such a role is empirically defined at any given time.

My findings are reliable to the extent that other researchers would interpret the case study similarly. Short of replication, this is difficult to assess. But since the two commitments are defined precisely and the case study examines each major decision point, it is reasonable to assume that others would reach similar conclusions.

Foreknowledge is defined by Eckstein as "the correct anticipation, by sound reasoning, of unknowns (whether the unknown has or has not yet occurred)"— in other words, the degree of explanatory power. In this study, foreknowledge is the amount of variance in foreign-policy adaptation explained.[6] Except for Hypothesis 4, each of the hypotheses was derived from a general argument without invoking examples from the NATO case. Since number 4 used some such examples, the degree of noncircular foreknowledge it provides is somewhat lower. Hypotheses 1, 5, and especially 2, on the other hand, provide fairly precise nonobvious predictions and thus somewhat more foreknowledge. Clearly, readers should recognize that my judgments vis-à-vis these two criteria are somewhat subjective.

Theories are parsimonious in direct proportion to the number and variety of observations they explain and in inverse proportion to the number and complexity of variables they employ.[7] My claims in this area are modest. To the extent that the argument is coherent, breadth has been sacrificed. I have attempted only what political scientists sometimes call "mid-range" theory. This book makes an argument about foreign-policy adjustment of *one* kind. Including medium and small states would make it quite difficult either to enumerate a short list of critical variables or make any general prediction about the loci of adaptation. Moreover, as explained in chapter 3, systematic explanations of foreign policy must confront problems of multiple, interacting causes. One deficiency of the argument herein may be its complexity.

Those interested mainly in the substance of U.S. NATO policy will focus on the argument's validity, or degree of empirical confirmation. In brief, this book claims that declining hegemons adjust at the margins and avoid renunciation of commitments wherever possible. According to Eckstein, a theoretical argument is valid "to the extent that a presumed regularity has been subjected, unsuccessfully, to tough appropriate attempts at falsification."[8] It cannot be said that

NATO policy is a tough test. America's role in Europe has been the core of postwar containment; one would thus expect cautious, slow adaptation to decline.

A better test might be trade policy. U.S. decision makers made essentially unconditional commitments to open markets for European and Japanese industrial exports to help those nations recover from World War II. As the United States became more open and its producers less competitive, domestic groups resisted such policies. It might have been predicted that those commitments would weaken as domestic pressures mounted and postwar reconstruction was finished. Yet, to explain the degree of protectionism—deviations from those commitments—one needs to examine the strategies through which those groups sought it, the nature of the relevant institutional structures, and the liberal ideas of policymakers.[9] There was less protectionism than would be expected from a model of declining hegemony, partly because policymakers clung to hegemonic commitments.

NATO commitments pose a weaker test because they have enjoyed solid, if not deep, public support. Since World War II, the American public has generally supported foreign commitments that either cost little or whose costs could be masked. NATO is expensive, but Americans have taken large defense budgets for granted since the Korean War and do not usually link them directly to European requirements. The case study was chosen for substantive interest and importance; readers should remember that assessing the validity of the theoretical argument was not my only objective.

The five hypotheses that comprise the argument were generally supported by the case study. Hypothesis 1 is the most counterintuitive in claiming that hegemons *knowingly* become overextended. While obviously not intrinsically desirable, it has been preferred to the alternatives. For example, although John Kennedy knew that the United States was overextended, he was essentially unwilling to pare back external involvements. To continue fighting in Vietnam, Lyndon Johnson accepted the troop rotation plan in Europe, changed the terms of the conventional commitment there by linking it to offset, and changed the terms of the gold-dollar link through the no-conversion pledge. Richard Nixon's Guam Doctrine, while a step in the other direction, still left the country with more obligations than it could honor below the nuclear threshold with the means at hand. This pattern continued through the 1970s, culminating in the Carter Doctrine.

There are three major reasons for this. First, because resolve reputation is valuable, great powers with many interests are strongly disposed against retrenchment or discriminating among commitments. Second, in a weak state, durable policy coalitions must include members of the legislature. For institutional reasons alone, congressional representatives often differ with the executive. Even if an optimal foreign policy would have entailed more retrenchment than occurred between 1960 and 1980, America's relatively wide policy coalitions seem to favor the risks of deterrence failure rather than the risks of allied bandwagoning.[10] Third, almost everyone assumes in the end that deterrence will *not* fail, or at least not simultaneously in too many places. That assumption has not yet been proved incorrect.

Hypothesis 2 held up well, with two exceptions. One, mentioned above, is easily explained. Johnson altered the terms of the troop commitment because doing so reflected the multiple substantive stakes involved and because he preferred to operate by consensus. The worsening payments deficit and growing pro-Mansfield sentiment in the Senate suggested a tough approach to Bonn, though Johnson would have preferred otherwise. This was no issue of principle for him and was initially reversed by the next administration.

The other exception *was* an issue of principle. The Kennedy administration sought a full conventional defense capability in Europe, even though this had never been a NATO objective.[11] The administration, especially McNamara, was unusually risk-averse about nuclear weapons and threats. Although FR under the nuclear threshold was taken to its logical conclusion, there was little enthusiasm by the end of the 1960s for similar capabilities above it. Compared to his successors, McNamara worried more about the risks of deterrence failure than the risks of alliance dissension. This was part of a coherent world view he has articulated often over the last two decades.

The next three administrations strongly reversed his emphasis. Each tried to revive first use through credible nuclear-war-fighting options. Their efforts, culminating in PD 59, were driven significantly by European requirements, since few thought basic deterrence was in jeopardy.

Hypothesis 3 is fairly straightforward and needs little additional comment. The "probabilistic" argument developed in Chapter 3 identifies policymakers' priorities on the basis of system-management tasks. Guidelines for monitoring the environment follow from them. The Johnson administration put aside nearly every consideration mentioned in Hypothesis 3 in its obsession with Vietnam, but this was the only notable exception. Otherwise, Washington kept its eyes largely on Soviet power, the West's capabilities and cohesion, and Europe's resolve.

Hypothesis 4 tells us that adjustment to hegemonic decline can follow more than one process or track within the same broad issue area. Of the two American commitments, the one involving troops was much more sensitive to the vicissitudes of legislative opinion about what the allies were doing and how much America could or should subsidize them. Every administration after Kennedy's took a tough line on burden sharing at some point for this reason. Not surprisingly, it has been much easier domestically for Washington to play the role of "benevolent" hegemon in areas where the societal costs were low and the allies had no obvious way to substitute their efforts for the hegemon's.

As stated in Hypothesis 5, hegemons prefer to act benevolently and therefore to adjust defensively and internally. Doing so minimizes allies' incentives to cut their dependency. Again, McNamara's pursuit of an undeclared NFU policy was the only significant exception. It asked Europeans to change behavior they found comfortable and had adopted partly at Washington's urging just a few years earlier. In contrast, Nixon, Kissinger, Schlesinger, and Brown emphasized the fundamentally adversarial character of extended deterrence *between* the two blocs and nudged the allies toward stronger conventional forces much more cautiously. In sum, defensive, internal adjustment usually occurs when there is broad internal agreement about ends and means. First use has endured essentially because Europeans have been willing to trust the United States and *neither* has been willing to pay for the conventional forces that would obviate the commitment.[12] In this context, Pentagon planning for nuclear war scenarios, many of which arise from attacks on allies or involve allied interest, has continued largely unhampered by Congress.

Policy coherence thus depends on a politically stable domestic environment in which long-term planning can occur. The Army, for instance, was reported in late 1989 to be planning to transform itself from a "heavy" service with an emphasis on defending Western Europe to a lighter, smaller, more flexible set of units oriented toward other crises. A diminished threat from the USSR and a radically different political configuration in central Europe had put NATO, its major postwar role, in question.[13] Of interest here is the adaptive time frame. A few weeks earlier, in response to these geopolitical changes, the services were directed to find hundreds of billions of dollars in budget cuts over the next several years. No one expected these new conditions to reverse in the near future. So despite lean times, the services had the luxury of formulating coherent plans to deal with them. This contrasted sharply with the situation they faced in the early 1970s.

More generally, what do chapters 4, 5, and 6 reveal about the extent and rate of hegemonic adaptation? Hegemonic theory postulates that as a hegemon's relative power declines, regimes will weaken because the leader will be less able and willing to maintain them. In essence, a study such as the present one should tell us whether this causal connection holds and why. Unfortunately, however, hegemonic theory provides only a weak explanation of policy adaptation. Its most specific prediction is that a declining hegemon will try to internalize the external benefits it provides to others. But some, such as extended deterrence, cannot be readily internalized; in general, the theory cannot tell us even when this incentive overrides contradictory tendencies toward risk aversion. Chapters 4 through 6, furthermore, constitute only a weak test. NATO policy, as mentioned earlier, is not a tough test of an argument about delayed adaptation. And even though the case study juxtaposes two specific issue areas within the broader one of European defense, it *is* essentially one case. This is mitigated somewhat by fairly good empirical confirmation for each hypothesis and by scrutiny of the two areas over twenty years.

What, then, do we know about hegemonic adaptation? From this case, it is apparent that declining hegemons face greater internal and external constraints as their relative advantages erode. This much foreknowledge we expect from a systemic theory. We know that hegemons are powerful enough to delay adaptation for considerable periods and that they prefer not to adjust, since this can induce allied "defections"—not necessarily to the adversary, which would be self-defeating, but to greater self-reliance. Following from this, we know that if hegemons must adjust commitments, they prefer to do so defensively. Even those few instances of offensive adjustment, such as Kennedy's "Grand Design," were defensively motivated, that is, aimed at a more viable hegemony. Most specifically, we know that hegemons prefer to adjust seriatim, beginning with the smallest changes, and that their ability to do so depends on control of the necessary policy resources.

What we do not know is the degree of external change or internal constraints that induces specific degrees or types of policy adjustment. In short, the theory of hegemonic stability is not a theory of foreign policy. But, as Keohane notes more generally about Structural Realism, "more attention to developing independent measures of intensity of motivation and greater precision about the concept of power and its relationship to the context of action" could be steps in that direction.[14] Chapters 4 through 6 can thus be considered a "heuristic" case study, one intended to refine and improve the argument.[15]

This could be done in several ways. More precise measures of geopolitical position and systemic change are necessary, although this will sacrifice parsimony. These systemic variables need to be linked theoretically to types of commitments or even to specific commitments. As for Keohane's other suggestion, if decision makers' cardinal utilities were inferred from another case(s), those data could be used to predict more precisely the sequence of adaptive changes outlined in Hypothesis 2. The critical ranges of variables, which indicate the kind of stress to which policies are vulnerable,[16] might serve as a surrogate measure of utilities. Depending on the accessibility of such data and the degree of decision-making detail necessary for confidence about the empirical tests, this could be a substantial project in itself.

In sum, little has changed in U.S. NATO policy since the 1950s. Kegley and Wittkopf argue that

The world has changed, but the basic tenets of American foreign policy have not. . . . American policy makers have possessed a consistent vision of the major characteristics of the international environment, a vision which has become institutionalized in the vast structure of federal bureaucracies that service American policies toward the outside world. As a result, precedent, habitual ways of thinking, and bureaucratic inertia have stifled consideration of radical policy alternatives. The problems of defining long-range goals have been avoided, and policy innovations have been rare. Consequently, the historical pattern of foreign behavior, while occasionally appearing on the surface to change, is marked by preference for gradual adaptation rather than fundamental reorientation.[17]

While partly true, this exaggerates the impact of inertia and downplays the extent to which containment, and NATO policy in particular, have rested on coherent, long-range goals. Goldmann convincingly argues that policies are typically stabilized first substantively and politically, and only then administratively.[18] Tasks, after all, must be assigned before bureaucracies can develop stakes in them, and the first step is a political one.

This suggests that an explanation of continuity in American policy toward European defense must begin with the political durability of the two commitments discussed in this book. NATO has endured because it simultaneously deterred the Soviets, anchored the Federal Republic of Germany to the West, and reassured the rest of Europe about both. These were the key tasks of the postwar order. The second and third have been as important as the first: as David Bruce, U.S. ambassador to Paris, averred in a telegram to Washington in 1951,

This [European army] . . . seems [to be] only solution of Ger[man] problem which will tie Ger[many] closely to West and offer hope for constructive and peaceful future for Europe. This goal appears so basic in relation to long-term security of United States that no effort should be spared to achieve it.[19]

When the European army failed to materialize, U.S. commitments became non-situational. In effect, they have been NATO's glue.

By 1989, their raison d'être was in doubt. Mikhail Gorbachev's unilateral gestures of rapprochement to the West including, most spectacularly, acquiescence in the demise of Moscow's Eastern European empire, convinced many that elaborate deterrence measures had become unnecessary. In all the tumult of that fall and winter when the Berlin Wall came down, one event struck particularly hard at the rationale for close military links to Western Europe. Gregor Gysi, the new head of the East German Communist party, actually asked Washington for help in keeping his country from being absorbed by Bonn![20] This signified an emerging fluidity in international alignments that threatened to make NATO irrelevant. As it turned out, Western Europe had before this begun acting in ways that made the alliance obsolescent. Before I discuss the developments of 1989, these longer-term changes deserve comment.

IMPLICATIONS: THE FUTURE OF AMERICAN NATO COMMITMENTS

For some time before Gorbachev's "New Thinking" in foreign policy began to affect Western perceptions of threat, NATO's European members had been inching toward greater self-reliance. Talk of a "European Pillar" that would function more assertively within NATO came increasingly from Europeans as well as from Americans looking for a reliable helpmate. These changes, to be sure, were very gradual, and easily missed by those inclined to see a helpless, demoralized, and divided Europe. While one can only speculate about might-have-beens, these developments could have produced pressures for a different U.S. role in Europe even without Gorbachev.

This occurred in several steps. First, Europe gradually discovered and felt confidence in its own cultural and political identity. One should recall the extent to which U.S. leadership was based on more than just power and confidence, especially during NATO's early years. It was also built on a pervasive sense in early postwar Europe that European ideas and political institutions had failed—discredited by two terrible wars, holocaust, and the apparent lack of a viable late-twentieth century model. There *was*, then, a sense in Europe after World War II that America had answers that the Old World lacked; the American perception of the late 1940s was not incorrect. As William Pfaff put it, "American political and social institutions fascinated Europeans in the 1940s because they seemed innovative and successful, while European institutions had failed. This is no longer so. It is the European institutions that seem in better health today."[21]

The changes, to repeat, were gradual. An important first step was the EEC, an attempt to transcend historic divisions and find a new European identity. A second was a loss of faith in the American model. America's seemingly endless struggles with civil rights, its Vietnam disaster, and a decade of discredited presidential leadership took their toll. Europe lost its complexes and confidence in American institutions during these years: "suddenly we were no better than they."[22] A third, more gradual still, was what many Europeans outside the doctrinaire right saw as an increasing American hedonism and narcissism, especially during the Reagan years. In Goldsborough's view, such a society will lose touch with others, such as those in Europe, in which group structures predominate and give meaning to individual pursuits. The undercurrent of hostility about Europe's spending on the welfare state at the expense of defense is part of this cultural gap.[23]

Resentments accumulated on both sides of the Atlantic. Although such individual crises as divergent responses to the 1973 oil embargo and the Soviet invasion of Afghanistan were papered over, deeper differences grew. Many Americans grew tired of European protectionism, lack of enthusiasm for a vigorous stance toward Moscow, and lack of support for non-European U.S. foreign policy goals. Among Europeans, Sergio Romano, quoted at the beginning of this chapter, spoke for many, especially those too young to remember the sense of trans-Atlantic solidarity during the difficult early postwar years.

Perhaps most alarming from Washington's point of view, even European elites sympathetic to America detected and began to adjust for the symptoms of U.S. hegemonic decline. By the 1980s, some European centrists believed that American elites had lost touch with the world's complexity, had adopted an increasingly egocentric and unilateralist view of U.S. interests, and were approaching East-West relations in ways that damaged European security.[24] And unlike past integrative efforts, the EEC'S 1992 single-market program is aimed less at building an entity to cooperate with or resist the U.S. and more at resisting the Japanese challenge.[25] A slow divorce was in the making.

One thus might have expected Europe to find its way by separating from its "parents." In defense, that separation has been painfully slow but increasingly evident. The idea that the French and British nuclear forces might form the basis for an independent European force was advanced in 1986 by the leaders of Britain's centrist political bloc, the Liberal/Social Democratic Alliance. It revived a 1962 proposal by the then Defense Secretary, Peter Thorneycroft.[26] The more recent initiative was motivated in part by internal politics: the Alliance parties were trying to steal the thunder of the Labourites, whose anti-nuclear program was driven partly by a desire for greater distance from the United States. But international factors were at work as well. In recent years, European defense cooperation, particularly between France and Germany, has flourished when America has been perceived as weak or undependable. The 1986 Reykjavik U.S.-Soviet summit, at which President Reagan was apparently willing to trade away all U.S. ballistic missiles and thus much of Europe's nuclear umbrella, and the INF agreement, which dealt away those missiles so painfully deployed, disturbed Europeans and set in motion further European cooperation.[27]

If it progresses, such cooperation will probably build on the 1963 Franco-German Elysée Treaty, which signified reconciliation between the former enemies and established a basis for closer relations. That relationship is now one of the new Europe's pivot points. Already in the 1970s and early 1980s, Bonn made clear that it would not subordinate Ostpolitik and its deepening relationship with East Germany to NATO cohesion. Moreover, Bonn's decreasing confidence in U.S. guarantees gave it an increasing incentive to broaden its contacts in the East.[28] This *could* be interpreted as incipient Finlandization, and was just what the French wanted to check or at least monitor through *their* collaboration with the Federal Republic.

But Bonn thus far has been willing to embed itself in other Western structures, and there is no indication that this will change. Under one scenario, a Franco-German defense community would develop and gradually absorb other members of the Western European Union (WEU). Some embryonic steps have already been taken. A bilateral Defense and Security Council was established in January 1988; other countries have been invited to join, a possibility that seems to interest Spain.[29] Paris and Bonn formed a joint combat brigade, although Paris remains reluctant to extend explicitly its nuclear umbrella over the Federal Republic.[30] And the Western European Union (WEU), formed to complement NATO in the 1950s as a Europe-only group but essentially moribund during most of the intervening years, came to life after Reykjavik. French Prime Minister Jacques Chirac noted in October 1987 that the superpowers were making decisions affecting European security without European participation. While this was hardly a new development, the WEU went on to approve a common "Platform on European Security Interests" that included the following:

• European integration will remain incomplete until a security dimension is added.

• WEU member states intend to reinforce the European pillar of the Alliance, enlarge their defense cooperation by all practical measures, improve their conventional forces, and *pursue European integration (including security)*. Britain and France will maintain the credibility of their nuclear forces.[31]

This initiative was noteworthy in at least two ways. It came from Europe, not Washington, and came in response to perceived American *weakness* and *indifference*, not leadership. It is hard to imagine a response more different from bandwagoning. Talk is cheap, of course. But developments of these kinds could further undermine the rationale for both U.S. commitments to NATO, or at least the level of American effort. The Franco-German relationship, especially if broadened and developed within the WEU, could replace NATO as an instrument to deter Moscow and anchor the Federal Republic to the West. These developments, to repeat, were germinating *before* the extraordinary changes that took place in Europe during 1989.

To conclude, some rumination on those changes is useful. The quotes at the beginning of this chapter usefully highlight their implications. Although not directly related to the substantive or conceptual material in this book, these changes imply a vastly different future U.S. role in Europe.

In December 1988, Gorbachev announced sizable unilateral cuts in Soviet conventional forces stationed in Eastern Europe. If Moscow had been interested only in diplomatic posturing, it could have publicized them and left the initiative for further cuts to NATO. Instead, the following spring, Warsaw Pact negotiators accepted in principle five "highly demanding" conditions for further progress in the Conventional Forces in Europe Talks (CFE).[32] Moscow agreed to cut asymmetrically to NATO levels, indicating to all but the most suspicious hawks that it no longer desired forces capable of intimidation or an offensive advantage.

Also by 1988, opposition groups in several Eastern European countries, notably Poland, were testing the limits of another aspect of Moscow's "New Thinking": repeated signals that each Warsaw Pact member could order its internal affairs as it chose. Gorbachev probably intended that this would bring reform-minded Communists to power. He soon found otherwise. During 1989, elections that had been promised in exchange for Soldarity's aid in Polish economic reconstruction dealt the Communists a crushing blow and led to the first non-Communist government in forty years. Similar elections were shortly promised in Hungary and Czechoslovakia; meanwhile, in both countries, the Communists gave up their constitutionally guaranteed leading role, reconstituted themselves as democratic parties, and prepared to contest free elections. The most dramatic events took place in East Germany. There, after weeks of emigration through Hungary, the government opened the Berlin Wall and finally the Brandenburg Gate, sparking instant and sustained speculation about reunification in both parts of the divided nation. By mid–1990, Albania had the only unreconstructed hard-line regime in the former Soviet European bloc.

NATO's opposite number collapsed sooner than anyone expected. As *The Economist* speculated in mid-November 1989,

A couple of weeks ago, the hope was that NATO and the Warsaw Pact would before long agree to a deal which cut the communist alliance down to rough equality with NATO, at NATO's present size or a bit below. Two weeks on, the Warsaw Pact may for practical purposes be ceasing to exist. . . . NATO could be negotiating with a burst balloon.[33]

Washington, needless to say, was caught flat-footed.

NATO's short-term responses indicated the resistance outside Germany to quick, fundamental change. NATO structures had served so long and dependably that Washington (and others) seemed at a loss as their rationale unraveled. The United States spent much of late 1989 and early 1990 trying to manage the turbulence diplomatically.

A major problem was that few were prepared for the surge in pan-German solidarity. Germans on both sides of the border drew together, setting in motion the disintegration of the postwar European order that had been based upon division. The European Council reaffirmed NATO's long-standing endorsement of "free self-determination" for Germany, while taking account, as emphasized by British Prime Minister Thatcher, of "all of our existing agreements and alliances." Washington meanwhile began trying to heal incipient tensions between Germans and the rest of the alliance. Because the conditions under which reunification might occur would greatly affect Bonn's status within NATO and the future of U.S. troops there, U.S. officials became "obsessed" with maintaining close consultations to prevent sudden moves toward the East. Washington also reiterated its support for stronger political and military integration among Europeans, again to anchor the Federal Republic.[34]

Gorbachev's diplomatic offensive and the major substantive changes in Soviet policy meanwhile put pressure on NATO and particularly the United States for a forthcoming CFE position. Bush's first response, presented to a NATO summit in May 1989, was cautious: a 10 percent reduction in U.S. forces stationed in Europe that would bring the total to about 275,000. U.S. CFE negotiators were instructed to reach a first-round agreement by May 1990, an optimistic deadline given the remaining disagreements between the two sides.[35] But no one foresaw protracted talks, and Bush was reported to have set a target of as few as 100,000 troops in Europe by the mid–1990s.[36]

These developments, as indicated earlier, forced the Pentagon to make two kinds of adjustments. It would have to make do with fewer forces and lower budgets; and the services, particularly the Army, would have to redefine roles and missions to reflect the reduced importance of European contingencies. SACEUR Gen. John Galvin believed that cuts in the range of 30,000 could be implemented in a year; his headquarters, assisted by computer war games, weighed the implications of various combinations of reductions. Some preliminary steps were taken: NATO exercises were sharply cut back, including those associated with the 1967 withdrawal-rotation program.[37] Even before the first CFE agreement was reached, Defense Secretary Cheney warned that "we are going to have to make some cuts . . . in force structure, close some bases, terminate some weapons systems."[38]

Reductions in Soviet ground and air forces along the general lines already agreed to would permit substantial cuts in American forces. While the United States now pledges to have 10 Army divisions, 100 tactical air squadrons, and a Marine brigade in Europe within 10 days of a Pact mobilization, Soviet cuts and demobilizations would provide at least three months warning of a major Pact military move. According to Lawrence Korb, a former Pentagon official and hardly a dove, active Army divisions and tactical air squadrons could then be cut in half.[39] Obviously, still deeper reductions in the approximately 380,000 Soviet troops in East Germany could allow the U.S. to cut further.[40]

Beyond even further rounds of CFE talks lay the long-term U.S. role in Europe. The main issue here is less how many troops remain or how high the nuclear threshold can be raised and more what the U.S. presence will mean. For example, if Europe takes its own defense more seriously, for whatever reasons, the trans-atlantic relationship will become much less hierarchical. This is a future for which NATO seems headed, as Americans turn somewhat more inward and divisions on the Continent heal, and one for which America must plan. What might it look like?

To begin, we might briefly consider the extended deterrence commitment. The height of the nuclear threshold has always depended on the conventional balance and conventional threat. The changes taking place in Europe suggest that the political and military salience of first use will significantly decline. Therefore, a key issue is the impact of conventional force reductions on the conventional balance. Initially, the impact of significant asymmetric cuts will obviously be beneficial to NATO and could allow a more relaxed nuclear posture. But symmetric reductions beyond that leave open whether NATO could effec-tively guard the Central Front region.Complex issues of force-to-terrain ratios are involved, and will not be discussed here in detail.

This problem clearly has a political dimension as well. Bonn has insisted that NATO be able to defend its territory right up to the border, even though this has been more costly and less flexible than a maneuver defense. If this political constraint were relaxed as the Warsaw Pact becomes politically in-capable of a coordinated, aggressive move toward the West, forward defense would become much less necessary, and with it the option of nuclear preemption.[41]

Since even the Pentagon admits that a war in Europe is less likely than any time since 1945,[42] incentives to "couple" America and Europe more closely by lowering the nuclear threshold will diminish. NATO might thus move gradually toward "No Early Use" as Soviet forces are cut. Under one suggestion, the U.S. would remove all its land-based nuclear battlefield weapons from Europe but retain the option of using central strategic systems first. This would ease German fears of entrapment in a Europe-only war while assuaging fears of abandonment.[43] It might also eventually allow France and perhaps Britain to take over the nuclear defense of central Europe through a gradually enlarged "extended sanctuary." Again, FR is "flexible" enough for such an adjustment:

as new U.S. strategic systems are deployed, targets formerly covered by LRTNF weapons will be covered by the former.[44]

What the U.S. troop presence means over the long term depends on what Europe becomes. Clearly, America retains considerable clout and can shape the new Europe to some extent. But as events unfolded with dizzying speed in 1989, it was evident that Washington would henceforth be more of a bystander rather than, as Acheson put it, "present at the creation." Not only did the Bush administration lack a blueprint, or seem nostalgic for Cold War simplicities; more profoundly, Europeans increasingly took matters into their own hands and indicated that the era of hegemonic dominance was over.

Europe at this writing is still so politically fluid that specific, long-range predictions about NATO or the U.S. role in European security are foolhardy. Germany's pivotal position, however, means that its role in Europe, its relationship with France, and NATO's future are inextricably intertwined. Two general scenarios seem plausible.

Likeliest at this point is the American and British preference for a scaled-down but still viable NATO that will absorb and anchor a new, united Germany. Gorbachev resisted this for months, proposing in turn that the new Germany be neutralized by treaty, that both NATO and the Warsaw Pact be dismantled, and then that Germany belong to both blocs. None of these was accepted by the West. In mid-June 1990 the Soviets, whose only remaining bargaining chip was their 380,000 troops in East Germany and who desperately needed Western economic help, conceded that a united Germany could be a full member of NATO. It was a stunning political coup for the western allies: just a few months before the Soviets had demanded neutrality as the price for German unity, a position they had held since 1952.

A package of measures designed to reassure Moscow was offered as compensation: its troops will be allowed to remain in what is now East Germany for some time, East Germany's economic obligations will be honored by the successor state, and NATO will probably abrogate first-nuclear use. Gorbachev also endorsed a wider role for the 35 member Helsinki-accords group known as the Conference on Security and Cooperation in Europe (CSCE), Moscow's only institutional link to Europe other than the moribund Pact. The Soviets hoped, not without reason, that CSCE might eventually supplant both blocs. Washington strongly disagreed with the latter, although other Europeans had more mixed feelings.

France is determined that the new Germany be firmly anchored in Europe and will apparently strengthen its commitment to various institutions, NATO among them, to make it happen. Former Prime Minister Jacques Chirac suggested that his country would again take a "direct part" in the defense of the Continent, including a Franco-British nuclear force. He insisted that DeGaulle rejected only American domination of NATO, not integrated defense per se.[45] Others, including French President Mitterrand and former NATO Secretary-General Lord

Carrington, have revived proposals for a specifically European "axis," "pillar" or EC group within or parallel to NATO.

Gorbachev's vision of a blocless Europe is another possibility. It is hard to see how NATO can endure indefinitely, even as a more "political" group, without the principal threat that catalyzed it; even so strong a supporter as British Prime Minister Margaret Thatcher admitted that NATO no longer has a "clear front line." Should such erosion occur, the Germans will likely precipitate it. Lothar de Maiziere, East Germany's first freely elected prime minister, surprised some who thought him little more than a mouthpiece for Helmut Kohl, his West German counterpart. His suggestion that CSCE could eventually replace both alliances will find support on the left and perhaps the center in the new Germany. To the extent that NATO is seen increasingly as a means to contain them, Germans may wish to create institutions without that particular connotation. How strong these sentiments will be is unknown, but persuading the Germans that NATO is a more appropriate forum for the kinds of issues Europe will face in the future will be a difficult and time-consuming process.[46]

America has not lost its role in Europe. Europeans realize that an alliance without America would be dominated by the Germans; their desire for a U.S. counterweight springs less from specific past German misbehavior than more general balance-of-power considerations.[47] During early 1990, Bush effectively emphasized that U.S. forces, unlike Moscow's were in Europe by invitation and that they provided continuity at a time of dizzying uncertainty and potential instability.

But that role will diminish over time, perhaps profoundly. As Alan Riding put it,

The unspoken focus of this debate [over NATO's and Europe's futures] is whether the United States should play a smaller—or at least a different—role in Europe. European governments still want the protection of Washington's defense shield. But while in the past, they accepted the United States as the dominant European power, today they want to be treated more as equals.[48]

For example, U.S. troops might eventually be placed under a European, perhaps French, Supreme NATO Commander.[49] This would severely test Washington's penchant for unilateralism. An even bigger change, amounting to a change of regime, is the impending renunciation of first use. Washington's nuclear capability and expertise have long been sources of hegemonic inequality; while power capabilities will remain skewed, this will matter less if Europeans can keep their own house in order. Clearly, the rationale for America's hegemonic role in Europe has passed.

Whither America's world role in the fluid global system now emerging? Can Americans define a strategic purpose for their foreign policy without a clear enemy, especially when domestic problems compete for increasingly scarce resources?

The Wilsonian tradition in U.S. foreign policy suggests that it will be difficult. Wilsonians believe that external conduct must reflect internal values, that the latter are immutable, and that foreign policy is thus about good and evil. But these deeply ingrained cultural predilections may be irrelevent if future challenges abroad are less ideological and predictable than those of the last four decades. Under these conditions, Americans may have trouble distinguishing friend and foe.

U.S. foreign policy need not become rudderless, but preventing that will require major changes in the way Americans think about the world. The United States, as a superpower, will retain geopolitically defined stakes in many places. However particular situations are resolved, security in Central America, the Middle East, and Southeast Asia as well as Europe will depend on some U.S. commitment. American stakes in certain kinds of regimes, relationships, and regional power balances derive from more than just superpower competition, though they may be harder to define in practice without a clear adversary.

Americans' attitudes toward international involvement have differed greatly from this classic balance-of-power conception. Deep strains of isolationism prevent many Americans from regarding sustained, non-ideological involvement abroad as a normal state of affairs. A major role abroad has been possible only in emergencies. If the Cold War was essentially an extended emergency, why should the familiar extroversion-introversion pattern not repeat itself?

International stability is never achieved once and for all; if an old challenge such as Soviet expansionism is tamed, others will replace it. As argued in chapters 2 and 3, a country as powerful as the United States has both permanent stakes in stability and the capacity to affect it. To do so usefully, Americans must begin thinking about international stakes and commitments in more contingent terms and give their leaders the flexibility to implement the requisite strategies. This is a plea not for renewed "hegemonic" leadership, since that era has passed, but for flexible involvement in a fluid world. Wilsonianism, though it provides internal purpose, is ultimately an unaffordable luxury.

NOTES

1. *New York Times*, December 1, 1989, p. 9.
2. Ibid.
3. *Wisconsin State Journal*, November 23, 1989, p. 1.
4. Eckstein, "Case Study and Theory in Political Science," in *Handbook of Political Science*, Fred I. Greenstein and Nelson Polsby, eds. (Reading, Mass.: Addison-Wesley, 1975), pp. 88–90.
5. Ibid., pp. 88.
6. The quote is from Ibid.; see also Kiell Goldmann, *Change and Stability in Foreign Policy* (Princeton: Princeton University Press, 1988), p. 224.
7. Ibid., p. 89.
8. Ibid., p. 88.
9. Judith Goldstein, "Ideas, Institutions, and American Trade Policy," in G. John

Ikenberry, David A. Lake, and Michael Mastanduno, eds. *The State and American Foreign Economic Policy* (Ithaca, N.Y.: Cornell University Press, 1988), p. 215.

10. On this general point, see Alan Lamborn, "Risk and Foreign Policy Choice," *International Studies Quarterly* 29, no. 4 (December 1985), p. 408.

11. Henry Kissinger, "A Plan to Reshape NATO," *Time*, March 5, 1984, p. 23.

12. Warner R. Schilling, "U.S. Strategic Nuclear Concepts in the 1970s," *International Security*, 6, no. 2 (Fall 1981), pp. 62–63.

13. *New York Times*, December 12, 1989.

14. Robert O. Keohane, "Theory of World Politics," in *Political Science: State of the Discipline*, Ada W. Finifter, ed. (Washington, D.C.: American Political Science Association, 1983), p. 526.

15. The best available discussion of heuristic case studies is Eckstein, "Case Study and Theory in Political Science," pp. 104–108.

16. Goldmann, *Change and Stability in Foreign Policy*, p. 59.

17. Charles W. Kegley, Jr., and Eugene R. Wittkopf, *American Foreign Policy: Pattern and Process*, 3d ed. (New York: St. Martin's Press, 1987), pp. 4, 7.

18. Goldmann, *Change and Stability in Foreign Policy*, pp. 70–71, 76.

19. David Bruce to Secretary of State Dean Acheson, July 3, 1951, reprinted in Martin F. Herz, *David Bruce's "Long Telegram" of July 3, 1951* (Lanham, Md.: University Press of America, 1978), p. 11.

20. *New York Times*, December 15, 1989.

21. Pfaff, "Reflections: Finlandization," *The New Yorker*, September 1, 1980, p. 30, quoted in James Goldsborough, *Rebel Europe: How America Can Live With a Changing Continent* (New York: Macmillan, 1982), p. 92.

22. Goldsborough, *Rebel Europe*, p. 91.

23. See Ibid., p. 93, and Eric Willenz, "Why Europe Needs the Welfare State," *Foreign Policy* no. 63 (Summer 1986).

24. John Palmer, *Europe Without America? The Crisis in Atlantic Relations* (Oxford: Oxford University Press, 1987), p. 5.

25. Hoffmann, "The European Community and 1992," p. 34.

26. Palmer, *Europe Without America?*, note 29, Chap. 1, p. 196.

27. Garnham, *The Politics of European Defense Cooperation* (Cambridge, Mass.: Ballinger, 1988), p. 70 and passim.

28. Christopher Layne, "Europe Between the Superpowers: New Trends in East-West Relations," in Ted Galen Carpenter, ed., *Collective Defense or Strategic Interdependence? Alternative Strategies for the Future* (Lexington, Mass.: D.C. Heath, 1989), pp. 55–56.

29. Garnham, *The Politics of European Defense Cooperation*, pp. 69, 70–71.

30. Ibid., pp. 62–63.

31. Ibid., p. 119 (emphasis added).

32. This is the assessment of Jonathan Dean, who headed the U.S. delegation to the Mutual and Balanced Force Reduction Talks from 1973 to 1981. See Dean, "Conventional Talks: A Good First Round," *The Bulletin of the Atomic Scientists* (October 1989), p. 28.

33. *The Economist*, November 18, 1989, p. 53.

34. *New York Times*, December 10, 1989, and December 11, 1989.

35. *Newsweek*, December 4, 1989, p. 44. Jonathan Dean observes that despite the best prospects for conventional cuts in decades, serious differences between the blocs remain. The Pact wants talks on tactical nuclear arms reductions to commence along with

the CFE negotiations; NATO, for obvious reaons, wants to delay them until a conventional agreement is implemented. And although NATO resolutely refuses to discuss limitations in naval forces as part of the CFE framework, and this is reflected in the agreed mandate, the Soviets have pressed Washington repeatedly on the issue and will clearly bring it up again. See Dean, "Conventional Talks," pp. 28, 29.

36. *Newsweek*, December 4, 1989, p. 44.

37. Michael R. Gordon, "The Military Math of Peace in Our Time," *New York Times*, December 17, 1989; *New York Times*, October 18, 1989.

38. *New York Times*, November 20, 1989, p. 14.

39. Lawrence J. Korb, "How To Reduce Military Spending," *The New York Times*, November 21, 1989, p. 23.

40. This figure is from *New York Times*, November 11, 1989. It is not clear whether it reflects Moscow's unilateral withdrawal of 50,000 troops announced in December 1988.

41. See *The Economist* November 18, 1989, p. 53.

42. *New York Times*, November 11, 1989.

43. Sharp, "Arms Control and Alliance Commitments," pp. 666–667.

44. *New York Times*, November 2, 1988. The comparison between nuclear and conventional force sizes discussed in Chapter 3 is pertinent here. As new American central strategic systems are deployed, older weapons such as B–52 bombers and Minuteman ICBMs are being assigned other missions, for example, delivery of conventional bombs or destruction of "softer" targets. In short, nuclear plenty entails substantial flexibility in the SIOP. Conventional forces, in contrast, are being substantially reshaped as the threat of war in Europe diminishes. For example, armored and mechanized infantry divisions will bear the brunts of cuts in Army units, partly so that sizable light forces for rapid intervention elsewhere can be maintained. See *New York Times*, December 12, 1989.

45. Flora Lewis, "NATO A la Francaise," *New York Times*, June 16, 1990.

46. "Bush Meets East German Leader and Pushes NATO Membership," *New York Times*, June 12, 1990; "Deferring to the Germans," *New York Times*, May 4, 1990.

47. Michael Howard, "The Remaking of Europe," *Survival* 42, no. 2 (March/April 1990), p. 105.

48. Alan Riding, "Redoing Europe," *New York Times*, April 15, 1990.

49. Lewis, "NATO A la Francaise."

Bibliographic Essay

This book draws upon large literatures dealing with NATO, U.S. security policy, and the causes and implications of hegemonic decline. I have also drawn more selectively from the literatures on foreign policy adjustment and analysis, on international relations theory, and on comparative case-study method. All works used in preparing this book are cited in the notes following each chapter. This essay highlights those that were most helpful.

GENERAL THEORY AND METHOD

Kenneth Waltz's *Theory of International Politics* (Addison-Wesley, 1979), a work with which every serious student in the field must contend, claims that rigorous theory must proceed from the system level. Robert Keohane's "Theory of World Politics," in Ada Finifter, ed., *Political Science: State of the Discipine* (APSA, 1983) provides a perceptive critique of Waltz and Robert Gilpin (cited below) along with a version of Keohane's institutionally oriented approach. Harold and Margaret Sprout, *The Ecological Perspective on Human Affairs* (Princeton University Press, 1965) outline the perspective they call "Environmental Probabilism," which forms the basis for some core ideas in chapter 3.

Arthur Stinchcombe's *Constructing Social Theories* (University of Chicago, 1987) provides several nonobvious ways to think about social causation. Its chapter on geopolitics was useful in working out the theoretical sketch about expansionism in chapter 3.

The increasing use of comparative case studies to build and refine international relations theory is a welcome development. Harry Eckstein's "Case Study and Theory in Political Science" in *Handbook of Political Science*, Fred Greenstein and Nelson Polsby, eds. (Addison-Wesley, 1975) is an indispensable reference.

Also very useful are Alexander L. George, "Case Studies and Theory Development," in *Diplomacy*, Paul Gordon Lauren, ed. (Free Press, 1979) and the literature he cites.

HEGEMONIC DECLINE AND THE DECLINE OF AMERICAN POWER

Interest in the latter has driven the raft of writing on the former, and much of the general literature is focused on America. Notable exceptions are Paul Kennedy's influential *The Rise and Fall of the Great Powers* (Random House, 1987) and Robert Gilpin's *War and Change in World Politics* (Cambridge University Press, 1981) and, to some extent, Robert O. Keohane's *After Hegemony* (Princeton University Press, 1984). David Calleo, *Beyond American Hegemony* (Basic Books, 1987), is more topical and less conceptual. Keohane's argument about hegemonic stability has influenced much work in the growing field of international political economy. See also his "Theory of Hegemonic Stability and Changes in International Economic Regimes," in *Change in the International System*, Ole Holsti et al., eds. (Westview, 1980). Duncan Snidal, in "The Limits of Hegemonic Stability Theory," *International Organization* (Augumn 1985), critiques Keohane's work and was helpful in delineating distinctions based on hegemonic motivations and the type of good provided.

The literature on American hegemonic decline tends either to assert that premise or argue against it. Calleo, in *Beyond American Hegemony*, does the former, as do Mark Rupert and David Rapkin, in "The Erosion of U.S. Leadership Capabilities," in *Rhythms in Politics and Economics*, William R. Thompson ed. (Praeger, 1985), and Kennedy, in "The (Relative) Decline of America," *The Atlantic*, August 1987. Bruce Russett's "The Mysterious Case of Vanishing Hegemony," *International Organization* (Spring 1985), takes the opposing, more controversial, position.

FOREIGN POLICY ADJUSTMENT AND ANALYSIS

Relatively few works focus explicitly on how governments respond to changing constraints and opportunities, although it is central to foreign-policy analysis. Among the best of those that do, see Aaron Friedberg, *The Weary Titan* (Princeton University Press, 1988), which looks at turn-of-the-century Britain, and G. John Ikenberry, *Reasons of State* (Cornell University Press, 1988), which scrutinizes the U.S. response to the 1970s oil crises. Ikenberry's distinction between offensive and defensive adjustment was particularly helpful in developing the argument of Chapter 2. John Lewis Gaddis's studies of U.S. containment policies, particularly *Strategies of Containment* (Oxford University Press, 1982), and "Containment and the Logic of Strategy," *The National Interest* (Winter 1987–88), were also very useful.

Some of the more general works dealing with the causes of foreign-policy choices also provided valuable help. Kjell Goldmann's *Change and Stability in Foreign Policy* (Princeton University Press, 1988), which explains why Bonn's détente with Moscow in the 1970s was more durable than America's, examines policy stability amidst pressures for change. Even more generally, Spiro J. Latsis discusses the situations under which "single-exit" choice models apply. See his "A Research Programme in Economics," in *Method and Appraisal in Economics*, Latsis, ed., (Cambridge University Press, 1976), and "The Limitations of Single-Exit Models," *The British Journal for the Philosophy of Science* 27 (1976). David Lake, in *Power, Protection, and Free Trade* (Cornell University Press, 1988), explicates the notion of a "foreign policy executive" that defines national objectives with regard to systemic power considerations. See also Stephen Krasner, "Are Bureaucracies Important?" *Foreign Policy* no. 7 (Summer 1972) on this point. Alan Lamborn, in "Risk and Foreign Policy Choice," *International Studies Quarterly* (December 1985) discusses the policy outputs of coalitions whose members have different preferences.

Literature that accounts for certain specific alliance patterns also falls in this category. On the notion that small states will "balance" rather than "bandwagon," see Stephen Walt, "Testing Theories of Alliance Formation," *International Organization* (Spring 1988); some may wish to consult his larger study, *The Origins of Alliances* (Cornell University Press, 1987). See also Patrick Morgan, "Saving Face for the Sake of Deterrence," in Robert Jervis et al., eds., *Psychology and Deterrence* (Johns Hopkins University Press, 1985), which argues that Americans have reassured themselves through Western Europe.

GENERAL WORKS ON NATO

The NATO literature is voluminous. Three good places to begin are Richard Barnet, *The Alliance* (Simon and Schuster, 1983), a comprehensive review of postwar relations among the industrialized countries; Robert Osgood, *NATO: The Entangling Alliance* (University of Chicago Press, 1962), an early work on the causes and implications of an integrated alliance; and David N. Schwartz, *NATO's Nuclear Dilemmas* (Brookings Institution, 1983), a judicious and comprehensive account of that area. Harlan Cleveland's *NATO: The Transatlantic Bargain* (Harper and Row, 1970), is also useful as a solid account of NATO's functions and institutional mechanisms from the viewpoint of an experienced, mid-level official.

Most works address more specific topics. Among the most informative and concise histories are Lawrence Kaplan's *NATO and the United States* (Twayne, 1988) and Timothy Ireland's *Creating the Entangling Alliance* (Greenwood Press, 1981). Daniel Charles's *Nuclear Planning in NATO* (Ballinger, 1987) is a readable and informative account of that problem. Simon Lunn, in *Burden-Sharing in NATO* (Routledge and Kegan Paul, 1983), provides a good overview of that topic. Josef Joffe, in "Europe's American Pacifier," *Foreign Policy* no. 54 (Spring 1984) emphasizes (and perhaps overemphasizes) the U.S. role in bringing about harmony within Western Europe in the aftermath of World War II. George F. Kennan's "Europe's Problems, Europe's Choices," *Foreign Policy* no. 14 (Spring 1974) is an insightful short critique of Finlandization scenarios as applied to Europe.

U.S. SECURITY POLICY

The voluminous literature on U.S. national security policy ranges from broad-scale historical works to partisan critiques and detailed analyses of specific strategies or weapons systems. What follows is a sampling of those I found useful.

Memoirs, for all their obvious limitations, indicate what policymakers either thought was important or wished posterity to believed they emphasized. Memoirs by Dean Acheson, Lyndon Johnson, Zbigniew Brzezinski and especially Henry Kissinger were helpful in this regard. Henry Brandon's *The Retreat of American Power* (Doubleday, 1973) comes from a Washington insider with unusual access in several administrations. Alain Enthoven and Wayne Smith's *How Much is Enough?* (Harper and Row, 1971) summarizes the view of the McNamara Pentagon. Martin Herz's *David Bruce's "Long Telegram" of July 3, 1951* (University Press of America, 1978) highlights Washington's concern about the German Question at NATO's inception. Frank Costigliola's "The Pursuit of Atlantic Community," in *Kennedy's Quest for Victory*, Thomas G. Paterson, ed. (Oxford University Press, 1989), is a fine account of that administration's European policy. Jane Stromseth's *The Origins of Flexible Response* (St. Martin's Press, 1988) is a detailed work on that topic, as is Gregory Treverton's *The "Dollar Drain" and American Forces in Germany* (Ohio University Press, 1978). Franklin Weinstein's "The Concept of a Commitment in International Relations," *Journal of Conflict Resolution* (March 1969), while broader in scope than other works cited in this paragraph, weaves them skillfully into his discussion.

On the first-use commitment, see Bernard Brodie, "What Price Conventional Capabilities in Europe?" *The Reporter*, May 23, 1963; Richard Smoke, "Extended Deterrence: Some Observations," *Naval War College Review* (September/October 1983); Daniel Arbess and Andrew Moravscik, "Lengthening the Fuse: No First Use and Disengagement," in *Fateful Visions*, Joseph S. Nye et al., eds., (Ballinger, 1988); Richard Betts, *Nuclear Blackmail and Nuclear Balance* (Brookings Institution, 1987); Enthoven and Smith, "What Forces for NATO? And From Whom?" *Foreign Affairs* 48, no. 1 (October 1969); James Thomson, "The LRTNF Decision," *International Affairs* (Autumn 1984); McGeorge Bundy, "The Bishops and the Bomb," *New York Review of Books* (June 16, 1983); George Ball, "The Cosmic Bluff," *New York Review of Books* (July 21, 1983). Jane M. O. Sharp, "Arms Control and Alliance Commitments," *Political Science Quarterly* (Winter 1985–1986) puts these issues in the context of the tension between abandonment and entrapment. Finally, Anthony Cordesman,

"American Strategic Forces and Extended Deterrence," in *U.S. National Security: A Framework for Analysis*, David Kaufman, et al., eds. (D.C. Heath, 1985), was extremely useful. Cordesman examines military hardware as well as the conceptual foundations of U.S. strategy in detail.

On nuclear strategy more generally, see Smoke, *National Security and the Nuclear Dilemma*, 2d ed. (Random House, 1987); Robert Jervis, *The Illogic of American Nuclear Strategy* (Cornell University Press, 1984); Scott Sagan, *Moving Targets* (Princeton University Press, 1989); Desmond Ball, "The Development of the SIOP, 1960–1983," in *Strategic Nuclear Targeting*, Desmond Ball and Jeffrey Richelson, eds. (Cornell University Press, 1986); Desmond Ball, "The Role of Strategic Concepts and Doctrine in U.S. Strategic Nuclear Force Development," in *National Security and International Stability*, Bernard Brodie et al., eds. (Oelgeschlager, Gunn and Hain, 1983); Warner Schilling, "U.S. Strategic Nuclear Concepts in the 1970s," *International Security* (Fall 1981); and, for a well-researched account that stresses the role of individuals and institutional loyalties, Fred Kaplan, *The Wizards of Armageddon* (Simon and Schuster, 1983). John Prados, in *The Soviet Estimate* (Princeton University Press, 1986), gives a detailed account of how the American intelligence community evaluated and the government responded to growth in Soviet strategic forces.

U.S. conventional forces have received less sustained attention from this general, political perspective. See Phil Williams, *The Senate and U.S. Troops in Europe* (St. Martin's Press, 1985), and Williams, *U.S. Troops in Europe* (Routledge and Kegan Paul, 1984). Lawrence Korb, *The Fall and Rise of the Pentagon* (Greenwood Press, 1979), discusses similar issues from a more general perspective. Robert E. Hunter, in "Will the United States Remain a European Power?" *Survival* (May–June 1988), brings these issues and those in the previous paragraphs succinctly up to date.

GOVERNMENT DOCUMENTS

Of the five administrations surveyed in the case study, only three presidential libraries—the Kennedy, Johnson, and Ford—were open to researchers when this study was initially drafted. Collections in the Kennedy and Johnson Libraries were especially useful. Researchers should look at aides' files and national security files as well as specialized groups of materials on particular topics.

The Secretary of Defense's annual report, or posture statement, is another often useful indication of high-level or at least institutional thinking. While of course the rationales in such documents are self-serving, they often indicate how the Pentagon believes continuing commitments can or must be upheld. The same applies to congressional hearings, on which I relied fairly heavily. Administration officials clearly say what they think congressional representatives want to hear, but they also use such platforms to send signals to interested parties abroad. I found the Foreign Affairs and Armed Services Committee hearings in both houses helpful in sorting through these issues.

Index

Acheson, Dean, 6, 7, 85, 88, 117, 121, 123
Adaptation. *See* Hegemonic adaptation
Adaptive preferences, 33; hypotheses, 61–62
Administration, 39
Afghanistan, 55, 183
Agenda formation, 38
American Century, achievement of, 39
American model, loss of faith in, 202
Anderson, Robert, 125
Anti-ballistic Missile (ABM) Treaty, 163
ANZUS pact, 43
Assured destruction (AD), 122, 138; and extended deterrence, 140; Soviet capability for, 139, 163. *See also* Extended deterrence; Mutual assured destruction
Atmospheric Test Ban Treaty (1963), 111
Atomic Energy Act (1946), 123

Balance of payments, 125–30; and offset, 177; and troops in Europe, 144–45; and Vietnam War, 137. *See also* Dollar; Offset
Balance of power, 187
Ball, George, 173–74
Berlin Crisis, 116
Betts, Richard, 9, 95
Bipolarity, 72
Bloc cohesion, 85

Bohlen, Charles, 7
Borders, for mapping threat, 76–77
Brandt, Willy, 151; and Ostpolitik, 153–54
Bretton Woods, 74, 113; demise of, 151–52, 178. *See also* Dollar; Exchange rates
Brezhnev, Leonid, 150
Brodie, Bernard, 116, 118, 120
Brosio, Manlio, 150
Brown, Harold, 168
Bruce, David, 201
Brzezinski, Zbigniew, 168, 174–75
Budget deficits: and Congress, 99; and U.S. influence, 84
Bundy, McGeorge, 90, 121; and balance of payments, 127; on existential deterrence, 173
Burden sharing, 22, 129, 138–39, 176, 186–87; attitude toward, 198; demand for, 184; and European resolve, 75; and nuclear risks, 22; politics of, 182
Bush, George, 9, 37; policy adjustments of, 62

Calleo, David, 19, 113
Capability indicators, 47
Carlucci, Frank, 9
Carter, Jimmy, 11, 45, 52, 101; Long Term Defense Program, 180–82, 188; nuclear strategy of, 167–68

Carter Doctrine, 21, 183, 188, 197
Case study, limitations of, 25–26
Central Command and Control, 123–25
Cheney, Richard, 205
Chirac, Jacques, 203, 207
Classical Realism, 71
Clay, Lucius, 88
Cleveland, Harlan, 90
Cognitions, causal importance of, 92
Cognitive arguments, shared images of Europe, 86–92
Cold War, 82, 87, 209
Commitments, 39, 57; adjusting, 61; and available capabilities, 18–21; conventional, 143–56, 188; interstate, 40; Overcommitment Conference on Security and Cooperation in Europe (CSCE), 207; redefining, 59; situational, 48–49; world view for, 46
Connally, John, 152
Consistency, and hegemon, 42–43
Controlled counterforce, 121–22
Conventional forces: and balance of payments, 125; costs of, 9; in Europe, 4, 163, 179–82; policies on, 101; reductions in, 129–31, 160–61 n.70; and rivalness, 182–87; and spatial rivalry, 95; and U.S. Senate, 8
Conventional Forces in Europe (CFE) negotiations, 23, 204, 205
Conventionalization, 168
Cooper, Richard, 128
Cordesman, Anthony, 140
Countermilitary targeting, 58, 169
Counter-recovery strategy, 167
Countervailing strategy, 168
Cuba, 80
Cuban Missile Crisis, 116

Decision makers, 86–87; and critical variables, 102
Decision making, 38–39, 156–57
Defense budget, 19–21; congressional cuts in, 147–48
de Gaulle, Charles, 59, 124
de Maiziere, Lothar, 208
de Rose, Francois, 37
Détente, and Third World, 148

Deterrence. See Extended deterrence
Dillon, Douglas, 125, 128
Discriminate Deterrence, 59
Dollar: in international monetary system, 16; overvalued, 152, 177; stopgap measures for, 126–29; weakening, 138. See also Bretton Woods; Exchange rates
Domino beliefs, 47–48
Dulles, John Foster, 112

Eastern Europe, political change in, 204–5
Eckstein, Harry, 55, 195–96
Economic power, 41; and military power, 51 (figure); and security, 50–51; U.S. decline in, 14
Economic vulnerability, 76; and geography, 77
Eisenhower, Dwight D., 8, 13, 25, 48, 115, 125
Enthoven, Alain, 119
Environmental probabilism, 82
Environmental variables, 71
Erhard, Ludwig, 145
Europe: beliefs about, 153–56; commitment to, 21–25; Finlandization of, 16, 86, 91, 120, 153, 154–55, 165, 175, 188, 203; forces in, 56–57; resolve of, 87, 177; security commitment to, 1; self-reliance of, 201; sense of failure, 202; shared images of, 86–92; and Soviet pressure, 11; tactical nuclear weapons in, 116, 119
European Community, single-market, 202
European Monetary System (EMS), 178
Europe-first policy, 149
Exchange rates, 73–74; floating, 152, 176, 177; policy rationale, 191–92 n.66. See also Bretton Woods; Dollar
Executive, in weak state, 97
Expansion: causes of, 79; and hegemons, 44–45
Extended deterrence, 3–4, 85, 101, 138, 156; adversarial character of, 199; and assured destruction, 140; between 1966–1973, 139–42; between 1974–1980, 165–76; commitment to, 206;

concepts of, 11; as public good, 94–
95; and troop deployment, 9. *See also*
Assured destruction; Mutual assured
destruction
Externalities, 67 n.97; internationalization
of, 54–55
External position, and commitments, 74

Finlandization. *See* Europe
First use. *See* Nuclear weapons
Fiscal constraints, 84
Flexible response (FR), 3, 37, 58, 171–
72, 173, 198; contradiction to, 187;
and conventional readiness, 143–44;
defined, 116; development of, 114–23;
NATO acceptance of, 141–42; as pru-
dent adjustment, 130. *See also* Nuclear
weapons
Ford administration, 11
Foreign policy: adaptation of, 34–38; de-
cision structure for, 49–50; Wilsonian
tradition in, 209
Foreknowledge, 196
Forward defense, 5
Fox, William T. R., 17
France: German phobia of, 7; on German
reunification, 207; and nuclear defense
of Europe, 206; nuclear weapons in,
123, 142
Franco-German Elysée Treaty, 203
Frankel, Max, 153
Free riding, 184
Fried, Edward, 178
Friedberg, Aaron, 20, 21, 46, 79

Gaddis, John Lewis, 37
Galvin, John, 205
Game theory, 184–86
Garnham, David, 174
Geographic exposure, as threat, 76
Geography, and economic vulnerability,
77
George, Alexander, 101
Germany: as economic powerhouse, 152;
European role of, 207; military pro-
curement of, 127; and nuclear nonpro-
liferation treaty, 142; rearmament of,
7; reunification of, 153, 205

Gilpatric, Roswell, 127, 129
Gilpin, Robert, 16, 54, 72, 74
Gold, and troop cuts, 146–47
Goldmann, Kjell, 71
Gorbachev, Mikhail, 84, 201; European
vision of, 208; external retrenchment,
43; on German reunification, 207
Gravel, Mike, 170
Gray, Colin, 172
Great Britain, nuclear force in, 123–24,
206
Guam Doctrine. *See* Nixon Doctrine
Guns of August, The (Tuchman), 123
Gysi, Gregor, 201

Halloran, Richard, 51
Halperin, Morton, 118
Harmel Report (1967), 37
Harriman, Averell, 111–12
Hegemonic adaptation, 2, 40–62, 73–74;
analysis of, 33, 199–201; choices in,
57–62; defined, 34; objectives of, 35–
36; and policy, 70; probabilistic framework for, 81–85; and structural arguments, 80
Hegemonic decline, 102, 207; adjustment
to, 198; cognitive model of, 56–57;
and conventional-forces commitments,
102; debate about, 17; existence of,
13–17; managing, 187; as systemic
change, 81
Hegemons: ascending, 72; and burden redistribution, 56; constraints on, 70,
83–84; cycles of, 62, 72; and economic activity, 18; global reach of,
180; leadership of, 74; model of, 54;
overextended, 18, 197–98; physical security of, 43; special case of, 38–40;
stability of, 73, 103; and superpowers,
44
Herrmann, Richard, 81
Herter, Christian, 124
Hillenbrand, Martin, 156
Huntington, Samuel, 14, 16, 20–21

Ikenberry, G. John, 35, 61
Incrementalism, 100–101
Information, 83

Innovation, 39
Intercontinental ballistic missiles
(ICBMs), number of, 164
Interest Equalization Tax, 128
Intermediate Nuclear Forces (INF)
Treaty, 23
International Energy Agency, 73
Isolationism, 1, 5–6, 23, 155, 209
Issue area, 93–101

Jackson-Nunn Amendment, 178
Japan, 152; defense priorities, 42
Jervis, Robert, 115, 173, 174
Johnson, Lyndon B.: and balance of payments, 127; and budget deficit, 138;
and eroding hegemony, 137; on European troop cuts, 146; on French nuclear weapons, 124; and nuclear
warfighting, 140; and overextension,
197, 198; on U.S. leadership, 130; and
Vietnam costs, 143

Kaufmann, William, 20, 21, 52–53, 115,
120–21
Kegley, Charles, 200
Kennan, George, 85, 153, 156
Kennedy, John F., 17; and Berlin Crisis,
119; economic orthodoxy of, 126; military buildup by, 111; on NATO strategy, 117; on nuclear war, 118, 119,
120; and overextension, 197, 198; *The
Rise and Fall of the Great Powers*, 52;
on troop cuts, 129, 130; on U.S. leadership, 130
Kennedy, Paul, 18, 50
Kennedy administration: and balance of
payments, 113–14; and decline, 26;
flexible response strategy, 58
Keohane, Robert O., 33, 74, 93, 128,
156, 200
Kindleberger, Charles, 74
Kissinger, Henry, 23, 37, 53–54, 174;
and controlled nuclear warfighting,
138; on European troop cuts, 151; on
extended deterrence, 141; on Soviet
Union, 163
Kohl, Helmut, 24, 208
Komer, Robert, 164, 181

Korb, Lawrence, 206
Korean War, 6, 88–89
Krasner, Stephen, 75
Kugler, Richard, 20–21

Laird, Melvin, 148, 160–61 n.70; on Eu-
ropean troop cuts, 151
Lake, David, 75
Lamborn, Alan, 49–50
Larson, Deborah, 81
Latsis, Spiro, 80
Legislative impact, 97
Levels-of-analysis issues, 71
Limited nuclear options (LNOs), 166–67,
174, 187–88. *See also* Nuclear
weapons
Lippmann, Walter, 18
Logrolling, 49
Long range theater nuclear forces
(LRTNF), 174–76

McCloy, John, 88, 145–46
McIntyre, Thomas, 170
MacKinder, Halford, 78–79
McNamara, Robert, 62 n.5, 94, 111,
114, 115; on allied defense efforts,
145; on controlled counterforce, 121;
on first use, 119, 122–23; on flexible
response, 117; on mutually assured de-
struction, 172–73; on nuclear war,
118, 120, 122, 138, 165, 198–99; on
tactical nuclear weapons, 119
Mahan, Alfred Thayer, 78–79
Mansfield, Mike, 154, 179; and European
troops, 144, 149–50
Mansfield Amendments, 91
Marshall, George, 8
Mayer, Martin, 128
Military, and policy coalition defection,
53–54
Military power, and economic power, 51
(figure)
Missile gap, 111
Mobilization, 38
Modelski, George, 38, 41
Morgan, Patrick, 89
Morgenthau, Hans, 168
Multilateral Force (MLF), 117, 124–25

Multiple-exit approaches, 80–81
Mutual assured destruction (MAD), 165, 172–74. *See also* Assured destruction, Extended deterrence; Nuclear parity

National Security Decision Memorandum (NSDM) 242, 165–66
Neutron bomb, 175
New Zealand, 43
Nitze, Paul, 47, 111
Nixon, Richard, 52; and controlled nuclear warfighting, 138; election of, 147; and eroding hegemony, 137; on Europe, 157; on exchange rates, 152; and overextension, 197
Nixon Doctrine, 52, 59, 148, 155, 157, 160 n.57
No First Use (NFU) policy, 24–25, 60, 118–19, 198–99. *See also* Nuclear weapons
Norstad, Lauris, 124
North, Oliver, 97
North Atlantic Treaty (NAT), 5, 88
North Atlantic Treaty Organization (NATO), 3; as allied consultation forum, 90; burden-sharing policy, 13, 50; commitments to, 197; conventional forces under, 118; endurance of, 195, 201; evolution of, 4–13; force goals of, 56, 112; future of, 207; game theory model of, 185–86; German participation in, 7; interoperability for, 181; after mid–1970s, 164–65; military spending, 182; nuclear forces within, 52, 57, 94, 141–42; Nuclear Planning Group (NPG), 142; nuclear procedures of, 11–12; on nuclear risk-taking, 23–24; priority for, 181; public support of, 153; resistance to change, 205; as security regime, 37; and Soviet threat, 199; and theater nuclear weapons, 169–70; U.S. commitment to, 26, 163, 200–201; U.S. control of, 96–97, 123; and U.S. retrenchment, 154
NSC-68, 6, 114
Nuclear parity, 157, 163–64; official definitions of, 11. *See also* Mutual assured destruction

Nuclear Targeting Policy Review (NTPR), 168
Nuclear threshold, 13; flexibility above, 120–23; lowering of, 206; raising, 115–20
Nuclear weapons: and allied burden-sharing, 22; ambivalence about, 130; as deterrence, 181; first use of, 3–4, 11, 57–60; flexibility of, 96; in France, 202–3; in Great Britain, 202–3; policy options for, 24; proliferation of, 85, 123; stalemate in, 112–13, 115; and strategy, 79, 139–42, 165–76; tactical, 11–12, 97, 116, 167, 180; as threat, 9–11
Nuclear Weapons Employment Policy (NUWEP), 166
Nunn, Sam, 22, 169–70, 176, 179–80
Nye, Joseph S., 93, 128, 156

Offset, 149, 157; agreements on, 144; bargaining for, 150; end of, 177–78. *See also* Balance of payments
Oil, 73
Opportunity costs, 54; of U.S. power, 17
Organizational arguments, 92–93
Ostpolitik, 153–54; and NATO, 203
Overcommitment, 157; as adaptation, 61; calculated, 53; consequences of, 51–52; and devolution, 62; risks of, 50. *See also* Commitments
Overdetermined outcomes, 54–57

Parsimony, 196
Pentagon, and gold budget, 127
Pershing II missiles, 175
Persian Gulf: commitments in, 21, 45, 182; Soviet intentions in, 176
Persian Gulf Doctrine, 52
Pfaff, William, 202
Policy: coalitions, 49; coherence of, 199; domestic determinants of, 49; explaining change in, 70, 71
Political behavior, theory of, 196
Pompidou, Georges, 152
Possibilism, 81–82
Potter, William, 93

Power: decline of, 2; and foreign policy
adaptation, 34; models of, 46–47
Presidential Directive (PD) 59, 168
Prisoners' Dilemma game, 184–85
Public goods, 93

Rapid Deployment Force (RDF), 56, 97,
183
Record, Jeffrey, 19
Reagan, Ronald, 13, 19, 202; defense
buildup by, 20, 53; election mandate,
25; at Reykjavik, 203
Regularity, 196
Relative size, and expansion, 76
Reliability, 196
Reputation, within hegemonic coalitions,
48
Reserves, and Vietnam War, 143
Resolve, 47; preoccupation with, 89
Retrenchment, causes of, 79
Reykjavik summit, 203
Riding, Alan, 208
Rise and Fall of the Great Powers, The
(Kennedy), 52
Risks: acceptance of, 21; and policy
choice, 49
Risk-taking, as commonplace, 55
Rivalness, impact of, 95
Rogers, Bernard, 19
Romano, Sergio, 202
Roosa, Robert, 127
Rosenberg, David, 96
Rostow, Walt, 144
Rusk, Dean, 94, 144; on European troop
cuts, 146; on nuclear war, 118
Russell, Richard, 8
Russett, Bruce, 14

Schelling, Thomas, 47
Schlesinger, James, 1, 50, 121, 165,
170, 179; on conventional forces, 176,
181; and nuclear strategy dialogue, 172
Schlesinger Doctrine, 166
Schmidt, Helmut, 174, 178
Schroeder, Patricia, 22
Scowcroft Commission, 47
Security systems, hegemonic, 41–54
Shared images, origins of, 87–90

Shultz, George, 177
Single-exit models, 80, 157
Single Integrated Operational Plan
(SIOP), 58, 101
Sino-Soviet split, 148
Skocpol, Theda, 36
Skybolt missile, 124
Snidal, Duncan, 74, 75
Southwest Asia, crisis in, 183
Soviet Union: European forces of, 5,
204; force reductions in, 205–6; global
reach of, 183; ICBMs of, 111, 115,
139; military power of, 164, 180; na-
val power, 180; nuclear forces of, 112,
137, 149; tactical nuclear weapons,
122
Spofford Compromise, 7
Sprout, Harold, 82
Sprout, Margaret, 82
SS–20 missile, 174
Stability-instability paradox, 115
State structure, 93–101
Stinchcombe, Arthur, 76
Strange, Susan, 14, 16
Strategic Air Command (SAC), 121
Strategic Arms Limitation Talks (SALT),
174
Strategic Arms Limitation Talks (SALT)
II Treaty, and NATO, 175
Strauss, Franz-Josef, 127
Structural power, 14–16
Structural realism, 103; and hegemonic
stability, 71–79; as theory of con-
straints, 83
Subsystemic arguments, of foreign pol-
icy, 85–101
Sulzberger, C. L., 89
Superpowers, and hegemon, 17, 44
Systemic arguments, of foreign policy,
71–85
Systemic-constraint model, 55, 81

Taft, Robert, 8, 23
Taylor, Maxwell D., 116
Technological change, and nuclear strat-
egy, 171
Technological superiority, erosion of, 84
Technology, in military planning, 52

Thatcher, Margaret, 205; on NATO, 208
Thorneycroft, Peter, 203
Trade, 114; free, 39–40, 74, 75
Triffin, Robert, 113
Truman administration, 5
Tuchman, Barbara, *The Guns of August*, 123
Turbulent Frontier, 45–46, 50

United States: balance-of-payments position, 113; as beneficent hegemon, 17; Central American policy of, 46; as declining hegemon, 26, 164; defense role of, 2–4; economy of, 16; European role of, 2, 7, 206, 208; first-strike capability, 112–13; foreign bases of, 43; foreign policy of, 209; imperial overstretch, 19; investment decline, 21; NATO policy of, 22, 89; nuclear assistance program, 142; nuclear invulnerability of, 112; nuclear parity with Soviet Union, 137; perceived weakness of, 204; as risk-averse, 188; trade policy, 197
United States Congress: and conventional forces, 186–87; impact on policy, 98–99; independence of, 179; isolationists in, 7–8; and nuclear strategy, 168–72

Validity, 196–97
Vance, Cyrus, 175
Vietnam War, 95, 179; budget effects of, 143–47, 164; impact of, 156; as nonnuclear flexible response, 137; as overextension, 147; and payments deficits, 128
Vulnerability, defined, 77

Waltz, Kenneth, 71–72, 85, 86, 97
Warsaw Pact, 204–5; force superiority, 117; standardized forces, 180
Warsaw Treaty, 43
Weaponry, diffusion of, 84–85
Weinberger, Caspar, 52
Western Europe, 112; postwar integration, 42
Western European Union (WEU), 203–4
Widman, F. Lisle, 191–92 n.66
Wittkopf, Eugene, 200
World product, shares of, 76